P9-DDP-015

DATE DUE

FEB 1 8 1974			
JAN 21 '88			
FEB 8 '88			
1/16/89			
JAN 17 1990			
JAN 31 1990			
APR 1 4 1997			
APR 20 1998			
GAYLORD			PRINTED IN U.S.A.

9603

THE GREEKS

BOOKS ON HISTORY BY

ISAAC ASIMOV

THE KITE THAT WON THE REVOLUTION

A SHORT HISTORY OF BIOLOGY

A SHORT HISTORY OF CHEMISTRY

ASIMOV'S BIOGRAPHICAL ENCYCLOPEDIA OF SCIENCE AND TECHNOLOGY

THE GREEKS

THE GREEKS

A GREAT ADVENTURE

BY ISAAC ASIMOV

HOUGHTON MIFFLIN COMPANY BOSTON
THE RIVERSIDE PRESS CAMBRIDGE

BLAIRSVILLE SENIOR HIGH SCHOOL
BLAIRSVILLE, PENNA.

938

To the memory of

JOHN FITZGERALD KENNEDY,

35th President of the United States

With few exceptions,
the decorations in this book are
adapted from Greek vase paintings.

SECOND PRINTING   C

COPYRIGHT © 1965 BY ISAAC ASIMOV

ALL RIGHTS RESERVED INCLUDING THE RIGHT TO REPRODUCE
THIS BOOK OR PARTS THEREOF IN ANY FORM.

LIBRARY OF CONGRESS CATALOG CARD NUMBER 65-12174.

PRINTED IN THE U.S.A.

CONTENTS

THE MYCENAEAN AGE

At the southeastern edge of Europe, jutting into the Mediterranean Sea, is a small peninsula we call Greece. It is mountainous and infertile, with a jagged coastline and narrow streams.

Throughout its history, Greece has always been surrounded by larger, wealthier, and more powerful states. In comparison to those neighbors, it has always seemed a small and unimportant land if one merely consulted the map.

And yet no land is more famous than Greece; no people have made a greater mark in history than the Greeks.

The Greeks who lived twenty-five centuries ago (the "ancient Greeks") wrote fascinating stories about their gods and heroes and even more fascinating stories about themselves.

They built beautiful temples, carved wonderful statues, wrote magnificent plays. They produced some of the greatest thinkers the world has ever seen.

Our modern notions of politics, medicine, art, drama, history and science date back to those ancient Greeks. We still read their writings, study their mathematics, ponder their philosophy, and stand in awe and wonder before even the ruins and fragments of their beautiful buildings and statues.

All of western civilization descends directly from the work of the ancient Greeks and the story of their triumphs and disasters never loses its fascination.

KNOSSOS

Well before 2000 B.C., tribes of Greek-speaking peoples began to drift southward from the northwest corner of the Balkan peninsula into the land that then became Greece.

At the time, the Greek tribes were still working with stone tools, for they had not yet developed the use of metal. However, lying to the south of the peninsula was the island of Crete.

Crete, with an area of 3200 square miles, is a little over half as large as the state of Connecticut, but was far more important in those early days than one might guess from its size. About 3000 B.C. its people were using copper and had begun to build efficient ships.

Surrounded by water as they were, the Cretan cities had to develop shipping in order to trade with the nations on the continental shores to the south and east. Navies were developed to protect those ships so that Crete became the first naval power in history.

By 2200 B.C., the island was united under a strong monarchy. For centuries the navy protected it from invasion. The cities on

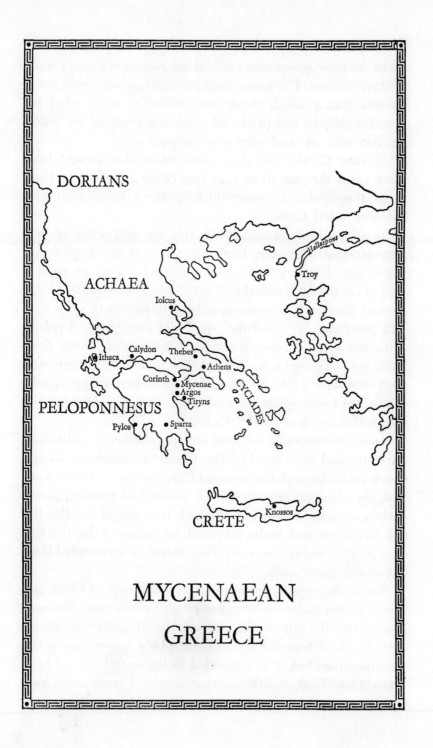

DORIANS

ACHAEA

Troy

Hellespont

Iolcus

Calydon   Thebes

Ithaca

Corinth   Athens

Mycenae

Argos

Tiryns

PELOPONNESUS

Pylos   Sparta

CYCLADES

CRETE   Knossos

MYCENAEAN

GREECE

the island grew prosperous and did not require the usual walls for their defense. The rulers built luxurious palaces, held great festivals during which there were elaborate rituals that included bullfights, and produced attractive works of art which one can still see and admire in museums.

The later Greeks had dim memories of this ancient land which ruled the seas when they first entered Greece. In their myths, they spoke of a powerful King Minos (migh'nos) who had once ruled Crete.

For a long time, historians felt this was just a legend and nothing more. However, beginning in 1893, an English archaeologist, Arthur John Evans, conducted a series of excavations in Crete which actually showed the buried remains of the great civilization that had once existed thousands of years ago.

In particular, he found the remains of a magnificent palace at the site of the ancient city of Knossos (noss'us) where King Minos was supposed to have ruled. The period when Crete was great therefore came to be called the Minoan Age (mih-noh'an) in honor of its greatest king. This age extends from about 3000 B.C. to about 1400 B.C.

Cretan civilization had spread out over the Aegean islands to the north and even reached the European mainland. As the Greek tribes learned the lessons of civilization from the Cretans, they became more powerful, established growing towns of their own and began to trade with their neighbors. But the Greeks always had to be prepared for invasions by the still uncivilized tribes of the north. They therefore surrounded their cities with great walls.

The southernmost portion of Greece is closest to Crete and therefore was under the strongest civilizing influence. This section (about the size of the state of Massachusetts) is almost entirely cut off from the rest of Greece by a narrow arm of the Mediterranean Sea. It is connected to the rest of Greece by a thin neck of land, or isthmus, that is some twenty miles long and, at some points, is only four miles wide.

This southern peninsula of Greece was called the Peloponnesus (pel"oh-puh-nee′sus) in ancient times. This means "Pelops' island" (for it is nearly an island) because a legendary King Pelops (pee′lops) had ruled there in early times.

In the northeastern area of the peninsula were a trio of important cities: Mycenae (migh-see′nee),* Tiryns (tigh′rinz) and Argos (ahr′gos). About forty miles to the south of these three cities is Sparta (spahr′tuh), and about twenty miles to the north is Corinth (kor′inth). On the west coast of the Peloponnesus was the city of Pylos.

Corinth is just at the southwestern end of the isthmus which is therefore known as the Isthmus of Corinth. The arm of the sea to the north of the Peloponnesus is the Gulf of Corinth.

Northeast of the isthmus were the cities of Athens (ath′enz) and Thebes (theebz) but in those early days, these cities just outside the Peloponnesus were relatively small and unimportant.

The Greeks of the mainland, growing stronger, were restless under Cretan domination, and they rebelled. We don't know the details of the rebellion but a memory remained to the later Greeks of an Athenian hero, Theseus (thee′syoos) who brought an end to the tribute Athens was paying to Crete.

The Greeks managed to defeat the Cretan navy and end the many centuries of Cretan dominion over the mainland. They were helped by some disaster, probably an earth-

---

* This is not either the spelling or the pronunciation used by the Greeks. The Greeks used an alphabet that is different from ours, and their spelling, if placed into the nearest English letters would be "Mykenai." The later Romans used the alphabet with which we are familiar, and "Mycenae" is their spelling. In the Latin language used by the Romans, "c" is pronounced like "k" and "ae" is pronounced like our long "i" as the Greek "ai" is. In English, we keep the Latin spelling but use our own rules of pronunciation where a "c" before an "e" is pronounced like an "s" and "ae" is pronounced like a long "e." In this book, I will use the Latin spelling and the English pronunciation because these are most familiar. Please remember, though, that this does not represent either the Greek spelling or the Greek pronunciation.

quake which destroyed Knossos about 1700 B.C. Finally, about 1400 B.C. the Greeks raided Crete and captured Knossos, destroying the palace. The palace was later rebuilt, but Crete never regained its power.

The Cretan language has never been deciphered, and inscriptions found in this language cannot be read. However, Cretan writing comes in several varieties. The earlier varieties, in use before 1700 B.C., are types of picture-writing. Afterward, the Cretans made use of writing that consisted, essentially, of wiggly lines (as our own handwriting does). The earlier variety of this line-writing came to be called "Linear A." The later variety, in use about the time of the destruction of Knossos, is "Linear B."

In 1953, the English archaeologist Michael Ventris managed to decipher Linear B, and found that it was a form of Greek. It didn't use the Greek alphabet, but the words were Greek.

The documents written in Linear B that have been deciphered consist of such things as inventories, receipts, work instructions and so on. There are no great works of art, science or history. Still, even the dullest business memos cast light upon the daily life of men and women and historians are glad to have them. The details of Minoan society are a little clearer, thanks to the work of Ventris.

Furthermore, it shows that the influence of the Greeks of the mainland was widespread even while Knossos was still in power. Probably Greek merchants filled the land, Greek ships were taking over trade, and the Cretans gradually lost control of their own island. The destruction of Knossos just put an end to something that was coming to an end anyway.

MYCENAE AND TROY

The Greeks of the mainland continued to expand their influence. The most powerful city of the time was Mycenae, so

that the period of Greek history from 1400 B.C. to 1100 B.C. is
called the Mycenaean Age (migh"see-nee′an).

The Mycenaean navies spread out over the Aegean Sea in
search of trade, and often they carried colonists or warriors to
extend their influence by occupation or force. They took over
Crete completely by 1250 B.C. They settled on the island of
Cyprus (sigh′prus) in the northeastern corner of the Mediterranean, 300 miles east of Crete. They even entered the Black
Sea to the northeast of the Aegean.

The later Greeks looked back to this Mycenaean Age as a
heroic period in which great men (supposedly the sons of
gods) performed mighty feats. The first penetration of the
Black Sea was described in the form of the story of Jason
(jay′son) who sailed the ship *Argo,* rowed by fifty
"Argonauts" northeastward. After overcoming great perils, this
ship reached the eastern tip of the Black Sea in order to gain
and bring back a golden ram's fleece. This "Golden Fleece"
could well be the storybook version of what the Argonauts
were really after, the wealth that comes with a successful trading expedition.

In order to get into the Black Sea, the Mycenaean ships had
to pass through narrow straits. First there was the Hellespont
(hel′es-pont), which in modern times is called the Dardan-
elles (dahr"duh-nelz′). In spots, this is less than a mile wide.

The Hellespont opens into the Propontis (proh-pon′tis) a
small body of water about the size of the state of Connecticut.
Its name means "before the sea" because in traveling through
it in either direction one next enters a large sea. The Propontis
quickly narrows into a second strait, Bosporus (bos′poh-rus),
which, in spots, is only half a mile wide. Only after passing
through the Bosporus does one enter the Black Sea itself.

Any people who dominated the narrow waters of the Hellespont and Bosporus were in a position to control the rich Black
Sea trade. They were able to charge fees for passage and good
high fees, too.

In Mycenaean times, the area was ruled by the city of Troy, which was located on the Asian coast at the southwestern end of the Hellespont. The Trojans grew wealthy and powerful through the Black Sea trade and the Mycenaean Greeks grew increasingly resentful of the situation.

Eventually, they decided to take over the straits by force and about 1200 B.C. (1184 B.C. is the traditional date worked out by the later Greeks) a Greek army laid siege to Troy and, in the end, destroyed it.

The Greek army, according to tradition, was led by Agamemnon (ag″uh-mem′non), king of Mycenae and the grandson of the Pelops after whom the Peloponnesus was named.

The story of portions of that siege was told (or put into its final form) by a poet whom tradition names Homer and who lived and wrote about 850 B.C. The long epic poem, the *Iliad* (after Ilium, an alternate name of the city of Troy), tells the story of the quarrel between Agamemnon, leader of the host, and Achilles (uh-kil′eez), the greatest warrior under his command.

A second poem, also supposedly by Homer, is the *Odyssey* which tells of the adventures that befell Odysseus (oh-dis′yoos), one of the Greek warriors, during his ten years of wanderings after the conclusion of the war.

Such is the greatness of the Homeric poems that they live on to this day and have been read and admired by every generation that followed Homer. They are considered not only the first but also the greatest of the Greek literary productions.

Homer's story is full of supernatural happenings. The gods interfere constantly in the progress of the battle and at times even join in the fighting. Up to a century ago, modern scholars dismissed the whole thing as a fable. They were pretty sure there never really was a city of Troy, and no siege, either. All of it, they decided, was Greek inventiveness and myth.

However, a young German, Heinrich Schliemann, born in 1822, read Homer's poems when he was young and was fascinated by them. He was sure they were real history (except for the gods, of course). It was his dream to dig in the ancient ruins where Troy had once stood and find the city that Homer had described.

He went into business and labored hard in order to amass the fortune he would need to conduct the investigation, and he studied archaeology so that he would have the necessary background. All went as he planned. He grew rich; he learned archaeology and the Greek language; and in 1870, he traveled to Turkey.

In the northwest corner of that nation was a little village that was his goal, for Schliemann's study of the *Iliad* convinced him that mounds nearby covered the crumbling ruins of the ancient city.

He began digging and uncovered ruins not of one city but of a series of cities one on top of another. He matched the descriptions in the *Iliad* with one of these cities and now no one doubts that Troy really existed.

In 1876, Schliemann began similar diggings at the site of Mycenae and uncovered traces of a powerful city with thick walls. It is as a result of his work that much modern knowledge of the time of the Trojan War and before has come to light.

ARGIVES AND ACHAEANS

In his poems, Homer uses either of two words to describe the Greeks: Argives (ahr'jivez) and Achaeans (uh-kee'anz).

These are clearly tribal names. Agamemnon's rule was centered over the cities of Mycenae, Tiryns and Argos. In Homer's time, Argos had become the most powerful of the three so it was natural for him to think of Agamemnon as an Argive.

Although Agamemnon led the Greek host, he did not rule over all the Greeks as an absolute king, for other regions had kings of their own. Nevertheless, the other kings, particularly in the Peloponnesus, deferred to Agamemnon as holding first place. The city of Sparta was governed by Menelaus (meh"neh-lay'us), Agamemnon's brother. What's more, Agamemnon supplied ships for the towns in the interior of the Peloponnesus which, having no access to the sea, had no ships of their own. The term Argives, therefore, might well include all the people of the Peloponnesus.

But what about the Achaeans? About fifty miles north of the Gulf of Corinth, there is a section of the Aegean coast that makes up the southernmost portion of a large plain once inhabited by a group of people called Achaeans.

Jason had been an Achaean, according to legend, and so was Achilles.

The Achaeans were not as much under Agamemnon's control, apparently, as were the Argives of the Peloponnesus. Achilles quarreled with Agamemnon and haughtily withdrew from the fight when he felt that his rights had not been respected. He acted as though he were an independent ally, rather than an underling.

The Achaeans, since they lived farther north than the Argives, had been less exposed to the civilizing influence of Crete and were more savage. Achilles is described as a man of anger, who has no hesitation in abandoning his allies in a fit of sulks. Then, when his rage is roused again by the enemy, he plunges into battle in the most ferocious manner.

One of the Achaean tribes called themselves the Hellenes (hel'eenz) and the region they lived in was Hellas (hel'as). Though they are casually mentioned in only a single verse in the *Iliad*, it is probably an indication of the early importance of the Achaeans that these names spread until they included all of Greece.

All through history, since Mycenaean times, the Greeks have called their land "Hellas" and have referred to themselves (whether they lived in Greece or outside Greece) as Hellenes. Even now, the official name of the modern Kingdom of Greece is Hellas.

Our words "Greece" and "Greek" are inherited from the Romans. It happened that a group of Hellenes had emigrated to Italy some time after the Mycenaean period. (The southernmost portion of Italy is separated from northwestern Greece by a narrow stretch of sea only about thirty miles across.)

The tribe which had emigrated to Italy called themselves the "Graikoi." In the Latin language of the Romans this became "Graeci." The Romans came to apply this name to all Hellenes whether they belonged to the tribe of the Graikoi or not. This, in English, became "Greek."

Scholars interested in Greek history use the older term, too. For instance, the earliest period of Greek history, up through the Trojan War and a little beyond is called the Helladic period (heh-lad'ik). What I have been calling the Mycenaean Age might also be called, therefore, the Late Helladic Period.

2

THE IRON AGE

THE GREEK LANGUAGE

While the Greeks of even the earliest times recognized the existence of separate tribes, they also realized that there was a kinship among all tribes that spoke Greek. Language is always important, for groups of people, however different in some ways, can communicate as long as they speak a common language. It gives them a common literature and an understanding of each other's traditions. In short, they share a similar heritage and feel a natural kinship.

The Greeks, therefore, eventually had a tendency to split all people into two groups: themselves, the Greek-speakers, and foreigners, who did not speak Greek. To the Greeks, the foreigners seemed to speak meaningless syllables, which might as well be "bar-bar-bar-bar" for all the sense they made (at least to the Greeks). The Greeks therefore called all non-Greeks *barbaroi* meaning something like "people who talk queerly." Our version of the word is "barbarian."

At first, this word did not mean "uncivilized"; it just meant "non-Greek." Syrians and Egyptians who had high civilizations of their own that were much older than the Greek civilization were, nevertheless, "barbarians."

In later centuries, however, Greek civilization reached great heights and the greatest thoughts of philosophers and literary men were placed in the Greek language. Greek developed a large complicated vocabulary and a flexible way of making up new words (to express new ideas) out of old ones. In fact, we still have the common saying "The Greeks have a word for it" which simply means that no matter what new idea you have, you can always find a word or phrase in the Greek language to express it. The modern scientific vocabulary draws very heavily on Greek to express terms and notions no ancient Greek ever heard of.

Compared with the Greek language, other languages usually seemed tame and dull. Compared with Greek civilization, other peoples seemed backward. Consequently as the centuries progressed, a barbarian (one who couldn't speak Greek) came to be considered altogether uncivilized. Uncivilized people tend to be cruel and savage and that has come to be the meaning of "barbaric" or "barbarous."

The Greeks, while recognizing the common language among themselves, also realized that there were several dialects of this language. Not all Greeks spoke Greek in exactly the same way.

In the Mycenaean age, the two most important Greek dialects included the Ionian (igh-oh′nee-an) and Aeolian (ee-oh′lee-an). It seems probable that in Agamemnon's time the Argives spoke Ionian Greek, while the Achaeans spoke a form of Aeolian Greek.

During Mycenaean times, however, there existed a group of

Greeks who spoke a third dialect, the Dorian (doh'ree-an). While Agamemnon, the Ionian, and Achilles, the Aeolian, were leagued together to destroy the city of Troy, the Dorians lived far to the northwest. Far from the influence of the advanced south, they remained backward and uncivilized.

THE PEOPLES

OF THE SEA

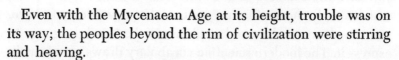

Even with the Mycenaean Age at its height, trouble was on its way; the peoples beyond the rim of civilization were stirring and heaving.

This happens periodically in history. Somewhere in central Asia, perhaps, there is a long series of years of good rainfall, during which crops and herds multiply and the population increases. This may then be followed by a series of years of drought, during which the increased population is faced with starvation. They have no choice but to surge outward in search of pasture for their herds and a better life for themselves.

The tribes which meet the first shock of the invaders must themselves flee outward and this sets a new group of people into motion. Eventually, large areas are filled with the disruptions of migrating tribes. It was this which happened in the Mycenaean Age.

The Dorians who, of all the Greeks, were farthest north, felt the pressure first. They moved south, pushing against Aeolian-speaking tribes, who had to move south in their turn.

One Aeolian tribe was called the Thessalians. Shortly after the Trojan War (1150 B.C. perhaps), they came spilling southward into that plain where the Achaeans lived of which

Phthiotis forms a part. There they settled down permanently so that ever since then the region (about the size of the state of Connecticut) has been called Thessaly (thes'uh-lee).

Another Aeolian tribe, the Boeotians (bee-oh'shanz), moved still farther south about 1120 B.C. to the smaller plain centered about the city of Thebes. This area came to be called Boeotia.

Under this pressure by their fellow Aeolians, the Achaeans were forced to move southward in their turn. They invaded the Peloponnesus and drove out the Ionian population, penning them in the area about Athens, which is on a peninsula that juts southeastward out of Central Greece. (Indeed, this may have happened even before the Trojan War and Agamemnon's army may have been forced into war in Asia by the pressure of upheavals in Greece itself.) Along the northern coast of the Peloponnesus, bordering on the Gulf of Corinth, is a region that came to be called Achaea as a result of this invasion.

Continuing pressure from the north forced both Ionians and Achaeans out into the sea. They spilled eastward and southward onto the islands and up against the surrounding coasts of Asia and Africa, devastating and disrupting the settled life they encountered.

They landed in Egypt, for instance, where the surprised Egyptians referred to them as "The Peoples of the Sea." Egypt survived the shock of their landing, but the invasion helped break down a great Egyptian empire which was then already in decline. (Homer, in the *Iliad*, describes Achilles as speaking respectfully of the capital of this Egyptian Empire as the richest city in the world.)

In Asia Minor the arrival of migrating Achaeans was even more disastrous. There, the great Hittite empire, already far in decline, was destroyed by the invasion.

Yet another party of Achaeans reached the Syrian coast via Cyprus and established themselves there. They were the Philistines (fih-lis'teenz) so important in the early history of the Israelites.

THE DORIAN INVASION

In Greece itself, bad enough was made worse by the fact that following the Achaeans came the still-savage Dorians. They paused for some years in an area in central Greece about fifteen miles north of the Gulf of Corinth. The town of Doris was there established by them.

You might think that the rude Dorian war bands would not have a chance against the organized armies of Mycenaean Greece, armies described with such admiration by Homer. However, this is not so.

For one thing, the Dorians had an important new weapon of war.

During the Mycenaean age, weapons were made of an alloy of copper and tin, which we call bronze. The heroes of the *Iliad* hurled bronze-tipped spears against bronze shields and wielded bronze swords, as was carefully described by Homer. Bronze was, at this time, the hardest metal easily available to the Greeks and the period in which it was used in warfare is known as the Bronze Age.

Iron was known at the time and men realized that it could be treated in such a way as to be harder than bronze. However, no methods were known for obtaining iron from its ores and the only iron that was available was the occasional find of metallic iron in the form of a meteorite. It was therefore treated as a precious metal by the Mycenaeans.

During the Mycenean Age, however, people in the Hittite dominions, about 750 miles east of Greece, had discovered methods of smelting iron ore and obtaining iron in sufficient quantities to make weapons. This knowledge gave them an important new war weapon. Iron swords could cleave right through bronze shields. Bronze-pointed spears and swords rebounded, blunted and harmless, from iron shields. Such weapons, even when available only in small numbers, helped the Hittites maintain their empire.

News of new inventions and techniques traveled slowly in those ancient days but by 1100 B.C., the secret of iron weapons had reached the Dorians, though not the Mycenaean Greeks. The result was that it was an iron-armed Dorian war band that defeated the bronze-armed warriors, and swept ever further south, crossing the Gulf of Corinth at a narrow point and invading the Peloponnesus about 1100 B.C.

The Dorians proceeded to establish themselves as permanent rulers in the south and east of the Peloponnesus. Sparta, as well as the old dominions of Agamemnon, fell to them. Mycenae and Tiryns went up in flames and were reduced to nothing more than obscure villages in later times. That marks the end of the Mycenaean age.

THE ISLANDS AND ASIA MINOR

When the Dorians completed their conquests in the Peloponnesus, the Ionians retained their grip on only one portion of mainland Greece. This was Attica (at'ih-kuh), the triangular peninsula on which Athens stands. As for the Aeolians, they retained not only part of the Peloponnesus but most of the Greek areas north of the Gulf of Corinth.

Times were nevertheless hard for everybody. The savage Dorians had destroyed rich cities and had uprooted settled populations. The level of civilization in Greece receded from the heights reached in the Mycenaean Age, and for three centuries an Iron Age of darkness settled over the land. It was iron because of the new weapons and iron because of the misery and poverty across the land.

Many Ionians and Aeolians fled the troubled mainland and migrated to the islands of the Aegean Sea. Most of these islands eventually became Ionian in speech, if they hadn't been that already. The nearest of these is Euboea (yoo-bee′uh), which is about the length, shape and size of Long Island, south of Connecticut. Euboea is the largest island of the Aegean and extends northwest and southeast just off the coast of Boeotia and Attica. It is quite close to the mainland and at one point a strait that is less than a mile in thickness separates Boeotia and Euboea. At this point, the city of Chalcis (kal′sis) was established. This is from the Greek word for "bronze" and Chalcis was probably a center of bronze-working. The one other important Euboean city was Eretria (eh-ree′tree-uh), about fifteen miles east of Chalcis.

By 1000 B.C. the Ionians had reached the eastern shores of the Aegean and had begun to settle along the coast, slowly pushing away or absorbing the native population.

The Greeks called this land to the east Anatolia (an″uh-toh′lee-uh) from their word for the rising sun, for, indeed, it lies in the direction of the rising sun to anyone coming from Greece.

It also received a name which may possibly have derived from an even more ancient term for the east. Some people think that the words first used to describe the lands to the west and east of the Aegean Sea were derived from *ereb* (west) and *assu* (east). These words are from the Semitic language of the people dwelling along the easternmost shores of the Mediterranean.

These Semites traded with Crete which lies south of the Aegean. To the Cretans the continental coasts would indeed be west and east and eventually the Semitic words would become Europe and Asia. (There is a Greek myth to the effect that the first human being to arrive in Crete was a princess from the easternmost shores of the Mediterranean. Her name was Europa and Minos was her son.)

At first, the term "Asia" was applied only to the land just east of the Aegean. As the Greeks learned more and more about the vast stretch of territory lying still farther east, the term spread out. Today it is given to the entire continent, the largest in the world. The peninsula east of the Aegean came to be distinguished from the large continent of which it formed part by being named Asia Minor (which is Latin for "lesser Asia") a name that is quite commonly used today.

The term "Europe" also spread to include the entire continent of which Greece forms a part. Eventually, it was discovered that while Europe and Asia are separated by the Aegean Sea and the Black Sea, they are not separated farther north, but form one large stretch of land sometimes referred to, as a whole, as Eurasia.

The Ionians who landed on the shores of Asia Minor, east of the islands of Chios (kigh'os) and Samos (say'mos), founded twelve important cities, and this section of the coast (plus the nearby islands) came to be called Ionia (igh-oh'nee-uh).

Of the Ionian cities, the most important was Miletus (migh-lee'tus). It is located just across a bay from the mouth of the Meander River (mee-an'der), a stream so famous for its winding course that the word "meander" has come to mean any irregular motion that varies constantly in direction.

THE CITY-STATE

The Dorian invasions broke down the structure of the Mycenaean kingdoms. In Mycenaean times Greece was ruled by kings, each of whom governed sizable areas, serving as both judge and high priest.

In the disorders following the Dorian invasion, however, the old Mycenaean kingdoms were destroyed. The people of each little valley on Greece's uneven surface, gathered together to try to defend themselves. They huddled within the walls of the local city when they were invaded and they might, if the occasion offered itself, issue forth from that city to raid some neighboring valley.

Slowly, the Greeks began to develop the ideal of the *polis* (poh'lis), a self-governing community consisting of a chief city with a small tract of farming land about it. To our modern eyes, the polis is nothing more than an independent city, and not a large one either, so we call it a "city-state." (The word "state" refers to any region not subject to outside control.)

It is important for people of the modern world, living as they do in giant nations, to get an idea of the small size of the Greek polis. The average city-state was perhaps fifty square miles in area, no larger than the city limits of Akron, Ohio.

Each city-state viewed itself as a separate nation and considered people from other city-states as "foreigners." Each had its own government, its own festivals and its own traditions. Cities even conducted wars against each other. Viewing Greece of this period is like watching a world in miniature.

To be sure, the city-states of a particular area often tried to join together into larger units. In Boeotia, for instance, Thebes, as the largest city, usually expected to be the leader and to decide policy. However, the Boeotian city of Orchomenus (awr-kom'ih-nus), about twenty miles northwest of Thebes, had been powerful in Mycenaean times and never forgot that. It therefore perpetually feuded with Thebes for mastery in Boeotia. The Boeotian city of Plataea (pluh-tee'uh), about nine miles south of Thebes, was also always hostile to Thebes.

Although Thebes managed to dominate Boeotia, its strength was frittered away in these internal struggles and any army which threatened Thebes could always count on the help of these competing Boeotian city-states. As a result, Thebes was never able to make its strength truly felt in Greece, except for one brief period to be described in Chapter 11.

The same was true of other regions. To a very large extent,

each city-state had its strength neutralized by its neighbors and almost all remained weak. The only two cities which managed to dominate sizable areas were Sparta and Athens and these were the "great powers" of the Greek world.

Yet even these were small. The territory of Athens was about as large as that of Rhode Island, the smallest state in the Union. The area of Sparta was equal to that of Rhode Island plus Delaware, the two smallest states of the Union.

Nor were populations very large. Athens, at its height, had a population of about 43,000 adult male citizens and this was simply tremendous for a Greek polis. Of course, there were also women, children, foreigners and slaves in Athens, but even so the total population could not have been more than 250,000, which is about that of Wichita, Kansas.

Even this seemed far too large to those later Greeks who tried to work out theories as to what a well-run city-state should be like. It was estimated that perhaps 10,000 citizens would be ideal and, in actual fact, most city-states had only 5000 citizens or less. This included "giant" Sparta, of whose population very few were allowed to be citizens.

Nevertheless, these tiny city-states worked out systems of government that were so useful, that they have proven far better adapted to modern times than did the simple, heavy-handed monarchies of the large oriental empires that surrounded Greece. Even today, we speak of the technique of government as "politics" from the Greek polis, and a person engaged in the business of governing is a "politician." (More obvious is the fact that the armed protectors of a city are its "police.")

The word "polis" is also used, occasionally, as a rather fancy suffix for the names of cities, even outside Greece and even in modern times. In the United States, three prominent examples are Annapolis, Maryland, Indianapolis, Indiana, and Minneapolis, Minnesota.

The Greeks always kept their ideal of the self-governing polis and considered this to be liberty even though that polis was governed by just a few men, actually, and though half the population might consist of slaves.

The Greeks fought to the death for their liberty, the only people of their times to do so. And although their notion of liberty isn't broad enough for us, it gradually broadened with the centuries, and the ideal of liberty, which now means so much to the modern world, is but the Greek liberty made broader and better.

Then, too, with hundreds of different city-states, each going its own way, Greek culture was able to develop an amazing color and variety. The city of Athens brought this culture to a height and in some ways is worth more than all the rest of Greece put together. Still, it is very likely that Athens could not have developed to such a pitch, if it had not been stimulated by hundreds of different cultures all within close reach.

As the polis developed, the office of king declined in importance. In a good-sized kingdom, there is enough wealth to supply considerable luxury and ceremony for the king and it is possible to establish an elaborate court. This sets the king apart from other people, even from ordinary landowners (and it is the landowners who are usually the "nobles" as opposed to the landless "people"). Such luxury and ceremonialism pleases the population which views it as a reflection of the might of the nation and therefore of their own power.

In a polis, however, so little wealth is available that the king is not much richer than other nobles. He cannot establish himself as something apart from others and he cannot expect to be treated with much consideration by the nobles.

Then, too, the necessity for a king vanishes in a polis. In a large state, it is useful to have one man who can make quick decisions for the whole kingdom. A polis, however, is so small that it is easy for individuals to get together and come to decisions, or at least to make known their preferences. They can choose a ruler who agrees with their decisions and overthrow him if he begins to go against those decisions. Or they can choose a new one every once in a while, just on principle, in order to keep an old ruler from becoming too powerful.

The general Greek word for a ruler was *arkhos*, from a word meaning "first," since the ruler is the first man in the state. A single ruler would be a "monarch" (one ruler). Through most of history, a single ruler was usually a king so that "monarch" has come to be synonymous with "king," even though an elected president, for instance, is also one ruler. A kingdom may therefore be called a "monarchy."

If, however, the real power lies in the hands of a few nobles, the heads of the more important landowning families, then we have an "oligarchy" (a few rulers). Thus, though Greece entered the period of the Dorian invasions as a group of a small number of good-sized monarchies, it emerged as a large number of small oligarchies. Even those city-states which retained their kings (as Sparta did, for instance) limited the power of those kings drastically and were actually run by an oligarchy.

Most people who are not part of the oligarchy tend to think of the few rulers as working mainly to keep themselves in power even if this meant disregarding the needs and desires of the common people. For that reason "oligarchy" has come to have a bad sound to us.

The oligarchs themselves, however, naturally thought well of the situation. They felt that the reason they were in power was that they were the most capable men, the best men. They therefore thought of themselves as "aristocrats" ("best in power") and a government run by them as an "aristocracy."

It was for an audience of oligarchs that Homer wrote the *Iliad*. Virtually nothing is known about Homer, except for traditions invented long after his time. There is a tradition that he was blind, for instance. A number of different cities claimed to be his birthplace but the Aegean island of Chios seems to be accepted by more people than any other place. Estimates as to when he lived vary over a stretch of no less than five centuries, but the best guess is about 850 B.C. (Actually, there is no real proof that Homer existed at all — but, on the other hand, *some-one* wrote the *Iliad* and *Odyssey*.)

The *Iliad* reflects the prejudices of 850 B.C. The heroes are all noblemen. There are kings, of course, but they are the kind of kings that developed during the centuries after the Dorian invasion and are not really Mycenaean kings. That is, they were "fathers of the people" who lived simply, did their own plowing, consulted the nobles before making decisions and were clearly "one of the boys."

On the other hand, the common people are not shown in a good light. In the *Iliad*, there is only one short scene in which a common man speaks. He is Thersites (ther-sigh'teez) and he raises his voice to object to the policy of Agamemnon. What he says makes good sense, but Homer describes him as deformed and scurrilous and allows him to be haughtily put down (with a blow) by the nobleman Odysseus while the army laughed. No doubt the oligarchic audience laughed also.

In the *Odyssey*, a later and gentler poem, there is Eumaeus (yoo-mee'us) a slave and lowly swineherd who is, neverthe-less, one of the most decent and lovable characters in the poem. And the suitors of Penelope (Odysseus's wife) who make rather nasty villains, are all noblemen.

The part of the common people was taken by the other ma-jor literary figure of this era. This was Hesiod (hee'see-od), who lived about 750 B.C. His parents emigrated from Aeolia in Asia Minor to Boeotia, and Hesiod was a Boeotian by birth.

He was a hard-working farmer and his major literary work is *Works and Days*. In this he teaches the proper management of a farm and the earnest moral of the book is the worth and dignity of labor.

A second important work, also attributed to Hesiod, is the *Theogony* (thee-og'oh-nee). The name means "birth of the gods" and it is Hesiod's attempt to organize the myths that must have been circulating among the Greeks at that time.

Hesiod's stories of Zeus and of the other gods (together with the less systematic tales of the gods in Homer) served as the basis of the official religion of the later Greeks.

THE BONDS OF UNION

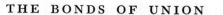

The development of the polis and the perpetual warfare that went on among the Greek city-states did not cause the Greek people to forget their common origin. There were always certain factors that held them together even through the most bitter wars.

They all spoke Greek, for one thing, so that they always thought of themselves as Hellenes as opposed to the non-Greek-speaking barbarians. For another, they had the memory of the Trojan War, when the Greeks acted as a single army; and they had Homer's magnificent poems to remind them of that.

Then, too, they shared a common set of gods. The details of religious festivals might vary from polis to polis, but all recognized Zeus as the chief god and paid reverence to the other gods as well.

There were religious shrines that were considered the common property of the whole Greek world. Of these the most important was in the region called Phocis (foh′sis) which lies west of Boeotia. In Mycenaean times, there was a town named Pytho (pigh′thoh), which lay at the foot of Mount Parnassus (pahr-nas′us) about six miles north of the Gulf of Corinth. A well-known shrine dedicated to the earth-goddess was located there and it was served by a priestess, known as the "Pythia." She was considered as having the gift of acting as the medium by which the wishes and wisdom of the gods could be made known. She was an "oracle." The oracle at Pytho is mentioned in the "Odyssey."

The Dorian war-bands devastated Phocis, and when they moved on to the Peloponnesus, Pytho changed its name to Delphi (del'figh) and made itself into an independent city-state. It now came to be dedicated to Apollo, god of youth, beauty, poetry and music, and to the Muses, a group of nine goddesses who, according to myth, inspired men with knowledge of the arts and science. (The word "music" comes from "Muse.")

As the centuries passed, the oracle at Delphi was more and more highly regarded. All Greek city-states, and even some non-Greek governments, would, from time to time, send deputations to seek the advice of Apollo. As each deputation brought gifts (Apollo not being immune to a bribe) the temple grew rich. Since it was sacred territory which men dared not attack or rob, cities and individuals would deposit treasures there for safekeeping.

The Phocian cities resented the loss of Delphi, particularly as it proved to be such a wonderful source of revenue, and for centuries kept trying to regain control of the oracle. The Phocian attempts caused a number of "Sacred Wars" (sacred because they involved the shrine) in later centuries, but in the end they always failed.

The reason for this was that Delphi could call upon other city-states to defend her. She became, in fact, a sort of international territory and was under the continuing protection of about a dozen of the neighboring regions (including Phocis.)

Other activities in which all the Greeks were concerned were the festivals that accompanied certain religious rites. These festivals might be enlivened by races and other athletic events. Because the Greeks also valued the products of the mind, competitions in music and literary productions might be carried on as well.

Chief among these competitions were the Olympian Games, which were held every four years. Tradition makes the game begin with a foot race run by Pelops (Agamemnon's grandfather) to win the hand of a princess. This would make it a Mycenaean festival to begin with, and perhaps it was. However, the official listing of winners begins in 776 B.C. and that is usually taken as the date at which the Olympian games began.

So important did these games become to the Greeks, that they counted time in four-year intervals called Olympiads, with 776 B.C. as the first year of the first Olympiad. By that system, 465 B.C. would be the third year of the seventy-eighth Olympiad, for instance.

The Olympian games were held in the town of Olympia, (oh-lim'pee-uh) in the west central portion of the Peloponnesus. The games were not named for the town, however. Both the games and the town were so named in honor of Olympian Zeus, the chief god of the Greeks, who was considered to dwell on Mount Olympus (oh-lim'pus).

This mountain is nearly two miles high and is the highest in Greece. It is located at the northern boundary of Thessaly, about ten miles from the Aegean Sea. Because of its height (and because the early Greek tribes may have worshipped in that vicinity before they moved southward) that mountain came to be considered the particular home of the gods. It is for this reason that the religion which takes the tales of Homer and Hesiod as the background is called the "Olympian religion" or "Olympianism."

Olympia was sacred because of the games and the religious rites in connection with those games so that treasures could be deposited there as well as at Delphi. Representatives of different city-states could meet there even when their cities were at war, so that it served as international neutral territory. In fact, during the Oympian games and for some time before and after, wars were temporarily suspended so that Greeks might travel to and from Olympia in peace.

The games were open to all Greeks, and Greeks came from all over to witness the games and to be contestants in them. In fact, for a city to be given permission to take part in the games was equivalent to its being accepted as officially Greek.

As the Olympian games grew important and popular and Olympia itself filled with treasure, there was naturally considerable competition among neighboring towns as to which was to have the right to organize and run the games. By 700 B.C. this honor had fallen to Elis (ee'lis) a town about twenty-five miles northwest of Olympia. It gave its name to the entire region, but throughout the course of Greek history, its only importance lay in the fact that it controlled the Olympian games. This it did, with brief interruptions, as long as the games lasted.

There were also other important games open to Greeks in general, but all were founded some two centuries after the first Olympiad. Examples are the Pythian games, which were held at Delphi every four years in the middle of each Olympiad; the Isthmian games held at the Isthmus of Corinth; and the Nemean games held at Nemea (nee'mee-uh) ten miles southwest of the Isthmus. Both the Isthmian and Nemean games were held at two-year intervals.

The winners of these games did not receive money or any prize that was valuable in itself but, of course, they got much honor and fame. Symbol of this honor was the wreath of leaves bestowed on the winner.

The winner of the Olympian games received a wreath of wild olives and the winner of the Pythian games received a wreath of laurel. The laurel was sacred to Apollo and such wreaths seemed a particularly meaningful reward for excellence in any field of human endeavor. Even today we speak of anyone who has achieved something important as having "won laurels." If, afterward, he sinks into sloth and does nothing more of importance, he is "resting upon his laurels."

3

THE AGE OF COLONIZATION

ADVANCE TO THE EAST

Slowly, during the three centuries that followed the Dorian onslaught, Greece recovered and regained its prosperity. By the eighth century B.C. it was about where it had been before the great invasions and was ready to climb higher in the scale of civilization than ever the Mycenaeans had gone.

Historians take, as a convenient date, the first year of the first Olympiad, 776 B.C., and mark this as the point from which the new and higher climb begins. This is said to open the "Hellenic period" of Greek history, a period which was to take in the next four and a half centuries and to include the most glorious era of Greek civilization.

As Hellenic times opened, returning prosperity meant serious problems for the Greeks. The population, multiplying
under the sun of good times, had outrun the capacity of the
limited land of Greece to supply food. Under such conditions,
a natural solution might have been for one city-state to make
war on its neighbors in order to seize additional land.

However, with one exception (to be considered in the next
chapter) none of the city-states was strong enough to do so
successfully. On the whole, they were too evenly matched to
make a career of conquest profitable. Their innumerable wars
generally ended in mutual exhaustion or in some small victory
which could not be followed up without arousing a whole
group of new enemies anxious to keep the victor from winning
too much and becoming too powerful.

Another possible solution, and the one adopted by almost all
the city-states, was to send part of the surplus population overseas, in order to establish new city-states on foreign shores.

This was a practical solution because the northern shores of
the Mediterranean Sea were inhabited, in those ancient days,
by poorly organized tribes at a low level of civilization. They
could not fight off the war-experienced Greeks.

Furthermore, the Greeks were interested for the most part
only in shorelines which, as experienced traders, they had already explored and where they had already formed commercial relations with the natives. The Greek colonists restricted
themselves to those shorelines where they engaged in shipping,
trade, and manufacture, leaving agriculture and mining to the
tribes in the interior. The Greeks were customers for foodstuffs,
timber, minerals and, in return, sold manufactured goods. This
was an arrangement that benefited both the Greeks and the
natives and the Greek cities usually remained in peace (at
least as far as the native interior was concerned).

By the opening of Hellenic times, the eastern shores of the
Aegean Sea had already been colonized and were filled with
thriving cities. The north, however, was still open.

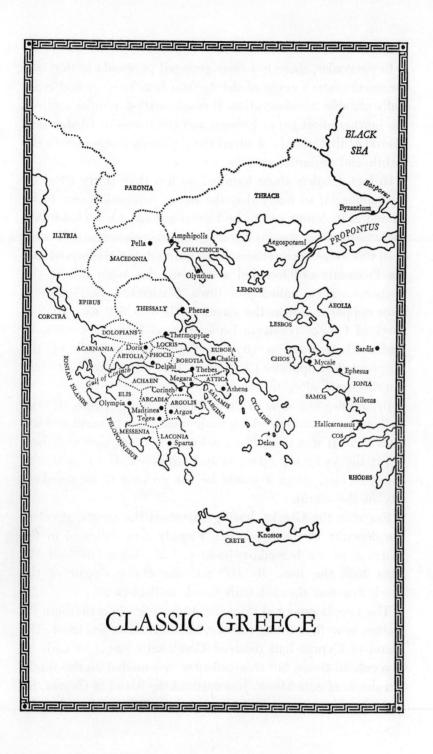

BLACK
SEA

Bosporus

PAEONIA

THRACE

Byzantium

ILLYRIA

Pella ●

Amphipolis

Aegospotami

PROPONTUS

MACEDONIA

CHALCIDICE

Olynthus

LEMNOS

AEOLIA

EPIRUS

THESSALY

Pherae

LESBOS

CORCYRA

DOLOPIANS

Thermopylae

Sardis ●

ACARNANIA

Doris ● LOCRIS

EUBOEA

CHIOS

Mycale

IONIAN ISLANDS

AETOLIA PHOCIS

Chalcis

Ephesus

Gulf of Corinth

Delphi

BOEOTIA

Thebes

IONIA

ACHAEN

Megara

ATTICA

Athens

SAMOS

Miletus

ELIS

Corinth

SALAMIS

CYCLADES

Olympia ●

ARCADIA

ARGOLIS

AEGINA

Mantinea ●

Argos

Tegea ●

Halicarnassus

PELOPONNESUS

MESSENIA

LACONIA

COS

● Sparta

Delos

RHODES

CRETE

Knossos

CLASSIC GREECE

In particular, there is a three-pronged peninsula jutting into
the northwestern angle of the Aegean Sea. This seemed especially suitable to colonization. It is only sixty-five miles north of
the northernmost tip of Euboea and the towns of Chalcis and
Eretria of that island colonized the peninsula thoroughly in the
eighth and seventh centuries B.C.

In fact, Chalcis alone founded no less than thirty cities on
the peninsula; so many that the entire peninsula came to be
named in its honor and to be known as Chalcidice (kal-sid'ih-
see).

In 685 B.C., Greek settlers sailed through the Hellespont and
the Propontis and founded a town on the Asian side of the
Bosporus. They called the town Chalcedon (kal'suh-don)
after copper mines in the vicinity. Then in 660 B.C., another
party of Greeks (under a leader named Bezas, according to
tradition) founded a city on the European side of the
Bosporus, just opposite Chalcedon. This was Byzantium (bih-
zan'shee-um) after the leader.

Byzantium was now in the position Troy had been. It controlled straits through which trade must pass. It could and did
grow rich. It was ruined as a result of warfare now and then,
but it always sprang up again and prospered. The time was to
come, in fact, when it would be the greatest Greek-speaking
city in the world.

But now the Greeks, having colonized the straits, stood at
the doorway of the Black Sea. Eagerly they followed in the
footsteps of the legendary Jason and his Argonauts, and Miletus took the lead. By 600 B.C. the entire circuit of the
Black Sea was rimmed with Greek settlements.

The Greeks emerged from the Aegean Sea in a southern direction as well, entering the vast Mediterranean Sea itself. The
island of Cyprus had received Greek settlements as early as
Mycenaean times, but now others were founded on the southern shores of Asia Minor. Just north of the island of Cyprus, for
instance, the town of Tarsus (tahr'sus) was founded by

Ionians as early, perhaps, as 850 B.C.

To the southwest of Tarsus, the city of Soli (soh'lee) was founded. Its name suffered a peculiar fate. Greeks who built cities in the midst of barbarians and who remained cut off from the main body of their countrymen were bound to develop peculiarities in language. When Greeks from the large, cultured cities of Greece itself met these colonists, they would be amused at the queer words, pronunciations and grammatical usage they would hear. For some reason, inhabitants of Soli in particular were made fun of for this reason. In fact, the Solians became so famous for their poor Greek that any piece of bad grammar is called a "solecism" to this day.

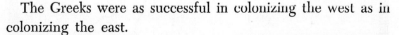

ADVANCE TO THE WEST

The Greeks were as successful in colonizing the west as in colonizing the east.

The sea to the west of Greece is called the Ionian Sea. This is not because of any connection with the Ionian-speaking Greeks but because of an involvement with the Greek myth concerning the nymph Io. The islands in that sea, just off the Greek mainland west of the Gulf of Corinth, are the Ionian Islands.

The main group of these islands, in a rough semicircle west of the Gulf, were Greek even in Mycenaean times. One of the smaller ones, Ithaca (ith'uh-kuh) was the legendary homeland of Odysseus, the hero of the *Odyssey*.

The northernmost of the Ionian islands, about seventy miles north of Ithaca, is Corcyra (kawr-sigh'ruh). This was not Greek until about 734 B.C. when, according to tradition, a band

THE
GREEK
WEST

ITALY

Rome

Cyme
Neapolis

TYRRHENIAN

SEA

MAGNA GRAECIA

Taras
(Tarentum)

Gulf
of
Tarentum

Sybaris

Croton

To Greece

Panormus

Messana

Lilybaeum

Himera

Rhegium

SICILY

Acragas

Catana

Carthage

Gela

Syracuse

Carthaginian
Greek

of settlers from Corinth landed there.

Across the Ionian Sea lies the southern tip of the boot-shaped peninsula of Italy. Just at the tip of the peninsula's toe, looking (on the map) for all the world like a football ready to be kicked, is a triangular island about as large as the state of Vermont. It is, indeed, the largest island in the Mediterranean Sea.

The Greeks sometimes called the island Trinacria (trih-nak'ree-uh) meaning "three-pointed." However, it was inhabited by tribes who called themselves "Sicans" and "Sicels" and the name, Sicily (sis'ih-lee), is derived from that.

During the age of colonization, the Greeks swarmed into Sicily and southern Italy and converted those lands into another Greece. In fact, some of these cities became in time more prosperous than any of the cities in Greece itself. The southern part of Italy is sometimes known (in Latin) as Magna Graecia (mag'nuh gree'shuh) or "greater Greece" because of that.

The Corinthians seem to have been among the first in Sicily. In 735 B.C., Corinthian colonists were founding the city of Syracuse (sir'uh-kyooz) on the eastern coast of Sicily.

In Italy, the first Greek town to be founded was Cyme (sigh'mee) much better known by the later Latin version of its name, Cumae (kyoo'mee). It is about one-third of the way up the west coast of Italy and represents the northernmost penetration of the Greeks. According to tradition, it was founded even before 1000 B.C., but this is quite impossible and represents Cyme's attempt to claim special antiquity. It was probably founded about 760 B.C. by settlers from Chalcis.

On the instep of the Italian boot, settlers from Achaea founded the town of Sybaris (sib'uh-ris) in 721 B.C. Sybaris extended its territory across the 300-mile thickness of the Italian boot at that point, to the northern shore. She became rich and prosperous and her luxury became famous among the Greeks. There is the well-known story of the man from Sybaris who had his couch strewn with rose petals but insisted that it was uncomfortable because one of the petals was crumpled. For this reason, the word "sybarite" is used nowadays to refer to any person devoted to extreme luxury.

Another group of Achaean settlers founded Croton (kroh-ton) in 710 B.C. This was on the toe of the Italian boot, about fifty miles southward along the coast from Sybaris. Despite the sistership of origin of the towns, Croton and Sybaris had the sort of traditional enmity which was often found between neighboring Greek city-states. This was one of the few cases in which one city-state won out with devastating completeness over the other. The victor was Croton and its victory, so the story goes, was at the expense of Sybarite luxury.

The Sybarites, it seems, taught their horses to dance to mu-sic so that their parades might be more impressive. In 510 B.C., they fought a battle with the Crotonites who, knowing this fact about the horses of Sybaris, advanced into battle with musi-cians playing. The Sybarite horses danced and the Sybarite forces were thrown into confusion. The Crotonites won, and destroyed Sybaris so thoroughly that there was a dispute in later centuries as to what the exact site of the town might have been.

On the inside of the Italian heel, the Spartans in 707 B.C. founded Taras, which eventually became the most important Greek city in Italy. It is far better known under its Latin name of Tarentum (tuh-ren'tum). This was the only town to be founded by Spartans overseas, for they were preoccupied (as will be explained in the next chapter) with a difficult war at home.

About 600 B.C., settlers from Cyme founded a new town a few miles southeastward along the coast and called it simply that, "Newtown." Of course, they used Greek, which made it Neapolis (nee-ap'oh-lis). In English, this has become Naples, though we still speak of an inhabitant of Naples as a Neapoli-tan.

Greek colonists penetrated even farther west than Italy. Phocaea (foh-see'uh), most northerly of the Ionian towns in Asia Minor, landed Phocian settlers on the northern coast of the Mediterranean, some 400 miles northwest from Cyme, and founded Massalia (ma-say'lee-uh) about 600 B.C. This is the modern-day Marseille (mahr-say').

EGYPT

Only the northern shores of the Mediterranean were freely open to Greek colonization. The other shores were occupied, not by backward tribesmen retreating cautiously in the face of sophisticated newcomers, but by civilizations older than Greece itself.

To the south of Asia Minor, across 350 miles of Mediterranean Sea, lay the fabled land of Egypt, already ancient even in Mycenaean times.

During Mycenaean times, Egypt had experienced a time of great military power and had established an empire that included large sections of nearby Asia. The Greeks had vague memories of this and in later centuries spoke of a conquering Egyptian king called Sesostris (see-sos'tris) who established a world-empire. This was an exaggeration, of course.

After 1200 B.C., however piratical bands of Achaeans ravaged the Egyptian shores (the "Peoples of the Sea"). These raids, too, are reflected in Greek legend, for Menelaus of Sparta is supposed to have landed in Egypt on his way home from Troy and to have remained there for seven years.

These raids weakened the already declining Egypt to the

point where never again was she a great military power. This turned out to be fortunate for the Greeks for it meant that during the dark centuries following the Dorian invasion, the Greek city-states were allowed to develop freely without interference from what might otherwise have been a powerful and aggressive Egypt.

Meanwhile, in Asia, about a thousand miles to the east of Egypt, a warlike people grew powerful. Armed, like the Dorians, with iron weapons, they made cruel war on surrounding people and began to establish an empire about 900 B.C. They called themselves "Ashur" after their chief god, but they are better known to us by the Greek version of that name — Assyria (uh-sir'ee-uh).

The Greeks caught only faint whispers of this fearful but faraway nation. For instance, they imagined, in later years, that the first Assyrian king was Ninus (nigh'nus) and that the Assyrian capital, Nineveh (nin'uh-vuh), was named for him. They also thought that he was succeeded by his beautiful, immoral and very capable queen, Semiramis (see-mir'ah-mis) who was supposed to have conquered the lands of the Assyrian Empire. Actually, these legends are worthless, but the kernel of it all was that Assyria was powerful for a time and that was true.

By 750 B.C., as Greek settlers began exploring and settling the northern Mediterranean shore, Assyria began pressing toward the eastern shore of the same sea, and by 700 B.C. they had reached it. The Egyptians feared this Assyrian advance and financed rebellions against Assyria which, however, were always defeated. In 671 B.C. Assyria decided to strike at the source of trouble and invaded Egypt. Resistance was weak, and Egypt was added to the Assyrian Empire.

At this point, Greece itself might have been in danger, but her luck held again. Assyria had stretched itself out as far as it could. It treated its enemies with horrible cruelty and the result was that it was hated by all the peoples that it ruled.

There were continuous rebellions, first in one place, then in another. For some years, all such rebellions were defeated, but it kept Assyria busy and the Greeks were safe.

Egypt itself rebelled on a number of occasions (and, through the next three centuries, Egyptian rebellions against the nations ruling it were often to involve the Greeks, sometimes disastrously). In 652 B.C. the Egyptians actually won freedom and entered one last period of independence. The Egyptian capital was now established at Saïs (say'is), near one of the mouths of the Nile River and this period of her history may be referred to as Saitic Egypt (say-it'ik).

Saitic Egypt was friendly to the Greeks, for she viewed them as possible allies against renewed danger from the east. The large oriental monarchies of the day had armies that consisted of many men, but they were poorly organized. They depended on the weight of numbers, rather than on carefully planned maneuvers, and also on cavalry — men on horses or in chariots. Casualties among the foot-soldiers were unimportant for they could easily be replaced; therefore, the foot-soldiers were lightly armed.

The Greeks, on the other hand, were broken up into small city-states at perpetual war with each other. The city-states had small armies which (in Greece's mountainous land) consisted almost entirely of foot-soldiers, and the victory depended quite a good deal on the fighting qualities of the individual man.

Virtually every Greek was trained to arms from childhood and, to make the most of the few valuable soldiers available, each was heavily armed. The foot-soldier carried spears and swords of good quality, had a strong helmet protecting his head, metal elsewhere over body and legs, and a heavy shield protecting all. Such heavily armed soldiers were called "hoplites" (hop'lites) from a Greek word for "weapon."

A band of hoplites could defeat a considerably larger group of poorly disciplined, light-armed Asian troops (as was proved

over and over again in later history) so that Greeks were always in demand as mercenary troops; as soldiers, that is, that
would serve foreign governments for pay.

The Greeks were often available for such service, for when
one city-state was defeated in war with another, men from the
defeated state might seek employment abroad rather than endure hard times at home. Then, too, sending out mercenary
bands abroad was another way of dealing with overpopulation
at home. For five centuries, Greek mercenaries were to play an
important part in the warfare about the rim of the Mediterranean Sea.

The Egyptians found the Greek hoplites useful in Saitic
times. They also encouraged Greek trade and even allowed
them to establish a trading post at the mouth of the Nile. This
post, founded in 635 B.C. by settlers from Miletus developed
into the city of Naucratis (noh'kruh-tis), a name which means
"ruler of the sea."

This marks the beginning of a Greek penetration into Egypt,
a penetration which was to reach a climax three centuries later.
The Greeks applied their own names to the objects they saw
and since, in later years, Greek was understood and the original Egyptian tongue was not, it was the Greek names that survived. This has given Egyptian history a curiously Greek
flavor.

The capital of the Egyptian empire of Mycenaean times was
"No" to the Egyptians, but to the Greeks it became "Thebes"
for some reason, though it had no connection at all with the
Boeotian city. In later centuries, it became Diospolis (digh-
os'poh-lis) or "city of the gods" because of its many temples.

Egyptian Thebes was four hundred miles up the Nile River.
Much closer to the mouth, about at the point where the river
spreads out into a delta, was an important city with an Egyptian name which the Greeks twisted into Memphis (mem'fis).
From another version of that name, the Greeks may have managed to obtain "Aigyptos" (that is, Egypt) which they applied

to the entire nation. The nearby city of On, later became He-
liopolis (hee″lee-op′oh-lis) or "city of the sun" because of
the temples to the sun-god which were located there.

The giant tombs built by early Egyptian monarchs were
called *pi-mar* by the Egyptians, but the Greeks changed
that to the more Greek-sounding "pyramids." The Greeks were
very rightly struck with admiration for these gigantic structures and listed them, later, as first among the seven most
wonderful man-made structures in the world. (These are
usually called "the Seven Wonders of the World.")

Near the pyramids is a huge structure in the shape of a lion
with the head of a man. The Greeks had among their list of
mythical monsters certain lions with women's heads, which
they called "sphinxes." They applied this name to the Egyptian
structure, which has been called the "Great Sphinx" ever since.

The Egyptians also set up tall, thin structures on which they
inscribed the praise of their victorious monarchs. The most important were set up about 1450 B.C. when the Egyptian empire
was at its height. The Greeks jokingly referred to these as "little spits" (*obeliskos*). We still call them "obelisks" in consequence.

The inscriptions on the obelisks and elsewhere were in the
ancient picture-writing of the Egyptians. To the Greeks, who
could not read it, these were signs of possibly mysterious and
powerful religious significance. They called the writing *hiero-
glyphics* (sacred writing) and we do the same today.

PHOENICIA

The Egyptians had never been seagoing people themselves.
They might protect their own land, but they did not dispute

the Greeks on the sea nor did they send out colonists.

This was not so in the case of another Mediterranean people. The lands washed by the easternmost portion of the sea were inhabited by a remnant of the people who, in the Bible, are called Canaanites. They were old hands at sea-faring and their ships penetrated the unknown even more daringly than did those of the Greeks.

In Greek times, the chief city of these eastern shores was called "Sur" (rock) by its inhabitants, because it had originally been built, about 1450 B.C., on a rocky island just off the coast. The Greek version of the name has come down to us as Tyre (tire).

Tyre's greatest source of prosperity was its dye-works. It obtained a red-purple dye from a shellfish off its shores by a process it kept secret. In those days, good dyes, which did not fade or run, were very scarce, and this "Tyrian purple" as it is still called was very much desired. The Tyrian merchants got good prices for it and flourished.

When the Greeks first met the merchants and seamen of Tyre, they were impressed by the colorful clothes they wore. They called them Phoenicians (fee-nish'ee-unz), therefore, from a word meaning "blood red" and they called the Tyrian land, Phoenicia.

The Phoenicians are to be found in Greek legend. According to these legends, the ancient king of Crete, Minos, was the son of the Phoenician princess, Europa (see page 18). Europa's brother, Cadmus, (cad'mus), was supposed to have reached the Greek mainland and to have founded the city of Thebes.

This may well represent Phoenician raids during Mycenaean times. Phoenicians settled in the island of Cyprus, which is only 200 miles northwest of Tyre, during the unsettled period after the Dorian invasions. Greeks had already settled there during Mycenaean times, and Greek and Phoenician cities (often at odds with each other) were to be found on Cyprus throughout Hellenic times.

The Phoenicians not only closed the eastern end of the Mediterranean to Greek colonization, they also closed the western end.

Even before the flood of Greek colonization had begun, Phoenician colonists had landed on the southern coast of the Mediterranean Sea about a thousand miles west of the Nile. Two cities were founded, the first being known to the Romans, centuries later, as Utica (yoo'tih-kuh) and the second, founded in 814 B.C., as (in our spelling) Carthage (kahr'thij).

Carthage flourished. It became overlord of the entire coast and, indeed, grew far more powerful than Tyre. For long periods it remained the largest and richest city of the western Mediterranean and no ships could enter that portion of the sea without Carthaginian permission.

What's more, Carthage began to establish areas of control in direct competition with the Greeks. The city is separated from the western end of Sicily by only ninety miles of sea. It is not surprising, then, that Carthaginians moved into western Sicily as the Greeks moved into the eastern portion of the island.

Throughout Hellenic times, the Carthaginians and Greeks battled each other to a standstill in Sicily. Neither was ever able to drive the other completely out of the island though each came close to it at times.

The Greek drive northwestward up the peninsula of Italy also ground to a halt and did not pass beyond Cyme, the first colony they founded. To the northwest of Cyme were the Etruscans (ee-trus'kunz).

Very little is known about the Etruscans. They might have reached Italy from Asia Minor originally but even that is uncertain. Their language is not understood and few remnants of their culture are left behind to study. They were absorbed by the Romans later on, and so thoroughly that just about nothing remains.

When the Greeks were settling Italy, however, the Etruscans were still powerful. And they resisted when the Greeks reached out for the large islands of Sardinia (sahr-din'ee-uh) and Corsica (kawrh'sih-kuh) which lay between Italy and the Greek settlement at Massalia.

The Phocians, who had settled Massalia, took the lead in settling the islands, about 550 B.C. About 540 B.C., however, the Etruscans, in alliance with the Carthaginians, defeated the Phocian fleet in a naval battle near Sardinia. It meant disaster and the Greek settlers were either killed or driven off the island. Sardinia was taken over by Carthage while Corsica fell to the Etruscans.

That battle marked the end of the Greek age of colonization. The available areas for settlement had been filled and the Greeks could spread out no further.

Though the Phoenicians and their colonists frustrated the Greeks in this respect, they did them, and the whole world, a great favor in another. They invented the system of expressing words by means of a few different symbols.

Earlier civilizations, that of the Egyptians, for example, had invented writing but used hundreds or even thousands of different symbols, each for a different word or, at the very least, for a different syllable. (The Chinese do this even today.)

The Phoenicians were the first to realize that it was quite possible to let each symbol represent a consonant only and that one could then get by with some two dozen "letters." Every word would be a combination of several letters.

The Phoenician invention may have been the only one of its kind. All other groups of men who have learned to write in this manner seem to have picked up the Phoenician letters, though sometimes in a very roundabout way.

The Greeks got their letters from the Phoenicians and admit it in their legends. It was Cadmus, the Phoenician prince who founded Thebes, who, according to the legends, introduced the system of writing with letters to the Greeks.

The Greeks made one change, though. They allowed some of

the letters to represent vowel sounds, so as to make the system simpler and clearer by making it possible to distinguish (to use an English example) among "cat," "cot," "cut," "cute," and "acute."

4

THE RISE OF SPARTA

LACONIA

By far the largest part of the effort of Greek colonization was born by the Ionian peoples of the Aegean islands and Asia Minor. Of the Dorian cities, only Corinth was deeply engaged in colonization.

Corinth, however, was located on the isthmus, looking both east to Asia Minor and west to Sicily. It was well situated for trade and through all of Hellenic times and even beyond was a prosperous city which, at times, had a strong fleet.

It was different with the other Dorian cities in the Peloponnesus. They retained the tradition of land conquest and did not turn readily to the sea. And of them all, the one with the greatest tendency to fight well on land and poorly on sea was Sparta.

Sparta, also called Lacedaemon (las"uh-dee'mon) after a mythical founder, is located on the Eurotas River (yoo-roh' tas) about twenty-five miles from the sea. It is thus an inland town.

In Mycenaean times, it had been an important city, but after it had been taken by the Dorians about 1100 B.C. it sank to insignificance for a while. Over the next three centuries it gradually recovered and indeed extended its influence over neighboring towns until by 800 B.C. Sparta was mistress over the entire valley of the Eurotas, a region called Laconia (la-koh'nee-uh).

The Dorian conquerors maintained themselves as the sole citizens of Sparta and of the areas over which it gained control. They were the only ones with any say in the government. This ruling class were the Spartiates (spahr'shee-ayts) and when Spartans are mentioned in this book, it is usually the Spartiates that are meant. They were always a minority of the total population of the area controlled by Sparta, and in later times they came to make up as little as 5 per cent or even less.

The only activities which the Spartiates considered honorable were war and government. Someone, however, had to carry on trade and industry and this fell to the lot of another small group, the *perioeci* (per"ee-ee'see). These were freemen who had no political power. They probably represented the pre-Dorian inhabitants of Sparta, who had prudently allied themselves with the invaders in time.

The mass of the population in Spartan territory, however, consisted of the conquered peoples who had made the mistake of resisting. They had been defeated and were then brutally enslaved. Among the first towns to suffer this fate had been Helos, whose unfortunate inhabitants had been enslaved en masse.

Eventually, the term *helot* (hel'ot) came to refer to any Spartan slave, whether he was a descendant of the people of Helos or not. Occasionally, a helot might be freed for good service to Sparta and allowed to join the ranks of the perioeci. On the whole, though, the helots were treated as creatures without human rights and were subjected to crueller treatment than any other slaves in the Greek world.

The Spartans, who were the most conservative of the Greek people, and the least given to change, kept their kings as long as the city had any form of self-government at all. What's more, the kingship was unusual, for Sparta differed from most governments, both Greek and non-Greek, in having two kings. It was a *dyarchy* in other words.

This came about, probably, because two separate tribes among the Dorians combined to conquer and occupy Sparta and agreed to allow the families of each chieftain to rule together over the combined forces. The Spartans themselves explained it by saying that the kings were descended from the twin sons of one of their very early monarchs.

With time, however, the Spartan kings were limited sharply in power. Their chief function consisted of leading the armies. They were generals, primarily, and had power only outside the boundaries of Sparta.

At home, the government was under the tight control of an oligarchy of thirty men. The two kings were included but as only two votes out of thirty. The other twenty-eight were chosen from among those Spartans who had reached the age of sixty. They were the *gerusia* (jee-roo'zhee-uh) from a Greek word meaning "old."

There were also five *ephors* (ef'awrz) who served as magistrates. They were the executives who saw to it that the decisions of the gerusia were carried out. At home and in peacetime, the ephors had more power than the kings and could fine or punish them for any actions that were against the law.

On the whole, this inefficient way of having a city ruled by two kings plus a group of oligarchs contributed to making Sparta traditionally slow-moving, nor did she ever make any attempt to streamline her government until the very end.

ARGOS AND MESSENIA

During the dark centuries, while Sparta was making herself mistress of the Eurotas valley, the strongest town in the Peloponnesus was Argos. This dominance was marked enough to make Homer refer to the Greeks of the Peloponnesus as Argives.

Argos was like Sparta, only less so. It had kings but gave them up at a time when Sparta still kept its own. It had a caste system but one that was not nearly so tight as Sparta's.

Argos reached the peak of her power under Pheidon (figh'don), who ruled about 750 B.C. Under him Argos came to control the Argolis plus the eastern shores of the Peloponnesus and the island of Cythera (sih-thee'ruh) off the southeastern tip of the Peloponnesus as well.

He was even able to exert important influence in the western Peloponnesus. For instance, in 748 B.C. he seized control of the Olympian Games, ousting Elis, and presided at the Games himself.

The Elians turned to Sparta for help and this is the starting point for a long and bitter rivalry between Sparta and Argos that lasted for centuries. Very little is known of the details of what followed but Sparta must have won, for the Elians regained their primacy at the Olympian Games and removed from the records the one over which Pheidon had presided.

After Pheidon's death, Argos weakened and Sparta was able to seize Cythera and the eastern coast of the Peloponnesus. Argos was confined to the Argolis and remained there brooding. The Argives never forgot they had once been supreme in the Peloponnesus and never forgave the Spartans for defeating them. For centuries, they had but one aim, to defeat Sparta. They joined every possible Spartan enemy and would not join any activity in which Sparta was the leader.

While Sparta was driving eastward to the sea, she was also moving westward, spurred on, perhaps, by the excitement of her help to Elis.

West of the Spartan territories, occupying the southwest corner of the Peloponnesus was Messenia (meh-see'nee-uh). In Mycenaean times, the chief town of the area was Pylos (pigh'los), noted for its excellent harbor. During the Trojan war, according to Homer, its king was Nestor, oldest and wisest of the Greek heroes.

The Dorians conquered Messenia as they had conquered Sparta, but in Messenia, the Dorians intermarried with the earlier peoples. They did not maintain their warlike activities and to the Dorians of Sparta they must have seemed to have grown soft.

The Messenians could not have been as soft as all that, however, for according to tradition, it took the Spartans two wars, each lasting twenty years, to conquer the Messenians. Little is known about the details of the two wars, for the Greek historians whose descriptions have survived lived long afterward and they included a number of tales that seem to be glamorous fictions.

The First Messenian War started about 730 B.C. when the Spartans suddenly marched into Messenia. After several years of fighting, the Messenians, led by their king, Aristodemus (uh-ris''toh-dee'mus), retired to Mount Ithome (ih-thoh'mee), a half-mile-high peak in the center of the country which, on future occasions, was also to serve as a Messenian stronghold. There, the Messenians held out for many years but about 710 B.C. were finally forced to surrender.

The Spartans, angered at the long resistance, ruthlessly made helots of the Messenians.

In 685 B.C., the Messenians, goaded beyond endurance, rose in revolt, under the leadership of Aristomenes (ar″is-tom′ih-neez). Later tales made Aristomenes a kind of superman who, almost single-handed inspired the Messenians to feats of great bravery and by clever generalship held the Spartans' superior forces at bay. Finally, after seventeen years, when a key battle had been lost because an ally had betrayed him, Aristomenes and a small devoted band left the country and sailed to freedom overseas. In 668 B.C., then, Messenia was once again prostrate.

As for the Messenian refugees, they are supposed to have gone to the corner of Sicily, where it almost touches Italy. There settlers from Chalcis had founded a city in 715 B.C. and called it Zancle (zang′klee) meaning "reaping hook" because the lowland rim on which it was built resembled a reaping hook in shape. The Messenians came to dominate the city and changed its name to Messana (meh-say′nuh) in honor of their enslaved native land.

THE SPARTAN WAY OF LIFE

The Messenian wars cost Sparta a high price also. A half-century of war, so hard-fought, had ground the military life deep into the Spartan consciousness. It seemed to them they never dared relax, especially when there were so few Spartans and so many helots. Surely if the Spartans ever relaxed, even slightly, the helots would rise at once.

Furthermore, the Messenian wars had developed the role of the hoplite. Military training had to be particularly hard to inure the soldier to wearing heavy armor and wielding heavy weapons. Fighting was not a trade for weaklings as the Spartans practiced it.

For that reason, the Spartans dedicated their lives to warfare. Spartan youngsters were inspected at birth to see if they were physically sound. If they were not, they were abandoned and allowed to die. At the age of seven, they were taken from their mothers and were brought up in barracks.

They were taught to endure cold and hunger, were never allowed to wear fine clothes or eat good food, were trained in all military arts and were taught to endure weariness and pain without complaint.

The Spartan code was to fight hard, follow orders without questions, and to die rather than retreat or surrender. To run away, a soldier had to throw down his heavy shield, which would otherwise slow him down; if he died, he would be carried home, in honor, upon his shield. Therefore, Spartan mothers were supposed to instruct their sons to return from war "with their shields or on them."

The Spartan adults ate at a common table, everyone bringing his share, all contributing from the substance produced from his lands by the labor of his helots. (If a Spartan lost his lands for any reason, he was no longer entitled to a place at the table, which was a great disgrace. In later centuries fewer and fewer Spartans were entitled to such a place as land became concentrated in fewer and fewer hands. This was a source of weakness for Sparta but only toward the end of her history did she try to reform the situation.)

The food at the common table was designed to fill a person and keep him alive, but nothing more. Some non-Spartan Greek, having tasted the porridge that Spartans ate in their barracks, is supposed to have said that he no longer wondered why Spartans fought so bravely and without the slightest fear of death. Such porridge made death welcome.

In later centuries, the Spartans maintained that this way of life originated with a man named Lycurgus (ligh-kur'gus) who lived, according to their tradition, sometime about 850 B.C., long before the Messenian wars. However, this is almost certainly not so and it is even doubtful that Lycurgus existed at all.

The proof of this is that down to about 650 B.C. Sparta does not seem to have been very much different from the other Greek states. She had her art, her music, her poetry. During the seventh century, a musician from Lesbos named Terpander (tur-pan'der) came to Sparta and did well there. He is supposed to have improved the lyre and is called the "Father of Greek music."

Most famous of all Spartan musicians was Tyrtaeus (tur-tee'us). By tradition, he was an Athenian but he may well have been a native Spartan. In any case, he lived during the Second Messenian War and his music was said to have inspired the Spartans to new feats of bravery when their ardor flagged.

It was only after the Second Messenian War that the deadly hand of utter militarism completely shut off all that was creative and human in Sparta. Art, music and literature came to a halt. Even oratory (and all Greeks have loved to talk from ancient times to the present day) was stopped, for Spartans practiced speaking very briefly and to the point. The very word "laconic" (from Laconia) has come to mean the quality of speaking pithily.

THE PELOPONNESUS

As the Greek age of colonization approached its end Sparta, which had taken practically no part in it, found itself in absolute possession of the southern third of the Peloponnesus. It was the largest by far of the Greek city-states, and, thanks to its way of life, the one most devoted to militarism.

The other Greek city-states of the Peloponnesus — or at least those that were still free — viewed the situation with great concern. Argos, of course, had tried to help Messenia during the Second Messenian War (anything to harm Sparta), but Corinth had been on the Spartan side (anything to harm Argos).

The towns immediately north of Sparta, in the central region of the Peloponnesus called Arcadia, were particularly worried. Of these, the chief were Tegea (tee'jee-uh), about twenty-five miles north of the city of Sparta, and Mantinea (man"tih-nee' uh) some twelve miles further north.

As usual, Tegea and Mantinea feuded with each other and with other Arcadian towns so that Arcadia as a whole remained weak. Now, however, under Tegean leadership they faced Sparta more or less united.

Sparta, after the long Messenian ordeal, was not willing to engage lightly in any serious wars, and for many decades the rivalry between Sparta and Arcadia was allowed to simmer. In 560 B.C., however, Chilon (kigh'lon) became one of the Spartan ephors. He was a dominating personality who gained a reputation for careful forethought and was later listed among "the Seven Wise Men" of Greece. According to some traditions, he even founded the ephorate, so it may be that under him the Spartan kings were first sharply limited in their powers.

Chilon demanded a strong policy, and Sparta quickly defeated the Arcadians who hastened to make their submission. Tegea was allowed to remain independent and her citizens, who must have feared being reduced to helots, were grateful indeed. The Arcadians remained loyal allies of Sparta for nearly two centuries and none was more loyal than Tegea.

That left only Argos, still dreaming of her old supremacy. In 669 B.C., while Sparta had been occupied in the Second Messenian War, Argos had actually won a battle against Sparta. In the century since, however, she had lain quiet, full of resentment and hate but not quite daring to move.

In 520 B.C. Cleomenes I (klee-om'ih-neez) came to one of the two Spartan thrones. Shortly after his accession, he

marched into the Argolis and near Tiryns inflicted still another
defeat on Argos.

The defeats of Argos made plain what had become a fact
after the victory over Tegea. Sparta was supreme over the entire Peloponnesus. One third it owned and the remaining two
thirds were either in alliance with it or cowered in fear of it.
Nowhere could a soldier move in the Peloponnesus without
Spartan permission. Indeed, Sparta was now the dominant land
power in all of Greece and for nearly two centuries it was accepted as the leader of the Greek world.

However, Sparta was not really suited to the task of leading
Greece. The Greeks were at home on the sea and Sparta was
not. The Greeks had interests from end to end of the Mediterranean and Sparta was interested (in her heart) only in the Peloponnesus. The Greeks were quick, artistic and free; and Spartans were slow-moving, dull, and enslaved either to each other
or to the military way of life.

In later years, the Greeks of other city-states sometimes admired the Spartan way of life because it seemed so virtuous
and seemed to lead Sparta to such military glory. However,
they were wrong to do so. In art, literature, music, love of life
— all that makes it worthwhile to be on the earth — Sparta
contributed nothing.

She had only a cruel, inhuman way of life to offer — de-
pendent on a brutal slavery of most of her population — with
only a kind of blind animal courage as a virtue. And her way of
life soon became more show than substance; it was her reputation that saved her for a while when her core was rotten.

She seemed strong as long as she won victories, but whereas
other states could withstand defeats and rise again, Sparta lost
her domination of Greece, as we shall see, after a single defeat.
The loss of one major battle was to expose her and dispose of
her. (And, oddly enough, she was to be more admirable in the
days of weakness that followed than during her period of
strength.)

5

THE AGE OF TYRANTS

FROM FARMING TO COMMERCE

The Greek colonization of the Mediterranean was part of a great change that was taking place in the way of life of some of the Greek cities. The fact of colonization also hastened that change.

In Mycenaean times, Greece had had a highly developed commerce, but after the Dorian invasions, life grew, for a time, simpler and poorer. The Greek population took to "subsistence farming." That is, each area grew what raw materials it needed. It grew grains and vegetables, kept cattle for milk, sheep for wool, swine for meat and so on.

Under such conditions, very little trade was required and cities were self-sufficient. However, especially in a rather infertile nation such as Greece, this meant that the standard of living sank low. Each city just kept itself *barely* self-sufficient and could not afford much of an increase in population. (When an increase did take place, that forced colonization.)

But trade was slowly reviving and the process of colonization hastened that revival. It became possible to import food from overseas, from Sicily or the area north of the Black Sea, for instance. Such areas were more fertile than Greece itself and food could be grown in greater quantities there and with less effort. To pay for such food imports, Greek cities took to industry, manufacturing weapons, textiles or pottery to exchange for the grain. Cities might also indulge in "specialty farming" and exchange wine or olive oil (for which Greece is well-suited) for grain.

A city which could grow just enough food to support a small population could manufacture enough material to buy a great deal of food from abroad and could then support many more people. Population therefore grew, particularly among those cities that were most active in trade and colonization.

Southwest of Athens, lying between Attica and the Argolis, is an inlet of the Aegean Sea which is called the Saronic Gulf (suh-ron'ik). In the midst of this gulf is the small island of Aegina (ee-jigh'nuh), about twice the size of the island of Manhattan. It is rocky and infertile and yet it was one of the Greek towns that grew prosperous and even powerful as a result of commerce. Aegina was, in fact, responsible for an important innovation.

In early times, men had traded by barter, exchanging goods, with each man giving up something he didn't need very badly for something he needed or wanted much more. It slowly became customary to use metals such as gold or silver in this trading. These metals were attractive, they didn't spoil or rust, and they were quite rare so that a little went a long way. In short, they made a useful "medium of exchange."

But in order to make it a fair trade, a certain agreed-upon weight of gold had to be exchanged for, say, a pair of cattle or a tract of land. This meant that merchants had to carry scales about on which gold or silver could be weighed. This could lead to many arguments as to whether the scales were honest and whether the gold or silver was pure.

Sometime in the seventh century B.C. the nation of Lydia in Asia Minor began producing government-sponsored nuggets of gold or silver, using metal of guaranteed purity and with each nugget stamped with its weight or value. The use of such "coins" made small transactions a good deal easier and added to the prosperity of everyone who made use of the invention.

This new system of coins traveled to Greece. There is a tradition that King Pheidon of Argos first made use of them, but this can't be so for he ruled a century too early. Actually, it was Aegina that first made use of coins in commerce on a large scale. Her prosperity increased, reaching a peak at about 500 B.C., and other city-states hastened to imitate her in this respect.

Oddly enough, increasing prosperity meant trouble. As more wealth poured into a city, a new class of powerful men arose, the rich merchants. The old landowning class did not always want to allow these newly rich people to share the political power, and this made for unrest.

Then, too, as money poured in, prices naturally rose so that there was an inflation. This meant that people who did not happen to share in the new prosperity, particularly the farmers, were actually worse off than before. They went into debt.

The new commerce also put a greater value on slaves. Many more slaves could be employed in factories making pottery or cloth than in the farms, and the merchants could afford such slaves, too. There was strong pressure, therefore, to enslave the debt-ridden farmers as punishment for not being able to pay their debts. The use of slaves made it hard for free artisans, who turned out manufactured products on a small scale to remain prosperous.

The introduction of coinage made the whole process take place more quickly and more drastically. Sometimes the old landowning oligarchy took in the new merchant class so as to have a strong ally, while the farmers and artisans combined in opposition.

Only Sparta managed to avoid the upsets and dislocations produced by commercial expansion. She forbade the use of money and the importation of luxuries. She kept to subsistence farming and the old way. This made for a low standard of living but that was considered a Spartan virtue and her government remained stable.

Elsewhere, however, a new bitterness and violence entered politics with a few rich "haves" facing a growing number of increasingly poor "have-nots." And the situation was worst precisely in those cities which were most engaged in trade.

TYRANTS IN IONIA

To make the popular dissatisfaction with the oligarchies felt, the people needed leaders. Often they would find one (sometimes one of the noblemen themselves; one who had quarreled with the others) who was bold enough to arm them and lead them in an uprising against their rulers. The leader would then, usually, obtain the sole rule for himself. In fact, it might be ambition for just this sort of rule that would lead him to fight the oligarchy in the first place.

He was not a king, for he had not inherited his office and therefore had no legal or sacred right to it. He was simply a "master," nothing more. The Greek word for that was *tyrannos* and to us this word has become "tyrant." (The expression "tyrant" is equivalent to what we might nowadays call a "dictator." We use "tyrant" now in an evil sense, meaning by it any ruler who is cruel and vicious, but to the Greeks it only meant a ruler who had not inherited his power. He might perfectly well be a kind and good leader.)

Tyrants first became numerous in Greek history between 650 and 500 B.C. The last half of the Age of Colonization is therefore also called the "Age of Tyrants." This is not a very apt title, however, for there were many cities in this period without tyrants and there were many cities afterward that did have them.

Often the tyrants proved capable rulers who brought prosperity and peace to their cities. Since they had gained power because of changing times and popular discontent, they adapted the government to the new ways as the wisest method of staying in power. The lot of the common people therefore usually improved under them. Tyrants tried to make themselves popular by beautifying the city (and thus employing artisans in the necessary construction work and gaining their support), introducing new festivals for the pleasure of the people, and so on.

Tyrants came into power early in Ionia, where commerce with the interior of Asia Minor flourished and where the new ways made themselves strongly felt. The most famous was Thrasybulus (thras"ih-byoo'lus) who ruled over the great colonizing city of Miletus about 610 B.C. Under him, Miletus reached the peak of its fame and power and was, indeed, the most flourishing and important city in the Greek world.

And under Thrasybulus, there now arose in Miletus a group of men who were more important in the long run than any number of tyrants.

The first of these was Thales (thay'leez) who was born in Miletus about 640 B.C. He is supposed to have been born of a Phoenician mother, and he is said to have visited Egypt and Babylonia. Presumably, he was able to bring back to Greece the lore and knowledge of the much older civilizations to the south and east.

From the Babylonians, for instance, he learned enough astronomy to be able to predict eclipses, and his prediction of an eclipse that took place in 585 B.C. astonished men and raised Thales' prestige to great heights.

He also borrowed Egyptian geometry, but here he made two fundamental advances. First he converted it into an abstract study, being the first man we know of to consider it as dealing with imaginary lines of zero thickness and perfect straightness, rather than with actual lines, thick and irregular, scraped in the sand, scratched on wax, or made up of stretched cords.

Second, he proved mathematical statements by a regular series of arguments, marshalling what was already known and proceeding step by step to the desired proof as inevitable consequence. This led to the development of geometry, and that was the greatest scientific accomplishment of the Greeks.

In the physical sciences, he was the first to study the manner in which amber attracted light objects when rubbed. The Greek name for amber is *elektron* and such an attraction came to be called the result of "electricity" in later centuries.

Thales also studied a black rock which could attract iron. The rock had been obtained from the nearby city of Magnesia and so it was referred to as *he magnetis lithos* (the Magnesian rock) and this gave rise to the term "magnet."

Finally, he speculated on what the universe might be made of, what its nature was, how it might have started. In doing so, he made two assumptions. First, he decided that there were no gods or demons involved but that the universe operated through unchanging laws. Second, that the human mind, by observation and thought, could work out what those laws might involve. All of science, ever since the time of Thales, operates on these two assumptions.

Thales was followed by others, in Miletus and in other cities of Ionia over the next century, and these are referred to as the "Ionian school." Thus, Thales' pupil, Anaximander (uh-nak''sih-man'der), born in 611 B.C. and a younger man, Anaximenes (an''ak-sim'ih-neez), also speculated on the nature of the universe. So did Heraclitus (her''uh-kligh'tus), born about 540 B.C. in the neighboring city of Ephesus.

None of the writings of these early inquirers survives. We know of them only through casual quotations of their ideas in the works of later writers.

The most famous of these first scientists was Pythagoras (pih-thag'oh-rus) who was born about 582 B.C. on the island of Samos just off the Ionian coast. He referred to himself as a "philosopher" (a lover of wisdom) and it is by this name that the Greek thinkers have become known.

In the time of Thrasybulus, the tyrant of Miletus, and of Thales, the scientist of Miletus, another tyrant ruled in the Aeolian island of Lesbos. He was Pittacus (pit'uh-kus) and he ruled over Mytilene (mit''ih-lee'nee), chief city on the island.

About 611 B.C., he led a revolt against a man who ruled as tyrant both badly and cruelly. Once that was done, he found that the only way to make sure that the city would get good government was to become tyrant himself. He finally accepted the office in 589 B.C. and ruled for ten years. In 579 B.C., feeling that his task was done and that, at the age of seventy, he could do little more, he resigned.

Pittacus ruled so well that in later centuries, when the Greeks made up their lists of the Seven Wise Men (that is, the seven politicians who carried the Greek world through the critical sixth century B.C. which saw the changeover from

obscurity to wealth and power) Pittacus was listed along with
Chilon of Sparta (see page 54). A third in the list was Thales
of Miletus, not because of his scientific ability, but because of
his wise political advice, which will be described later. Still a
fourth "Wise Man" was Cleobulus (klee"oh-byoo'lus) who
ruled as tyrant over a city on the island of Rhodes about 560
B.C.

Under Pittacus, the island of Lesbos had a period of great
cultural development. About 600 B.C., the Greek lyric poet,
Alcaeus (al-see'us) was prominent on the island. He wrote
love songs and also political poems denouncing rulers he
considered evil. Pittacus thought it prudent to exile him during
the tyranny, but the poet returned after Pittacus resigned.
Alcaeus was no hero in physical combat, however, for what is
most frequently said of him is that once, in battle, he "threw
away his shield." That is, he ran away.

Also on Lesbos at this time was Sappho (saf'oh), a poetess,
and the first great female literary figure in history. Perhaps we
might consider her the greatest as well as the first, if we could
see her work. Unfortunately, it is almost all lost; however,
many of the ancient Greeks considered her the equal of
Homer, and their taste can usually be relied on.

TYRANTS ON THE MAINLAND

The Greek mainland had some notable tyrants among the
commercial towns. The city of Megara, on the Isthmus, was
under the rule of the tyrant Theagenes (thee-aj'uh-neez)
from about 640 B.C. onward. He had an aqueduct constructed
that would bring fresh water into the city, an example of the

manner in which tyrants made themselves popular by useful projects.

In nearby Corinth, thirty miles southwest of Megara, there was an even more successful example of tyranny. This was Cypselus (sip'sih-lus) who gained the Corinthian tyranny about 655 B.C. and passed it on thirty years later to his son, Periander (per"ee-an'der).

Periander was even more sucessful and capable than his father, and under him Corinth reached the peak of its importance and became the most cultured town in mainland Greece. It was the most commercially successful, too.

Under Periander, culture flourished. The poet Arion (uh-righ'on) was invited to his court. (Around this poet, legends later clustered — such as his having been brought back to land by a dolphin after he had been thrown into the sea by pirates.)

At this time the Greeks began to build temples of stone rather than of wood and Corinthians developed the technique of building in stone to a high pitch.

They did not use arches, but supported heavy roofs on a line of pillars. Corinth led the way by devising sturdy, simple pillars, with flutes or vertical grooves running their full length, to make them seem taller and more graceful, and with the tops un-ornamented. Such pillars are of the Doric order. In Ionia, taller and more slender pillars were used and the tops were somewhat ornamented. These formed the Ionic order. (In later centuries, pillars that were still taller and more slender and ornamented to a tasteless extreme, were termed the "Corinthian order," but this came when Greek art had passed its peak.)

Periander died in 586 B.C., having reigned successfully enough to be enrolled among the Seven Wise Men. He was reputed to have ruled with great cruelty, particularly in the latter part of his life, but the evidence is largely from the oligarchs whom he had exiled and who were, naturally enough, prejudiced against him. He was succeeded by a nephew, who was soon overthrown, and with that the tyranny at Corinth came to an end.

About 600 B.C. the tyrant, Cleisthenes (klise′thih-neez) ruled over the town of Sicyon (sish′ee-on) some ten miles northwest of Corinth.

Cleisthenes made an important mark for himself north of the Gulf of Corinth. This came about as follows: The Phocian town of Crisa (krigh′suh), near Delphi, attempted to seize control of the oracle in 590 B.C. This promptly led to the "First Sacred War," for the members of the group of city-states which controlled Delphi combined to punish Crisa.

Cleisthenes led the force which defeated Crisa. The offending town was completely destroyed and a curse was pronounced against anyone who tried to rebuild it or to cultivate her territory. As a memorial to the victory, Cleisthenes established the Pythian games (see page 28) about 582 B.C.

SAMOS

Perhaps the most remarkable of the early tyrants was Polycrates (poh-lik′ruh-teez), who became tyrant of the island of Samos about 535 B.C. For years he was very successful and all he did prospered. He built himself a hundred ships and conducted piratical raids the length and breadth of the Aegean Sea, of which he made himself master.

As was usual with tyrants, Polycrates encouraged culture and public works. He had an aqueduct built, hiring a man of Megara, Eupalinus (yoo″puh-ligh′nus), to do the job. The Greeks always emphasized abstract thought and paid little attention to their own record as practical engineers, so that little survives about men like Eupalinus, which is a great pity.

Polycrates formed an alliance with the king of Saitic Egypt. The king at the time was Ahmose II (ah'mose), who ruled from 569 to 525 B.C. He is better known by the Greek version of his name, Amasis (uh-may'sis).

Amasis was an admirer of Greek culture. He kept a Greek bodyguard, sent gifts to the temple at Delphi, and allowed the trading station at Naucratis to become a city. He was pleased to be in alliance with a clever and powerful Greek ruler whose navy might be useful to himself.

Amasis was superstitiously nervous, however, over Polycrates' unvarying good fortune. The Egyptian king felt the gods were saving up something horrible for the tyrant, in order to restore the balance. Amasis therefore advised Polycrates (according to a story the Greeks told later) to throw away some thing of value. This would create bad fortune for himself in a small way and, by restoring the balance, quiet the gods and prevent anything really bad from taking place later.

Polycrates listened to the advice, took a valuable ring and threw it into the sea. Some days later, a fish was brought into the palace for the tyrant's table and when it was cut open, there was the ring. Amasis, upon hearing this, realized that Polycrates was doomed and broke off the alliance. Sure enough, about 522 B.C. Polycrates was lured to the Ionian mainland, taken by an enemy and put cruelly to death. (Amasis, having died three years earlier, did not witness this.)

The reign of Polycrates had an important consequence in the history of science. When he became tyrant, Pythagoras the philosopher (according to the story) felt he could no longer remain in his native island, for the philosopher was an oligarch in his sympathies. He left Samos in 529 B.C. and emigrated to the city of Croton in southern Italy. He carried with him the scientific tradition of the Ionians and there, in the Greek west, it took root, though Pythogoras broke with the thoroughgoing straightforwardness of Thales. Instead he founded a cult marked by secrecy, asceticism and mysticism.

Still, Pythagoras and his followers managed to achieve important scientific advances. They were the first to study the "theory of numbers," working out the relationships among the numbers, and showing, for instance, that the square root of two could not be represented as an exact fraction.

They went on to initiate the study of sound, showing that the strings of musical instruments delivered sound of higher pitch as they were made shorter, and that the notes produced by two strings were particularly harmonious if the lengths were related to each other in certain very simple ways.

They studied astronomy, too, and were the first to suggest that the earth was a sphere. They even theorized that it might move through the heavens. Pythagoras, himself, is also supposed to have discovered the famous Pythagorean theorem which states that the sum of the squares of the sides of a right triangle is equal to the square of the hypotenuse.

The Pythagorean movement did not confine itself to science and mathematics, however. It achieved important political power and exerted its influence on the side of oligarchy. When the oligarchs in Croton were thrown out, Pythagoras was exiled too. Pythagoreanism lasted as a political movement for two more centuries but grew continually weaker.

In this period of Greek history, tyrannies did not endure long. For one thing, whereas a king was supported by law, tradition and religion, a tyrant could rely on none of these things. He had achieved his rule by force and it might be taken back by force. For that reason, tyrants had to be ever watchful and suspicious and frequently took to ruling with great harshness and cruelty. (This is the reason that the word "tyrant" has come to mean a particularly wicked ruler today.)

Then, too, Sparta, the most militarily powerful state in Greece, set its face firmly against tyrannies. Sparta was and remained oligarchic and objected to any disturbance of oli-

garchies elsewhere. It was Spartan influence that helped bring
an end to the tyrannies at Corinth and Megara.

Sparta also brought about the end of a tyranny in Athens.
This proved to be an event of prime importance in the history
of Greece and, indeed, of the world, and to it we will turn.

6

THE RISE OF ATHENS

THE BEGINNINGS

In very ancient times, there was nothing particularly distinguished about Athens or about Attica, the triangular peninsula on which the city was located. It was mentioned in the *Iliad* but it was not a conspicuous city among the Greek forces. Its leader, Menestheus (mee-nes'thyoos), was of minor importance.

In the centuries after the Trojan War, Attica managed to survive the Dorian invasion and the disorders that followed. It was the one portion of mainland Greece to remain Ionian.

Slowly, through those early centuries, all of Attica was united. This was not because Athens gained an absolute domination over the other town of Attica as Sparta did over the other towns of Laconia. Nor did it head an Attic Confederation as Thebes headed a Boeotian Confederation. Instead, Athens tried something unique that laid the foundation of its future greatness. It expanded itself into one big city that included all Attica. A person born in any part of Attica was considered as much an Athenian as if he had been born in the city itself.

According to Athenian legend, this had been accomplished by the Mycenaean hero, Theseus, father of the Menestheus of the Trojan War. However, it is very unlikely that the union of Attica was brought about by one man at one time. It is much more likely that it was brought about gradually over the generations. By 700 B.C., anyway, Attica was unified.

The last portion of Attica to be brought into the union was Eleusis (ee-lyoo'sis) in the northwest corner of the peninsula, about fourteen miles from the city of Athens.

At Eleusis, certain religious rites were practiced and passed on to Attica and the Greek world. This type of ritual was actually more important to the Greeks than was the Olympian religion of Homer and Hesiod. The Olympians represented an official religion which was written about by poets and literary men. It did not really offer an emotional ritual and it offered no promise for the future. In the *Odyssey*, when Odysseus visits Hades, the shade of Achilles is made to say, mournfully, that it is far better to be a slave on earth than a prince in the realm of the dead. That was scarcely solace enough to individuals whose life on earth *was* slavelike. They wanted the promise of something better after death at least.

The Eleusinian rites (and others of the same sort) were designed to bring the worshipper close to certain agricultural gods such as Demeter (dih-mee'ter), or Dionysus (digh"oh-nigh'sus), or to legendary heroes such as Orpheus (awr'fyoos). The rites modeled themselves on seasonal changes; on the manner in which grain died in the fall but left seed that grew again in the spring. It was a drama of death and rebirth and, like the grain, Dionysus and Orpheus died and were reborn, while Demeter's daughter, Persephone (per-sef'oh-nee) descended into Hades each fall and returned each spring.

Originally, such rites may have been designed as "sympathetic magic" to make certain that the ground would be fertile and the harvest plentiful. Eventually it was applied to human beings who, by participating in such rites, were assured of themselves undergoing the same cycle, of being reborn to glory after death.

The details of the rites had to be kept secret on pain of death. The Greek word for secret is *mystes*. Consequently, such rites came to be called "mysteries" or "mystery religions." The "Eleusinian mysteries" were the most famous in the Greek world, and the most secret. Although they continued for over a thousand years, outsiders never discovered the details of the rites.

The mystery religions left their mark on the modern world. Centuries later, when Christianity rose to dominate the western world, it included many features of the mystery religions.

During the dark centuries after the Dorian invasion, Athens, like most of the other cities of Greece, turned from its kings to an oligarchy.

According to Athenian tradition, it was in 1068 B.C. that the kingship came to an end. The last king, Codrus (cod'rus), was desperately battling off a Dorian invasion from the Peloponnesus. An oracle had stated that that army would win whose king died first. Codrus deliberately allowed himself to be killed so that Athens might remain Ionian. So good a king, the Athenians decided, should have no successor, for none would be good enough. (This story, however, is almost certainly a romance and nothing more.)

The Athenians also say that in the times after Codrus an *archon* (ahr'kon), meaning "ruler," was in power instead of a king. At first the archon served for life and the office was passed on from father to son among the descendants of Codrus, so that the office differed from that of king only in title.

Eventually, the archonship was fixed for a term of ten years, and did not necessarily pass from father to son, although it was confined to members of the royal family. Later, it was thrown open to the remaining noble families.

Finally, in 683 B.C., Athens was made into a full oligarchy. It was ruled by a body of nine men, chosen each year from among the nobles. One of them was the archon, but he didn't have much honor, except that the year was named after him. Another was the *polemarch* (pol'ee-mark) who had the supreme command of the army.

The nobles also had complete control of the Areopagus (ar'ee-op'uh-gus), meaning "hill of Ares" (the god of war) from its place of meeting. This was the council which acted as a supreme court over political, religious and legal questions.

DRACO AND SOLON

After 700 B.C., however, Athens was sharing in the commercial revival and the oligarchy grew increasingly unpopular. The examples of tyrants in other cities was before the eyes of the Athenians. In particular, Megara, the neighbor of Athens to the southwest, came under the rule of Theagenes (see page 63) and was doing very well.

An Athenian noble named Cylon (sigh'lon) was married to the daughter of Theagenes. It occurred to him that if he moved boldly enough he might make himself tyrant of Athens, particularly since he could count on his father-in-law, the Megarian tyrant, to help him. On a certain feast-day in 632 B.C., when the

Athenians were busy with their celebrations, Cylon with some other nobles and a band of Megarian soldiers seized the Acropolis (uh-krop'oh-lis).

The Acropolis (height of the city) was the central fortress of the city. It was, as the name implies, on a hilltop and, in primitive days, had been the first site of settlement at Athens for it could be easily defended by determined men against the enemy who would have to climb laboriously up its slopes.

Ordinarily, anyone who possessed the Acropolis would be in a strong position, but Cylon found himself without supporters. His Megarian helpers alienated the people. The oligarchy might be unpopular but the people were not quite ready to get rid of it at the price of throwing themselves under foreign domination.

Athenian forces surrounded the Acropolis. They made no attempt to storm it; just waited for the company of men on top to be starved out. Cylon himself managed to escape but the rest of the band were forced, finally, to surrender on the pledge that they would not be killed.

In that year, the archon of Athens was Megacles (meg'uh-klees) a member of one of the most powerful families of the city — the Alcmaeonidae (alk''mee-on'ih-dee). Megacles felt it would be wiser to kill the band and have done with traitors, despite the pledge. He persuaded the Athenians to do this.

Once the deed was done, the Athenians grew worried. They had broken a pledge that had been solemnly sworn to before the gods. To prevent a curse from falling on the entire city, Megacles and others of his family were tried for sacrilege and expelled from the city. This is referred to as the "curse of the Alcmaeonidae" and it was to have important consequences in later Athenian history.

The destruction of Cylon's band wasn't a final victory, either. It involved Athens in a war with Megara and, under Theagenes' firm leadership, Megara prospered and Athens did badly.

Dissatisfaction grew. No government which is unsuccessful in war can be popular. In addition, the common people were convinced that the nobles, who alone controlled the Areopagus, were being unfair in their administration of the traditional laws. These laws were not in writing and as long as that was so, it was hard to demonstrate that a particular decision was against tradition. The cry rose for a written code of law, therefore, one that would offer something definite to stand on.

The first law code in Athens was drawn up by a nobleman, Draco (dray'koh), in 621 B.C. The name means "dragon" and Draco lived up to his name, for the code as he wrote it was harsh indeed, and one-sidedly in favor of the oligarchs.

A creditor could take ownership of the body of a debtor and enslave him if the debt were not paid. The death penalty was set for a variety of crimes against property, even small ones. For instance, it meant death to steal a cabbage and when someone, horrified at this, asked why, Draco is supposed to have answered, "Because I could think of no more severe punishment."

Draco's laws, it was said, were written in blood, not ink. It was for this reason that the word "draconian" has come to mean inhumanly harsh and severe.

Still the mere fact that the laws were in writing was an advance, for once this was so, they could be studied and their severity and injustice was made plain. A drive began to change and improve them.

As the new commercial economy disrupted Athenian life more and more and poor farmers were enslaved in droves, the situation grew more dangerous. There was the example of Corinth where Periander had just inherited the tyranny from his father and was ruling with an iron hand, and destroying the members of the noble houses.

The Athenian nobles were intelligent enough to see that it might be better to lose some privilege in peace, than to lose everything by force.

ATTICA

EUBOEA

BOEOTIA

Chaeronea

Thebes

Delium

Chalcis

Eretria

Tanagra

Leuctra

Plataea

ATTICA

Decelea

Gulf of Corinth

Isthmus

Megara

Eleusis

Marathon

Corinth

Athens

Piraeus.

SALAMIS

AEGINA

Among them was Solon (soh'lon) a nobleman of the old royal family, who had made himself rich in trade and was a skillful poet to boot. Well-born, wealthy and talented, he was also a man of wisdom, kindness and decency, who took no pleasure in injustice.

In 594 B.C. he was made archon and given the task of revising the laws. This he did with such good results that he well earned the right to be included on the later Greek list of the Seven Wise Men. (What's more, the word "solon" has come to be used as a synonym for "law-maker" and in the United States is frequently used to mean a congressman.)

Solon began by abolishing all debts so that people could start fresh. He forbade the custom of enslaving people for debts and those who had already been enslaved were freed. Those who had been sold outside Attica were brought back at the public expense.

Then he repealed all of Draco's death penalties except that for murder. Furthermore, he set up new courts drawn from among the ordinary citizens. People who, coming before the noble-dominated Areopagus, felt themselves unjustly treated, might then appeal to the people's courts, where they might expect a more sympathetic hearing.

Solon also attempted certain economic reforms. He tried to arrange for lower prices by a variety of methods. He discouraged the exportation of food and encouraged the immigration into Athens of skilled workers from other Greek cities.

In addition, he reorganized the Athenian government and gave the ordinary people a larger voice. Instead of having a few oligarchs choose all the office-holders and decide all questions, an Assembly was set up to make the laws and the members of the Assembly were drawn from all the people.

By allowing the common people to participate in the meetings of the Assembly, Solon had taken an important step toward "rule by the people"; that is, "democracy."

To be sure, Solon moved only partway toward democracy.

The Athenian people were still divided into four classes on the basis of wealth, and the archons could only be drawn from the two upper classes. The lower classes still had no rights except that of sitting in the Assembly.

What's more, the only type of wealth recognized was that of land. The skilled artisans, however prosperous, were not admitted to the ruling group.

Even the first steps toward democracy were infinitely valuable. Solon's laws were an immense improvement on the situation as it had existed before. The danger of violent revolt receded for a moment, for Solon had shown that there was an alternative to oligarchy other than tyranny. Athens offered democracy as an alternative and for that alone she deserves the eternal gratitude of the modern world.

PISISTRATUS

But there was still the war with Megara, now half a century old. It had died down to a simmer, especially after the death of Theagenes, but there was no complete peace.

In particular the question of Salamis (sal'uh-mis) rankled. It was a small island in the Saronic gulf just off the point where the western shores of Attica curved and merged into those of Megara. It was only a mile or so offshore and could be seen on the horizon from either Eleusis or Megara. In the time of Draco and Solon, it belonged to Megara.

The Athenians, however, felt they had a claim to it and cited the *Iliad* in their support. In that book, Salamis was rep-

resented by the hero Ajax (ay'jax), second only to Achilles as
a warrior. From some verses in the poems (which Megara
claimed were spurious) Athens deduced that there was a special relationship between Ajax and the Athenians and that Salamis was therefore part of Attica.

However, Athenian attempts to seize the island had failed
and it seemed almost as though they were giving up the whole
matter. Indignantly, the aging Solon spurred them on. Fortunately, Solon's second cousin, Pisistratus (pigh-sis'truh-tus)
was polemarch. Charming and capable, he led the Athenian
forces in the successful conquest of Salamis in 570 B.C. and annexed it permanently to Attica. The long war with Megara was
brought to a successful end, and Megara remained a minor
power thereafter, nevermore to be a threat to Athens.

But there were internal threats. Solon's reforms were by no
means accepted as final by all Athenians. There were the noble
families still. Under the guidance of Miltiades (mil-tigh'uh-
deez) they hoped to regain their old power.

Opposed to them were the middle classes who accepted Solon's reforms. This latter group was led by one of the Alcmaeonidae. Solon had permitted the family to return despite the
curse (see page 73) but they remained outcasts among the oligarchs. Because of that, and out of gratitude to Solon, they remained democrats thereafter.

There were also Athenians who felt that Solon had not gone
far enough. Pisistratus, the successful conqueror of Salamis put
himself at their head and others were ready to follow the glamorous general.

Pisistratus gathered a bodyguard about him on the pretext
that there were assassination attempts on him and then, in 561
B.C., he seized the Acropolis. More fortunate than Cylon, Pisistratus was able to establish himself as tyrant of Athens, at least
for a while.

Solon lived just long enough to see this happen, dying in 560
B.C. at the age of about seventy. He must have had a feeling

that his life work was ruined.

Actually, it was not. Pisistratus' rule was not firm enough for him to attempt despotic government even if that had been in character for him. In fact, on two different occasions he was temporarily deprived of power. He had to move very carefully therefore. At home, he kept Solon's laws and even liberalized them. Abroad, he kept the peace with his neighbors.

Nevertheless, he ventured into a military stroke in the north. Athens had become a land of specialized farming, growing grapes and olives (which were most profitable) and importing grain from the Black Sea. It was important for Athens to protect the shipping lanes between herself and the Black Sea, for it was her "life-line." In particular, she needed to control (as far as possible) the straits between the Aegean Sea and the Black Sea.

Some decades earlier she had been able to establish a post at Sigeum (sigh-jee'um) near the site of ancient Troy on the Asian side of the Hellespont. This had been Lesbian territory and the tyrant, Pittacus of Lesbos, defeated the Athenian forces and drove them out of the place. Now, under Pisistratus, Sigeum was reconquered.

Then, too, he sent an Athenian force to the Thracian Chersonese (ker"soh-nees') to help the natives in a war they were fighting. The Thracian Chersonese (meaning Thracian peninsula) is a narrow tongue of land, about sixty miles long, on the European side of the Hellespont. (In modern times, it is called the Gallipoli peninsula.)

As leader of the force he chose Miltiades, his old political foe. No doubt Pisistratus felt well rid of him. The Athenians were victorious and by 556 B.C. Miltiades had established himself as tyrant over the peninsula. Thus Athens was in control of both sides of the Hellespont and her lifeline was that much more secure.

Pisistratus, as was typical for tyrants, was a patron of culture. He had the books of Homer carefully edited and put into the form in which we now have them. He built new temples on the Acropolis and began the process which, in another century, was to make it one of the marvels of the world.

He also introduced new festivals and made old ones more elaborate. In particular a new festival in honor of Dionysus was established. Included were processions of satyrs, representing mythical creatures that were half man, half goat. These sang *tragoidea* ("goat-songs") in praise of Dionysus.

Such "goat-songs" were usually rollicking, boisterous songs, but as time went on, poets began to write serious verses for use in the festival — even grand and moving ones. In stately poetry, they retold the old myths and used them to question the ways of the universe. And these are still called "goat-songs" for we speak of them, in English, as "tragedies."

Originally, the tragedies consisted of choruses singing in unison or in parts. However, in Pisistratus' time, an Athenian poet named Thespis (thes'pis) had the courage to write pieces for the Dionysiac festival in which the chorus was kept quiet, now and then, while a single character sang alone, telling and enacting a story from the old myths. This man was the first actor and nowadays we still sometimes refer to an actor, half-humorously, as a "thespian."

Pisistratus died in 527 B.C., a gentle and good-natured tyrant to the end.

CLEISTHENES

After the death of Pisistratus, his two sons, Hippias (hip'ee-as) and Hipparchus (hih-pahr'kus) succeeded to the

tyranny and ruled together in brotherly fashion. For some
years they carried on the policies of their father, and Athens
continued to be a city that encouraged art. Poets and drama-
tists from all over the Greek world came to Athens, where they
were assured of support and help from the cultured tyrants.
For instance, the poet Anacreon of Teos was invited to Athens
by Hipparchus after the death of the poet's earlier patron,
Polycrates of Samos.

However, the years of gentle tyranny in Athens were coming
to an end. Two young Athenians, Harmodius (hahr-moh′
dee-us) and Aristogeiton (uh-ris″toh-jigh′ton) had a private
quarrel with Hipparchus, one that had nothing to do with the
tyranny really, and in 514 B.C. decided to assassinate him. It
would have been madness to assassinate one tyrant and leave
the other alive to avenge the deed, so they plotted to kill them
both.

The scheme did not work out as planned. The plotters got
the notion that they had been betrayed and, in panic, struck
prematurely. They managed to kill Hipparchus but Hippias escaped and, of course, took his revenge. Harmodius and Aristogeiton were executed.

The assassination embittered Hippias. After thirteen years of
pleasant rule, he had learned the unpleasant facts of life, that
tyrants live in daily danger. He grew suspicious of everyone
and began a reign of terror.

The Athenians grew rebellious under the tyranny and this
meant there was a chance for the Alcmaeonidae, whom Pisistratus, in the latter part of his rule, had sent into banishment
once more. The head of the house was now Cleisthenes, the
grandson of Megacles (see page 73).

Cleisthenes began by ingratiating himself with the authori-
ties at Delphi, building a beautiful temple for them at his family's expense. This induced the oracle to advise the Spartans to
help the Athenians gain their freedom. This the Spartans were
perfectly willing to do. Now that they were the supreme mili-

tary power, they had ended all tyrannies on the Peloponnesus and had re-established oligarchies. It was in their interest to do the same in Attica.

In 510 B.C. the Spartan king, Cleomenes I, marched into Attica, defeated Hippias and drove him into exile. The Spartans did not do this for nothing, of course. Before leaving, they insisted on Athens' officially joining the list of Spartan allies. Cleomenes undoubtedly expected an oligarchy would be re-established at Athens.

However, Cleisthenes and the Alcmaeonidae, thanks to the old curse, were democrats, and they pushed not only for Solon's constitution but for a further advance in the direction of democracy. The oligarchs, seeing that the people were largely on the side of Cleisthenes, called for Spartan help again, pointing out that the Alcmaeonidae, being under a curse, ought to be expelled.

Back came Cleomenes in 507 B.C. and out went the Alcmaeonidae. This time, however, Cleomenes had underestimated the situation. He was too proud of his Spartans, perhaps, and too contemptuous of what he must have considered the Athenian rabble. His force was too small, therefore, really to do the job, and a rising of the general population beseiged him at the Acropolis. Frustrated, Cleomenes agreed to leave and returned to Sparta.

Cleisthenes was brought back in triumph and was able to establish a new political system. He divided Attica into a complicated system of groups that altogether ignored previous divisions into tribes and classes. His purpose was to prevent people from thinking of themselves as members of those old divisions. The new artificial groups had no hold on their affections so that nothing was left for them but to think of themselves merely as Athenians.

He also increased the extent of the involvement of the poorer classes in the government. (And yet, despite the increasing liberty in Athens, there remained slaves in Attica as every-

where in the ancient world. Slaves had no rights and were
sometimes treated with harsh brutality in even the most enlightened Greek cities. This is a blot on Greek civilization that cannot be explained away — not just that slavery existed, but that
so few Greeks ever saw anything wrong with it.)

In after years, the Athenians turned the overthrow of the tyranny into a grand drama. They played down (in embarrass-
ment) the part of the Spartans and, instead, made great heroes
out of the Athenian assassins, Harmodius and Aristogeiton, although their plot had failed and had been undertaken for un-
worthy personal reasons. The Athenians also played up the
cruelty of Hippias and helped make the very name "tyrant"
hated.

And, to be sure, it did seem as though the fall of the tyranny
and the establishment of the democracy filled the Athenians
with a vast energy and self-confidence that carried all before it.
Fortune seemed to smile at almost everything they did for the
next century.

For instance, they came to the aid of the small Boeotian
town of Plataea just north of the Attic boundary. Plataea considered itself as inhabited by men descended from those who
lived there before the Boeotian occupation of six centuries earlier (see page 15). They therefore refused to join the Boeotian
confederacy or acknowledge Theban leadership. Athens helped
them make this refusal stick.

The Thebans made ready for war and their chance came in
506 B.C. Cleomenes, brooding over his loss of face in Attica the
year before, decided to crush the Athenians properly. He mar-
shaled his Peloponnesian allies and marched on Attica from the
south, while Thebes attacked from the north. Chalcis, anxious
to destroy a trade rival, joined the Thebans.

Athens seemed doomed to destruction but Corinth stopped
to consider that possibility. Her commercial rival, since the
days of Periander a century earlier, had been Aegina. Surely to
destroy Athens was simply to play into Aegina's hands, since

Athens was a long-standing enemy of Aegina.

Consequently, Corinth suddenly refused to march with Sparta. Rather than break up the Peloponnesian alliance, Cleomenes, once again frustrated, returned home without striking a blow.

The Athenians now turned against the Thebans who had been left in the lurch by their Spartan allies. They defeated the Thebans and confirmed Plataean independence. The sullen Thebans did not forget this and were to maintain a bitter enmity to both Plataea and Athens during all the next century.

The Athenians defeated the Chalcidians even more handily and forced Chalcis to cede to Athens a strip of territory on the island of Euboea just across the narrow strait from northern Attica. This was settled by Athenians and made into a part of Attica and the colonists had the full rights of Athenian citizenship.

But the dangers that Athens had surmounted under Cleisthenes were minute in comparison to those which were to threaten next, from outside the Greek world altogether.

For 500 years — ever since the Dorian invasions — the Greeks had been fortunate in having to face no major empire. The feeble Egyptians and the over-extended Assyrians were no threat, while the Phoenicians and Carthaginians merely nibbled at the outskirts.

However, all during the age of tyrants, great events were shaking the east, and by Cleisthenes' time, a gigantic realm peered at Greece from over the eastern horizon, and all of Greece seemed to be at its mercy.

To see how this came about, let us turn to the east.

7

ASIA MINOR

PHRYGIA

During Mycenaean times, a group of people called Phrygians (frij'ee-anz) moved into the northwestern portion of Asia Minor. They were there at the time of the siege of Troy for they are mentioned in the *Iliad* as allies of Troy.

Their power grew during the disorders that followed the Dorian invasion. Indeed, the Phrygians might have been among the Peoples of the Sea and it was probably they who brought about the destruction of the Hittite Empire. By about 1000 B.C., the Phrygians had extended their rule over nearly the entire western half of Asia Minor. They did not, however, seriously interfere with Greek colonization of the Aegean coast. Rather, they seemed attracted to Greek culture and cultivated Greek friendship. Their later kings even entered Greek legend.

The Greeks say that a Phrygian peasant, named Gordius (gawr'dee-us), was surprised to see an eagle perch on his oxcart. He was told this was an omen signifying he would be king. Sure enough, the old king had just died and an oracle pointed to Gordius as the successor.

Gordius dedicated his cart to Zeus and tied one portion of it to another in a very intricate knot, called, for centuries afterward, the "Gordian knot." Whoever could untie the knot, the legend went, would conquer all Asia. (We will hear of this knot again.)

Gordius established a new capital, Gordium (gawr'dee-um), three hundred miles inland from the Aegean Sea, and under his descendants, Phrygia continued prosperous. The last important king of Phrygia was known as Midas (migh'das) to the Greeks. He ruled from 738 to 695 B.C. and figures in the well-known legend of the "golden touch." He was granted the power of having everything he touched turn to gold; a power which he quickly repented of having, when first his food and water, then his daughter (whom he incautiously embraced) turned to gold. The legend probably reflects Phrygian prosperity in the time of Midas.

In the later centuries of Phrygian power, the still greater realm of the Assyrians had been established to the southeast of Asia Minor. But the Assyrian grip reached only weakly into Asia Minor. Phrygia, by paying tribute, was left to itself.

However, trouble was brewing in the north, beyond the Black Sea. On the plains of what is now the Ukraine, there lived a people in Mycenaean times whom Homer referred to as the Cimmerians (sih-meer'ee-unz). Their name lingers even yet on the map, for the peninsula now known as Crimea may get its name from this ancient tribe.

The Cimmerians might have remained on their plains in peace, but about 700 B.C. central Asia discharged another human flood as it had done (perhaps) five centuries earlier when the Dorian invasions had been sparked. This time, tribes of horsemen, whom the Greeks called Scythians (sith'ee-unz), thundered westward into Cimmeria and the Cimmerians fled before them. For centuries afterward, the plain north of the Black Sea was known as Scythia.

The Cimmerians, fleeing from the Scythians, lunged across and around the Black Sea. They invaded Asia Minor, destroying the Phrygian power permanently. Midas is supposed, according to legend, to have committed suicide in the aftermath of a disastrous defeat.

LYDIA

Rallying against the Cimmerian invaders were a group of tribesmen called Lydians (lid'ee-anz) which hitherto had been under the domination of the Phrygians. Under a strong leader, Gyges (jigh'jeez), a Lydian kingdom was established in 687 B.C. and the fight against the Cimmerians was carried on.

Gyges maintained a long war against the Cimmerian raiders and eventually had to turn to outside help. He sought the assistance of the Assyrian Empire.

In 669 B.C., the last great king of Assyria, Ashurbanipal (ah"shoor-bahn'ee-pal) had come to the throne. The Assyrian Empire was being ripped apart by constant rebellions and in 660 B.C. Saitic Egypt succeeded in breaking loose (see page 39). Nevertheless, Ashurbanipal accepted the Cimmerian challenge.

A great battle was fought at which the Cimmerians were defeated and their main power broken. Skirmishes continued, however, and in one of these, in 652 B.C., Gyges was killed. The Lydian kingdom had by that time been well established and Gyges' descendants remained on the throne.

The grandson of Gyges was Alyattes (al″ee-at′eez) and he came to the throne in 617 B.C. He mopped up the last of the Cimmerians and by 600 B.C. those nomads disappeared from history. With the Cimmerians taken care of, Alyattes went on to absorb all of Asia Minor west of the Halys River (hay′lis) which, flowing north, divides Asia Minor into roughly equal halves. The capital of Lydia was established at Sardis (sahr′dis) only fifty miles inland from the Aegean Sea.

The fact that the Lydian capital was closer to the sea than the old Phrygian capital was an indication that Lydia was more interested in the coast than Phrygia had been. Indeed, Gyges had already made hostile gestures toward the Greek cities there, but the Cimmerian troubles had prevented him from taking too strong a stand.

Alyattes was in a far better position and so he moved westward.

Thales of Miletus (see page 61) warned the Ionian cities that the only way they could hope to withstand the Lydian armies was to combine into a "Pan-Ionian Council" that would guide Ionia in a united defense against the Lydians. It was this advice which earned for him inclusion on the list of the Seven Wise Men.

However, the Ionian cities did not take Thales' advice and, as a result, they fell under Lydian domination, one by one. For the first time, Greek cities submitted to "barbarian" rule. One Ionian city, Smyrna, was actually destroyed by Alyattes and was made into a Lydian port. Only Miletus managed to retain its independence.

What with peace and the tribute paid it by the Greek cities, Lydia, as Phrygia had done earlier, grew rich and prosperous.

It was Lydia, in fact, that invented coinage (see page 58).

Fortunately for the Greek cities, the Lydian yoke was a light one. After Alyattes died in 560 B.C., he was succeeded by a son, Croesus (kree'sus), who was in complete sympathy with the Greeks and was almost a Greek himself in his manner of thought.

Croesus was forever consulting Greek oracles, especially the one at Delphi. He sent rich gifts to Delphi; more elaborate ones, by far, than any the Greek cities themselves would have been able to afford. To such an extent did the reputation of his wealth spread over Greece that to this day we speak of any very wealthy man as being "as rich as Croesus."

Like Midas, two centuries earlier, Croesus seemed to have the golden touch; and, like Midas again, he was not fated to finish his reign in peace. Again trouble was brewing — in the east, this time.

MEDIA AND CHALDEA

The effort Assyria had made to defeat the Cimmerians took almost the last of its strength. Babylon, Assyria's richest possession, took advantage of the situation to rebel. It had been the center of large and brilliantly civilized empires as long ago as 2000 B.C. and it could never reconcile itself to domination by the rough Assyrians of the north. However, its rebellions were always crushed bloodily. With considerable strain, Ashurbanipal managed to subdue Babylon one last time in 648 B.C.

Ashurbanipal held Assyria together while he lived but in 625 B.C. he died and his weak successors didn't have a chance. Rising against the Assyrians were the Medes (tribesmen dwelling in the mountainous areas east of Assyria) under their native ruler Cyaxares (sigh-ak'suh-reez), who had just come to power.

Babylon also rebelled once again. It had come under the control of a tribe, originally Arabian, called the Chaldeans (kaldee'unz) and a Chaldean leader Nabopolassar (nab"oh-pohlas'er) was at their head.

Assyria was sinking under the onslaughts of Scythian raiders from the north, and the combination of Mede and Chaldean was the last straw. In 612 B.C., Nineveh was taken and utterly destroyed and by 605 B.C. the last remnants of the Assyrian forces were gone so that the cruel, hated empire was wiped off the face of the earth forever.

Assyria fell apart so rapidly after the death of Ashurbanipal, that the far-off Greeks, who heard only dim rumors of the fall, imagined Ashurbanipal was still king at the time (or possibly confused him with a brother). The Greeks called him Sardanapalus (sahr"duh-nuh-pay'lus) and described him as a weak, luxury-loving king, who set fire to his palace and perished in the flames when his city was taken.

With Assyria gone, Nabopolassar and Cyaxares divided the loot. Nabopolassar took the main portion of the Empire — Babylonia, Syria and Phoenicia — while Cyaxares took the more extensive but relatively undeveloped lands to the north and east.

It was only after the establishment of Nabopolassar's Chaldean Empire that the Greeks came to know Babylon. Men such as Thales and Pythagoras are supposed to have visited the land and to have brought back Babylonian learning in the field of astronomy. The word "Chaldean" came to mean an astrologer or magician for that reason.

The Chaldean Empire reached its height under Nabopolassar's son, Nebuchadrezzar (neb"yoo-kad-rez'er) better known by the Biblical spelling of Nebuchadnezzar. He succeeded to the throne in 605 B.C. and ruled for over forty years.

He is best known for two actions. First, he destroyed the Kingdom of Judah and carried off the Jews to their "Babylonian captivity." Secondly, he tried to humor his wife, a Median princess, who longed (amid the flat plains of Babylonia) for the hills of her homeland. Nebuchadrezzar therefore built a series of terraced gardens to give the illusion of hills and these are the famous "Hanging Gardens of Babylon." The Greeks eventually listed them among their Seven Wonders of the World.

As for Cyaxares, the ruler of the Median Empire, he cautiously extended his realm westward until it reached first the Black Sea and then the Halys River. On the other side of the Halys was Lydia, where Alyattes was then king.

War between the two for power in Asia Minor was inevitable and it raged for some years. The climax came a generation after the fall of Nineveh, when Mede fought Lydian in one of the oddest battles in history.

As the armies fought, an eclipse took place (the eclipse that had been predicted by Thales, see page 61). In ancient times, only a few astronomers had any notion as to the natural cause of an eclipse and to people generally, it was a sign of the displeasure of the gods and one of the most terrifying of omens of disaster.

So impressed with the eclipse were the armies that the battle ended at once. Peace was arranged, the armies returned home, and the Lydians and Medes never fought again.

Astronomers now understand the movements of the heavenly bodies well enough to be able to calculate backward and find exactly when there had been an eclipse of the sun over Asia Minor at about the time of that Lydian-Median battle. They find that it took place on May 28, 585 B.C. This battle, then, is the very first event in history which can be dated, with certainty, to the exact day.

Shortly after the battle, Cyaxares died, and in 584 B.C. his son, Astyages (as-tigh'uh-jeez), succeeded. It was a generation of peace, for while Astyages reigned Pisistratus ruled over

Athens and Croesus came to power in Lydia.

The peace, however, was an illusion. A new conqueror was on the scene.

PERSIA

About 500 miles southeast of Media is a region called Fars which, to the Greeks, became Persis and, to us, is Persia (per'zhuh). In language and culture, the Persians were closely related to the Medes.

In 600 B.C., or thereabouts, a child was born to the leader of a Persian tribe. He was named "Kurush" (meaning "sun") but he is better known to us as Cyrus (sigh'rus), the Latin spelling of the Greek version of his name. Later legend made him the grandson of Astyages but this may not really be so.

Cyrus succeeded to his father's rule in Persia in 558 B.C. and by 550 B.C. he had raised a revolt against the Median king which was successful. He overthrew Astyages and became absolute ruler of what might now be called the Persian Empire.

Once Cyrus became lord of the Persian Empire, he was ready to take up Media's quarrel with Lydia where it had been interrupted by the eclipse a generation before.

Lydia was not backward in accepting the challenge. Croesus felt that with the east in turmoil as a result of the change in kings, he had an excellent opportunity for extending his power eastward. He consulted the Delphic oracle to make sure and the oracle assured him that: "If Croesus crosses the Halys, he will destroy a mighty empire."

The oracle carefully refrained from saying which mighty empire was to be destroyed and Croesus did not ask. He flung himself across the Halys, where Cyrus met him in battle. The Lydian horses were upset by the odor of the Persian camels and, in the confusion, Cyrus won a complete victory. He pursued the Lydians across the Halys and in 546 B.C. took Sardis. The mighty empire that had been destroyed was Croesus' own and Lydia never again formed an independent kingdom.

This is the most famous example of an oracle consisting of a double-meaning statement which can be considered true whatever happens. Such statements are called "oracular" or "delphic" in consequence.

With Lydia destroyed, what of the Greek cities on the coast? Once again, they were unable to unite. One Ionian, Bias (bigh'as) of Priene (prigh-ee'nee), a town just across the bay from Miletus, suggested a policy of flight. He proposed that all the Greeks take to their ships and sail west to Sardinia which was just then being opened to Greek settlement. (Bias was later included on the list of the Seven Wise Men and with him, all seven have now been mentioned.)

Most of the Ionian Greeks remained where they were, however, and one by one, the cities were taken by the generals of Cyrus. Again, Miletus was the only one which retained a semblance of independence.

But even before the Greek cities had been taken care of, Cyrus had already turned south toward bigger game. Nebuchadrezzar had died in 562 B.C. and the Chaldean empire was now in weak hands. It had tried to help Croesus but that had done it no good, and the conquering Cyrus destroyed it easily in 538 B.C. Cyrus then went on to extend his lands eastward to the very borders of India and China. He died in 530 B.C., well advanced in years, but still engaged in war and conquest.

(Thus, it came about that a portion of the Greek world became part of a gigantic land-empire. It became possible for Greeks to travel securely over thousands of miles of continental domain. One Greek who took advantage of this was Heca-

taeus (hek″uh-tee′us) of Miletus, who was born about 550
B.C. He traveled widely through the Persian Empire and wrote
books on geography and history which, unfortunately, have
not survived. He was the first, however, according to statements by later writers, to whom history was more than a tale
of legends of gods and heroes. In fact, he took a skeptical and
downright scornful view of myths, which is what one would expect of an Ionian.)

Even after Cyrus' death, Persian conquests continued. His
son, Cambyses (kam-bigh′seez), felt Egypt to be his proper
prey since it was the one portion of the old Assyrian Empire
that still remained independent.

Egypt had been independent for 150 years now, and her
king, Amasis, the friend of the Greeks and the one-time ally of
Polycrates of Samos (see page 65), watched the rise and growing power of Cyrus with great alarm. He died in 525 B.C. just as
Cambyses was preparing to launch his attack. The Persian invasion was completely successful and Egypt became part of the
Persian Empire.

While Cambyses was in Egypt, however, a rebellion broke
out at home. Hurrying back to take care of matters, Cambyses
died in 522 B.C., possibly by accident and possibly by suicide.

There followed four years of confusion and civil war during
which there was constant danger that the Persian Empire, after
being established for but a single generation, might fall to bits.

However, the most capable member of the Persian royal family managed to seize control in 521 B.C. as Darius I (duh-righ′
us). By exerting much energy and skill, Darius held the Persian
Empire together and crushed all rebellions, particularly a very
dangerous one in Babylonia.

He then realized it was time to halt the period of uninterrupted Persian conquest, until he had organized what had already been won. This was not an easy task. A Greek polis ten
miles across might be easy to administer, but the Persian Empire was large, even by modern standards, for it was 2500

miles across from east to west. It stretched across mountains and deserts at a time when the only method of land-travel was by horse or camel.

Darius divided the Empire into twenty provinces, each being placed in charge of a *shathrapavan* or "protector of the realm." To the Greeks and, therefore, to us, this word became *satrap* (say'trap) and a Persian province became a *satrapy* (say'truh-pee).

Darius also improved the roads of the Empire and built new ones in order that the different portions could remain in efficient communication. He organized a corps of riders to carry messages along those roads. He adopted the Lydian invention of coinage. Under him, as a result of all this, the Persian realm experienced a growing prosperity.

With the Empire at peace, Darius felt he could now turn his mind to expansion. Cyrus had taken vast areas in Asia and Cambyses had added lands in Africa. To Darius there was left Europe.

In 512 B.C., the Persian army, under Darius, crossed the straits into Europe and advanced into Thrace, the area north of the Aegean Sea. Once again, Persian armies were successful and the Persian Empire was extended up the western coast of the Black Sea to the mouth of the Danube River. (Greek historians later reported that Darius had crossed the Danube in unsuccessful pursuit of the Scythians but this is almost certainly fiction.)

New Greek areas fell to Persia in this campaign. The Thracian Chersonesus, taken by Miltiades for Athens a half-century before (see page 79), came under Persian domination. Even some of the Aegean islands in the north, such as Lemnos (lem'nos) and Imbros (im'bros), became Persian.

Darius returned to Persia from his European conquests, fully expecting to live out his successful reign in peace. And this would probably have happened, were it not for the foolish behavior of Miletus and Athens.

8

THE PERSIAN WAR

THE IONIAN REVOLT

The Ionian Greeks were quite unhappy under Persian dominion. They weren't actually enslaved, to be sure. Still, they
had to pay an annual tribute; they had to endure the rule of
some tyrant installed by the Persians, with a Persian representative at hand, usually, to keep an eye both on the tyrant
and the town.

In some ways this was not much worse than it had been under the Lydians. However, the Lydian capital had been but
fifty miles away, and the Lydian monarchs had been all but
Greeks themselves. The Greeks and Lydians had understood
each other.

The Persian monarchs, however, held court in Susa
(soo'zuh) 1200 miles to the east of Ionia. Darius had even
built himself a new capital city, which the Greeks called Persepolis (pur-sep'oh-lis) or "city of the Persians" and this was
300 miles farther away still.

The distant Persian kings knew nothing of the Greeks and
were far outside their influence. They adopted the autocratic
ways of the Assyrian and Chaldean monarchs who had pre-
ceded them and the Greeks felt uncomfortable indeed with the
oriental fashions of their new masters.

By 499 B.C., then, the Ionians were ready for a revolt if they
could find a leader. They found one in Aristagoras (ar″is-
tag'oh-ras) who was in charge of Miletus while his brother-in-
law, the tyrant, was at Darius' court. Aristagoras had fallen out
of favor with the Persians and there was a good chance he
might end up in serious trouble with them. One way of avoiding that was to head a revolt against them and perhaps end up
as master of an independent Ionia.

The Ionian cities responded eagerly to Aristagoras' prompt-
ing and drove out their tyrants as so many Persian puppets.
The next step was to get help from the independent Greek cities across the Aegean.

Aristagoras first visited Sparta, the strongest military power
in Greece, and attempted to persuade Cleomenes to send help.
Cleomenes, upon learning that it was a three-month overland
journey from the sea to the Persian capital, ordered Aristagoras
to leave at once. No Spartan army was going to march that far
from home.

Aristagoras tried Athens next and there he had better luck.
In the first place, Athens was still laboring under the excitement of the new-won democracy and her successes in war afterward. Secondly, the rebelling cities in Asia Minor were fel-
low-Ionians and fellow-democrats. Thirdly, Hippias, the exiled Athenian tyrant was in Asia Minor at the court of one of
the Persian satraps and there was no telling when the Persians

might not make an attempt to restore him to power. This the Athenians would not tolerate and it seemed wise to try a "preventive war."

(It is about this time that Cleisthenes fell from power in Athens. Why this happened is not known, but one good possibility is that he was opposed to this Ionian adventure and advised against it. He and the Alcmaeonidae came to be looked upon as pro-Persian and for half a century afterward had little power in the city's government.)

Aristagoras returned to Miletus in triumph to say that Athens would send ships and men, and all preparations were made for what came to be known as the Ionian revolt.

Only Hecataeus, the geographer (see page 93) refused to be caught up in the general excitement. He advised against any such attempt as being foolish and hopeless. He said that if the Ionians were absolutely determined to revolt they should first build a fleet that would secure the control of the Aegean; that was their only hope for success. Otherwise the Persians would simply cut them off. The Ionians had not listened to Thales (see page 88) or to Bias (see page 93) on earlier occasions and they did not listen to Hecataeus now.

In 498 B.C. twenty ships arrived from Athens and five more from Eretria, which had been allied to Athens ever since Athens had defeated Eretria's neighbor and rival, Chalcis, eight years earlier. With the revolt actually in progress, other Greek cities rose, too, in Thrace and Cyprus as well as in Asia Minor. All the northwestern tip of the Persian Empire was on fire.

The first action seemed to promise success. Aristagoras led the Milesians and Athenians eastward, caught the Persians in Sardis (the old Lydian capital) by surprise, took and burned the city, then dashed back to Ionia.

But what good did that do? What was one town in the vast Persian Empire?

When the army returned to the Ionian coast, they found a Persian force waiting for them. The Ionians were defeated and

the Athenians decided it was not their fight after all and returned home. But the damage was done — Athens was in for
it.

Darius was furious. He was an aging man now, over sixty,
but he was still not the type of person with whom one might
safely meddle. He collected Phoenician ships and seized control of the Aegean Sea, which was precisely what Hecataeus
had warned the Ionians would happen if they neglected naval
preparations. Now the Ionians were cut off from Greece and
were faced with inevitable defeat. Aristagoras fled to Thrace
and died there shortly afterward.

The Persian-Phoenician fleet had destroyed Greek resistance
at Cyprus and now it stood off the shores of Miletus. In 494
B.C., the Ionian ships that ventured out were destroyed and the
revolt was over. The Persians entered Miletus and burnt it,
though they treated the other Greek cities with comparative
leniency. The power and prosperity of Miletus was over for
good; it never regained its previous position.

Darius next sent his son-in-law Mardonius (mahr-doh'nee-
us) into Thrace to reconquer that area. This was done and by
492 B.C. Thrace was once more Persian. Mardonius might then
have proceeded southward but his fleet was battered in a
storm in the Aegean Sea and he thought it wisest to end matters for the moment and return to Persia.

That left mainland Greece. Darius did not intend to let anyone escape who had done him harm. There was a score to settle with those puny Greek towns who had sent ships against his
empire and had dared help burn one of his cities. Even if he
had been disposed to forget, old Hippias, once the tyrant of
Athens, was at Darius' court now, urging the Persian monarch
to proceed against Athens, and hoping to regain his power in
that fashion.

Athens and all Greece trembled at the prospect.

For the first time, the eyes of a powerful Asian ruler were
looking with menace at the heart of Greece itself. The storm-

clouds that, for a century, had been approaching from the east were now hovering over the Greek heartland and the storm was about to break.

THE BATTLE OF MARATHON

While Darius was preparing his blow, he sent messengers to the various Greek cities that were yet free and required them to agree to Persian overlordship. Only thus could they expect to save themselves from the coming doom. Most of the islands of the Aegean, which could expect no help from anyone against the Persian fleet, submitted at once.

One of the islands, Aegina, felt such enmity to Athens over their trade rivalry (as the Corinthians had foreseen, see page 83) that they agreed to submit to Darius even before the messenger asking for such submission had had a chance to arrive. Athens was to remember this act of enmity.

Some cities on mainland Greece also considered discretion the better part of valor and submitted. One which did not was, of course, Sparta. Sparta was stronger than ever now. In 494 B.C. just as the Ionian revolt was failing, Argos had risen against Sparta once again and Cleomenes I had again defeated her, this time near the ancient town of Tiryns. Cleomenes was even winning a private feud with Demaratus (dem″uh-ray′tus) the other Spartan king and in 492 B.C., Demaratus was forced into banishment and had to flee to the court of Darius. With the aura of victory clinging about him, Cleomenes was not going to submit to the demands of some barbarian.

There is a story that when Darius' messenger came to ask for earth and water as a sign that Sparta would accept the overlordship of Persia on land and sea, the Spartans threw the messenger into a well and said, "There, have both at once!"

Athens could do nothing but wait now. One Athenian, however, had vision. That was Themistocles (thee-mis'toh-kleez). He was archon of Athens in 493 B.C. and to him it seemed as it had seemed to Hecataeus of Miletus five years earlier that in order for Greek cities to resist the Persian giant, they had to control the sea.

Athens did not have a strong fleet and it would take money to build one, an expense the Athenians might not be willing to undertake. Athens was not even a seaport, being five miles from the shore. Themistocles did what he could. He fortified a spot on the shore which later became the city of Piraeus (pigh-ree'us). This was to be the home base of a fleet that he hoped someday would exist. Meanwhile, though, Athens was going to have to withstand the shock of invasion without the protective screen of an adequate fleet.

By 490 B.C. Darius' expeditionary force was ready. It was not a very large one, but it was large enough, in Darius' estimation, for the job that needed doing. It sailed directly across the Aegean, taking such islands as seemed likely to make trouble. It seized Naxos (nak'sos), for instance, in the south-central Aegean, then bore northwestward to the island of Euboea.

On that island was Eretria which shared with Athens the guilt, in Darius' eyes, of having helped burn Sardis. Eretria was taken and burned, while Athens looked on and dared not send help. It needed every man for its own defense.

And, in fact, while Euboea was being taken by one part of the Persian force, another part was landing in Attica. They were being directed by Hippias himself who guided them to a small plain on the east coast of Attica, near the village of Marathon (mar'uh-thon).

Athens had sent for help, meanwhile, to the one other city which was not afraid to fight the Persians — Sparta. A professional runner, Phidippides (fih-dip'ih-deez) was sent the hundred-mile distance, for haste was essential.

Unfortunately, the Spartans were the most tradition-ridden city in Greece and it was traditional with them not to start any great project until the moon was full. It was nine days before the full moon when Phidippides reached them, and they refused to budge for nine more days. Cleomenes might have forced the Spartans to move if he had been in power, but shortly after he had forced out his fellow-king, the ephors, moved to jealousy over Cleomenes' growing power, had forced him into banishment also.

Yet Athens did not have to face the Persians quite alone. Plataea was grateful for Athenian support against Thebes (see page 83) and sent a thousand men to join 9000 Athenians against the enemy.

The small Greek army was ruled by a polemarch and ten generals. One of these generals was Miltiades, the nephew of the Miltiades who had conquered the Thracian Chersonese and made himself tyrant there. The younger Miltiades had succeeded his uncle as tyrant and submitted to Darius during the Persian king's Thracian expedition. However, his actions during the Ionian revolt had been on the anti-Persian side so, for safety's sake, he slipped out of the Chersonese after the revolt had been crushed and returned to the Athenian mother-city.

Now it was Miltiades who was the heart and soul of Athenian resistance. Some of the generals felt it was useless to fight and that perhaps a reasonable surrender might be arranged. Miltiades would have none of that. Not only was it necessary to fight, but he insisted on an attack. He had had experience with Persian armies and he knew the Greek hoplite was superior in both armor and training to the Persian.

Miltiades' eloquence won out and on September 12, 490 B.C., the Athenian army, under Miltiades' direction, dashed forward against the Persians at Marathon.

The Persians reeled back under the shock. For some reason, they had made the mistake of sending their cavalry back to their ships and now they had no horsemen to withstand the

Greek charge. The Persian foot-soldiers died in droves, unable to strike back past the heavy shield of the Athenian hoplite. They could do nothing, in fact, but try to battle their way back to their fleet — completely beaten. According to the Athenian report later (possibly exaggerated) the Athenians lost 192 men in the battle, while the Persians lost 6400.

The Persian fleet might still have carried what was left of the army around Attica and attacked Athens directly. However, their morale was broken and news reached them that the Spartan army was on its way. They decided they had had enough and sailed back across the Aegean, carrying Hippias with them. The old man's chance of re-establishing the tyranny was gone forever and he disappears from history.

Meanwhile, the Athenians waited for news of the battle. At any moment, they might expect to see fleeing soldiers with Persians in hot pursuit; the city would be burned, they themselves killed or enslaved. The Athenian army, victors at Marathon, knew well that their people were in agonizing suspense and they had to send a runner back to the city with the great news. According to tradition, it was the same Phidippides that had run for help from Sparta.

Now he ran from Marathon to Athens at top speed; reached the city, barely managed to gasp out the news of victory, and died.

The distance from Marathon to Athens is a little over 26 miles. In honor of this run of Phidippides, "marathon races" are run as sporting events over distances of 26 miles, 385 yards. The world record for such a race is 2 hours, 14 minutes and 43 seconds, but no one knows how long it took Phidippides to run the very first marathon.

The Spartans arrived at the battlefield shortly after the battle. They viewed the field and the Persian dead, spoke in high praise of the Athenians and returned home. Had they had the gumption to ignore the full moon, they would have been in the battle and taken the major credit for the victory, and the subsequent history of Greece might have been different.

Indeed, this Battle of Marathon has always struck the imagination of the world. It was David versus Goliath, with little David winning. Furthermore, for the first time, a battle was fought on which our whole modern way of life seemed to depend.

Before that September day in 490 B.C., there had been many great battles; but to us today it doesn't seem to make much difference whether Egyptian beat Hittite or vice versa, whether Assyrian beat Babylonian or vice versa, whether Persian beat Lydian or vice versa.

Here it was different. If the Athenians had lost at Marathon, Athens would have been destroyed and then (many people think) Greece might never have gone on to develop the peak of its civilization, a peak whose fruits we moderns have inherited. To be sure, Sparta would have fought, even if it had remained all alone, and it might even have kept its independence. However, Sparta had nothing to offer the world, except a horrible militarism.

The Battle of Marathon is, therefore, a "decisive battle" and many consider it the first decisive battle of history as far as the modern western world is concerned.

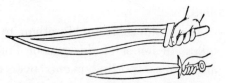

AFTER MARATHON

Darius was furious at the news of Marathon and had no intention of giving up. He made ready to prepare still another expedition against Athens, a much larger one. In 486 B.C., however, while he was still getting ready, he died, in ultimate frustration, with the Athenians still unpunished after all.

Yet the enemies of Darius scarcely fared better. Miltiades was, of course, the hero of the hour, but his success, apparently, turned his head. It seemed to him that he could go on now to become a conquering hero. He persuaded the Athenians to place men and ships under his command and, in 489 B.C., he led them out to attack Paros (par'os), an island just west of Naxos. The excuse was that they had contributed a ship to the Persian fleet.

Unfortunately, he failed in his attack and returned home with a broken leg. Nothing fails like failure. The indignant Athenians tried Miltiades for improper conduct during the campaign and fined him heavily. Soon afterward, he died.

As for Cleomenes I, the Spartan king who had lifted Sparta to undisputed mastery over the Peloponnesus and to the military leadership of Greece, his fate was even worse. He had been recalled from exile but in 489 B.C. went mad and had to be confined under guard. He managed, however, to get hold of a sword and with it, killed himself.

Yet the quarrel between Greece and Persia did not come to an end just because the old generation passed away. New men came to power and carried on the fight.

Succeeding to the Persian throne and to the dream of revenge against the Athenians was Darius' son, known to the Greeks and to us as Xerxes (zurk'seez). Xerxes rushed his father's plan on toward completion, but the Egyptians rebelled in 484 B.C. Xerxes lost several more years of time smashing the revolt, and those years proved crucial.

After the Battle of Marathon, Athens took additional steps toward the completion of the democracy. The various governmental offices which Cleisthenes had thrown open to all Athenian freemen, were now to be filled by lot so that all freemen had a truly equal chance at them. The power of the archon and polemarch was reduced and the popular assembly was made supreme. The only weapon left the upper classes was the Areopagus. That "supreme court" was to remain theirs for another quarter century.

Furthermore, the Athenians introduced a novel system to

prevent the possible establishment of a new tyranny. Once a year, an opportunity was offered for a special kind of vote.

In this vote, the citizens gathered in the marketplace, each with a small piece of pottery. (Pottery was cheap and pieces of broken pots could be picked up anywhere.) The name of any citizen believed to be dangerous to the democracy was scratched on the piece of pottery, which was then placed in an urn. When the voting was over, the urns were emptied, the names counted, and provided a total of more than 6000 were cast, the man who got the most was exiled.

The exile was not in disgrace and he did not lose his property. After ten years he could return and take up where he had left off. In this way, though, the Athenians hoped to avoid the establishment of a tyranny and, also, to make some final decision on the general direction to be taken by the city.

The Greek word for a piece of pottery was *ostrakon,* so the vote of banishment is called "ostracism" and the person banished is said to be "ostracized." The Athenians kept the custom for less than a century and it has never been tried elsewhere.

Ostracism was first used in Athens in 487 B.C., when a member of the family of Pisistratus was sent into exile. However, the most important ostracism in history took place five years later and the results fully justified the custom. The vote came about as a result of a dispute in Athens as to the proper method to prepare against a new invasion.

Of course, the oracle at Delphi was consulted and, according to the later story, the results were very bad; complete disaster was predicted. The Athenian questioners, horror-stricken, asked if there were not a single ray of hope, and the priestess of the oracle replied that when all else was lost, the "wooden wall alone shall remain unconquered."

Back went the Athenians to report this and at once there arose a controversary as to what the wooden walls might be.

One of the prominent Athenian leaders of the time was Aristides (ar″is-tigh′deez). He was a nobleman who rather dis-

trusted the new democracy. Nevertheless, he had been an associate of Cleisthenes, he had fought at Marathon, and he was
famous for his absolute honesty and integrity. In fact, he was
widely known, both in his lifetime and ever since, as Aristides
the Just.

Aristides maintained that the wooden walls referred to by
the priestess were just that: wooden walls. He held that the
Athenians should build a strong wooden wall about the Acropolis and hold out there even if all the rest of Attica was destroyed.

To Themistocles (see page 101) this was simply nonsense.
To him, a fleet was everything. He maintained that the wooden
walls were a poetic way of referring to the wooden ships of a
fleet. A new kind of ship was coming into use in those days, the
trireme (trigh′reem). It had three banks of oars which meant
that more rowing men could be squeezed into such a ship than
in the more old-fashioned type. Triremes were speedier and
more maneuverable than the older ships.

"Build triremes!" insisted Themistocles. Such triremes would
be invincible and from within the wooden walls of such a fleet,
the Persians could still be destroyed, even if they took all of Attica and stood upon the Acropolis itself.

If the need for ships was questioned there was the war with
Aegina that was going on. Athens was set on punishing Aegina
for her eagerness to help Darius but Aegina had the strongest
fleet in Greece and both Athens and Sparta combined could
not bring Aegina to a decisive defeat.

Of course, triremes were expensive to build, but Athens' fab-
ulous luck was holding. At the southeastern tip of Attica, silver mines were discovered in 483 B.C. while Xerxes was bogged
down in Egypt. The Athenians were suddenly rich.

There was a strong temptation for the Athenian citizens to
vote themselves shares in the silver so that each one might be
the richer by a small sum of money. Themistocles was horrified
at this. What good would a few extra coins in each pocket do

the city? On the other hand, if all the money were invested in a navy, 200 triremes could be built.

Aristides opposed this as a waste of money and for months the argument mounted while the rebellion in Egypt was being put down and the danger was looming closer and closer. In 482 B.C. Athens took the step of holding an ostracism-vote in order to choose between Aristides and Themistocles.

Aristides lost and was sent into exile, while Themistocles remained and was placed in charge of the Athenian defense. Under his direction, the fleet was built.

A famous story is told about this vote. An Athenian who could not write asked Aristides (whom he did not recognize) to write his vote for him.

"Whose name shall I write?" asked Aristides the Just.

"The name of Aristides," said the voter.

"Why?" asked Aristides. "What harm has Aristides done you?"

"None," came the reply. "I am just tired of hearing everyone call him Aristides the Just."

Aristides wrote his own name in silence and left.

Nevertheless, the ostracism saved Athens. There is no doubt in modern minds that if the ships had not been constructed, Athens would have been lost, whatever kind of wall had been built around the Acropolis; and with it would have been lost a bright hope of humanity. Aristides was a noble and honest man, but in this matter, he was simply wrong; and Themistocles was right.

If Xerxes had not had Egypt blow up in his face at just the wrong time and had been able to strike at Greece sooner, before the silver mines had been discovered and the Athenian triremes built, the history of the world might have been altogether different.

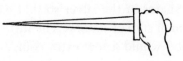

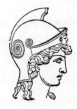

By 480 B.C., Xerxes had quieted Egypt, completed his preparations and was on the march. Ten years had passed since Marathon and Xerxes remembered it well. He was determined not to make his father's mistake and trust in too small a force.

Later on, Greek historians exaggerated the size of the army Xerxes led and claimed that the Persian host amounted to as many as 1,700,000 men, all told. This seems quite impossible, for such a large force could not have been fed and maneuvered in the Greece of that era. The true size of the Persian army could not have been more than 300,000 and was probably no more than 200,000. Even so, such an army was difficult enough to feed, supply, control and maneuver. Xerxes might have done better with a smaller force.

Xerxes himself accompanied the army, which showed the importance he attached to the campaign. With him, he also brought Demaratus, the exiled king of Sparta. The army crossed the Hellespont and marched across Thrace and into Macedonia.

Macedonia, which now enters the current of Greek history, gave little indication at this time that a century and a half later it would fill the world with its fame. Located north of Thessaly and the Chalcidice, Macedonia was a kingdom that was semi-Greek. Its people spoke a Greek dialect and its rulers had picked up Greek culture, but the Greeks themselves usually thought of the Macedonians as barbarians.

Macedonia had, in fact, not shared in the Greek advances since the Dorian invasion, but remained a kind of Mycenaean kingdom, and the notion of the city-state was foreign to her. When Darius had invaded Europe, thirty years earlier, Macedonia had submitted to his overlordship, but had retained her own kings and her own laws. Now that Xerxes was passing through, the Macedonian king, Alexander I, had to renew that submission. He was forced to join the Persian force though his sympathies, according to the later tales, remained with the Greeks.

Once past Macedonia, Xerxes turned southward and began the march into Greece itself.

While Xerxes was beginning his invasion, the Greek cities came closer to combining against a common enemy than they had ever done before, or were ever to do again. The Greek union took shape in the form of a congress held at the city of Corinth in 481 B.C. The leading position at this congress of Greek city-states was held by Sparta, of course, but in second place was Athens, because of the great prestige she had won at Marathon. Argos refused to join, because of her hatred for Sparta; and Thebes was only half-hearted at best because of her anger against Athens over Plataea.

The congress decided to send for help to outlying sections of the Greek world; to Crete, to Corcyra and to Sicily. Crete was helpless and squabbling and no help could be expected from her. Corcyra had a good fleet which would have been valuable on the Greek side, but Corcyra was out of the way of harm and felt no need to undergo any risk. She remained neutral.

It was from the western portion of the Greek world, Sicily and Italy, that help was to be received, if from anywhere. It was rich and prosperous and there the age of tyrants was in full swing. (In fact, Sicily and Italy continued to experience the rule of tyrants for a couple of centuries after they had grown uncommon in Greece itself.)

At the moment, the most successful of the tyrants was Gelon (gee'lon) who came to power in Syracuse. In 485 B.C., Gelon concentrated all his efforts on increasing the wealth and power of Syracuse and succeeded, for from his time onward, for nearly three centuries, Syracuse was the richest and most powerful city in the Greek west.

It seemed natural, then, for the Greeks of Greece itself, flinching under the threat of Xerxes, to turn to Syracuse for help. Gelon is supposed to have agreed to supply that help provided he was placed in full control of the United Greek forces. This, of course, the Spartans would never allow and so the offer fell through.

Actually, Gelon may not have made the offer seriously for he was about to have his hands very full. For a hundred years, the Greeks in eastern Sicily had been carrying on sporadic warfare with the Carthaginians in western Sicily. In Gelon's time, the Carthaginians had found an energetic leader, Hamilcar (ham'il-kahr). He proposed to lead a large Carthaginian force against the Greeks and drive them out of the island once and for all.

Greek historians claimed, afterward, that the Carthaginians acted in cooperation with the Persians; that there was some sort of agreement between the two lands to crush the Greek world between them.

That may possibly be so, and if so, it was clever strategy, for each half of the Greek world was forced to fight its own enemies separately. Neither could find help among the seriously endangered cities of the other.

THERMOPYLAE AND SALAMIS

With all pleas for help failing, Sparta and Athens had to do what they could alone. The Persians, in moving southward, would advance on Thessaly first, and the Thessalian envoys at the Congress of Corinth pleaded for help, pointing out that if no help were sent, they would have to submit to the enemy.

The Greeks did indeed send forces to northern Thessaly. There, in combination with Thessalian cavalry, they planned resistance at the Macedonian border. King Alexander of Macedonia warned them, however, that the Persian force was too large to be withstood and that the Greeks would be uselessly sacrificed if they remained where they were. The Greeks could not help but agree and they retreated. Thessaly and all of northern Greece promptly surrendered.

For the small Greek army to make a successful stand, a narrow space was required, one into which only small contingents of the large Persian army could be sent. The Greeks could then fight the Persians on even terms and in that case, the hoplites could be relied upon to win.

There was such a place, the Pass of Thermopylae (thermop'ih-lee) at the northwestern boundary of Phocis, about 100 miles northwest of Athens. This was a narrow tract of level ground between the sea and sheer mountain walls. At that time, the pass was no more than fifty feet wide in some places. (Nowadays, the area has silted up and the stretch of level land between mountain and sea is much wider.)

In July of 480 B.C., Xerxes' large army moved down to Thermopylae and facing them there were 7000 men under the leadership of Leonidas (lee-on'ih-das), king of Sparta. He was the half-brother of Cleomenes I and had succeeded to the kingship after Cleomenes' death.

Demaratus, the exiled King of Sparta, warned Xerxes that the Spartans would fight fearlessly, but Xerxes could not believe that so small an army would give battle. However, the 7000 Greeks held the pass firmly. They fought the Persians on equal terms in those narrow confines and, as they had confidently expected, did more damage than they suffered.

Days went by while Xerxes grew desperate. But then the Persians, through the help of a Phocian traitor, discovered a narrow path that would lead over the mountain to the other side of Thermopylae. A detachment of the Persian army was sent over this pass to catch the Greeks from the rear.

The Greeks realized that they were going to be surrounded and Leonidas quickly ordered a retreat. Not for himself, of course, or for the 300 Spartans who were the backbone of the army. If Spartans had retreated they would have been disgraced for life. Death was preferable to that. About 1100 Boeotians also remained behind with Leonidas since their territory would be quickly overrun if Xerxes forced the pass. Of the Boeotians, 400 were from Thebes, while the remaining 700 were from Thespiae (thes'pee-ee), about seven miles west of Thebes.

The Thebans are supposed to have surrendered in the fight that followed, but the Spartans and the Thespians, a mere thousand men, surrounded as they were and with escape hopeless, stood their ground. They struck and killed while they had the strength to stand and, in the end, died to the last man.

The stand at Thermopylae heartened the Greeks with its heroism and has inspired lovers of freedom through all the centuries since. Nevertheless, it was a Greek defeat and the Persian army, though badly stung, was able to resume its advance.

The Greek fleet, which had been stationed at Artemisium (ahr"tuh-mizh'ee-um) off the northern tip of Euboea, fifty miles east of Thermopylae had held off the Persian fleet in sporadic fighting. Now, with the news of Thermopylae, the Greek ships felt it wiser to move southward. Xerxes advanced on land and sea, therefore.

Attica lay helpless before the Persian hosts. On or about September 17, 480 B.C., the army of Xerxes occupied and burned the city of Athens itself. Xerxes stood upon the Acropolis and finally, after twenty years, the burning of Sardis was avenged.

The occupation was of an empty land, however, for Xerxes captured an Athens that contained no Athenians. The entire population of Attica had been removed to nearby islands, and the Greek ships, including the spanking new Athenian triremes (which made up more than half the fleet) waited between Salamis and the Attic mainland. The Delphic prophecy was coming true, for though all else had been taken, the wooden walls of the fleet remained; and while those were intact, Athens was not yet defeated.

Although the Greek fleet was largely Athenian, the admiral in charge was the Spartan, Eurybiades (yoo"rih-bigh'uhdeez) for Greeks generally felt safe only under Spartan leadership in those critical days.

The Spartans, however, were unsure of themselves at sea, and Eurybiades had no vision wider than the defense of Sparta itself. He wanted to move southward to protect the Peloponnesus, the one portion of Greece not yet conquered.

The Athenian leader, Themistocles, argued against this so vehemently that Eurybiades lost his temper. He raised his staff of command.

Themistocles, in a passion of anxiety, threw his arms wide and cried, "Strike! — But listen!"

The Spartan listened to Themistocles' fevered arguments and to his earnest threat to pack all the Athenian families into the Athenian triremes and to leave for Italy. Sparta might then see how long it would remain safe without the protection of a fleet.

Reluctantly, Eurybiades agreed to stay. Themistocles feared, however, that the wavering Spartan might change his mind again and so he prepared a master stroke. He sent a message to Xerxes, proclaiming himself a secret friend of the Persians, and advising him to trap the Greek navy quickly before it could escape.

The Persian king fell for this. After all, Greece was riddled with traitors who were trying to save themselves in case of what seemed a certain Persian victory. A Phocian had helped Xerxes trap a Greek army at Thermopylae; why should not Themistocles be helping him to trap a Greek fleet?

Xerxes promptly ordered the Persian ships moved to close both entrances from the narrow water between Salamis and the mainland. Within the strait the Greek fleet was trapped.

As Themistocles foresaw, the commanders of the ships argued all night, with some of them still bitterly demanding that the fleet retreat southward. In the night, however, Aristides the Just reached the ships from Aegina. He had been at Aegina since his ostracism but in the time of great danger, Themistocles himself had moved that Aristides be recalled since Athens needed all its men.

Aristides told them their fleet could not move out of the strait without fighting and the commanders, as day broke, were thunderstruck to see that this was so. Willy-nilly, they had to fight.

But it was Thermopylae all over again and with a happier ending. The Persian king found that in the narrow strait he could not use his full fleet, but could only send in a portion of his ships at a time. The Greek triremes were far more maneuverable and they could turn and dodge and pounce so that the Persian ships were almost helpless victims. The Greek fleet won a complete and one-sided victory.

At the battle of Salamis, on or about September 20, 480 B.C., the Persian fleet was destroyed, and Greece was saved. Three days after Xerxes had stood upon the Acropolis in triumph, he saw his plans ruined. Without a fleet, he could invade the Peloponnesus only through the narrow isthmus and he had had enough of fighting in narrow passageways. In fact, he had had enough altogether. Taking about one-third of the army, he left for Persia. He left the fighting in Greece to his brother-in-law Mardonius (the reconqueror of Thrace in the time of Darius, see page 99) and, as for himself, never returned to Greece again.

There is a charming story (perhaps not true) that after Salamis, the happy Greek commanders met to vote and determine who among them deserved most credit for the victory. Every single commander, says the story, voted for himself in first place; and every single commander voted for Themistocles in second place.

THE BATTLE OF HIMERA

Meanwhile, what of the Carthaginian danger in Sicily?

The Carthaginian general, Hamilcar, was slain by a daring Greek raiding party even as he stood at the altar, sacrificing to the gods and asking for victory in the coming battle. With Hamilcar dead, the opposing armies then met in 480 B.C. at Himera on Sicily's north coast. Here the Greek army won a smashing victory and the Carthaginian menace was ended for nearly a century.

The tradition grew up that the Battle of Himera was fought and won on the very same day as the battle of Salamis, so that on one day, the Greeks, east and west, were saved from destruction. This, however, sounds too good to be true.

Gelon, more famous and powerful than ever as a result of this victory, died two years later, in 478 B.C. His younger brother, Hiero I (high′er-oh), who had fought valiantly at Himera, succeeded to the tyranny, and under him Syracuse continued to prosper and grow in power.

Hiero faced still another dangerous enemy, the Etruscans. Fifty years earlier, the Etruscans, in alliance with the Carthaginians, had defeated a Phocian fleet off the island of Corsica (see page 44) and this had put an end to the era of Greek colonization. Since then, the Etruscans had been pushing southward in an attempt to take over the Greek settlements in southern Italy.

The city of Cyme, most northerly of the Greek city-states in Italy, bore the brunt of the Etruscan pressure. As they lay under siege, they called out to Hiero for help. A Syracusan fleet

sailed northward and defeated the Etruscans at the battle of
Cyme in 474 B.C. The Etruscans were worse off than either the
Carthaginians or the Persians for, unlike the other two, they
never recovered from this Greek defeat. They declined steadily
and slowly disappeared from history.

Sicily and Italy, in those years, formed a center of Greek
science. Ionia, under the accumulation of disasters — first the
Persian conquest and then the disastrous failure of its revolt —
had lost the scientific leadership of the Greek world. Its
thinkers emigrated to other areas (with Pythagoras, see page
62, the best-known example) bringing knowledge and intel-
lectual stimulation with them.

In addition to Pythagoras, for instance, there was the emi-
grant Xenophanes (zee-nof'uh-neez). He had been born in
Colophon (kol'oh-fon), one of the Ionian cities, about 570 B.C.
He left the Persians behind and emigrated first to Sicily then to
southern Italy. He is best known for his suggestion that the
existence of seashells on mountain heights indicated that regions of the earth, now high in the air, might once have been
under the sea.

Xenophanes founded the "Eleatic school" of which there
were two more important representatives in the following century. Parmenides (pahr-men'ih-deez), born in Elea (ee'lee-uh),
a town on the southwest Italian coast, about 539 B.C., was a
Pythagorean who developed a complex theory concerning the
nature of the universe, but only fragments of his writings survive. He had an important disciple, Zeno (zee'noh), born in
Elea about 488 B.C., who carried further Parmenides' idea that
the senses were not a reliable method of attaining truth. He
claimed that only reason could be used for the purpose.

Zeno tried to demonstrate this by presenting Greek thinkers
with four famous ways of showing that what we thought we
saw could not be so. (An apparent truth which is not truth is a
"paradox.") The best known of Zeno's paradoxes is one called
"Achilles and the tortoise."

Suppose Achilles can run ten times as fast as a tortoise and that the tortoise is given a ten-yard head start in a race. It follows then that Achilles can never overtake the tortoise because while he covers the ten yards separating them, the tortoise will have moved ahead one yard. When Achilles runs that one yard, the tortoise will have moved a tenth of a yard and so on. Since our senses, however, clearly show us a fast runner overtaking and passing a slow runner, our senses must be false (or the reasoning must be).

These paradoxes have proved extraordinarily useful to science. They have been refuted but their refutation made it necessary for scientists to investigate closely the very processes of reasoning themselves. Zeno is considered the founder of "dialectic," the art of reasoning for the sake of discovering truth and not merely to win an argument.

Still another Greek scientist of Italy was Philolaus (fil"ohlay'us) who was born in Tarentum or Croton about 480 B.C. He was a disciple of Pythagoras and the first to speculate that the earth was not necessarily fixed in space, but might move. He suggested it circled a "central fire" of which the visible sun was only a reflection.

As for Sicily, its greatest philosopher of the period was Empedocles (em-ped'oh-kleez). He was born about 490 B.C. in Akragas (ak'ra-gas) on Sicily's southern coast. He helped overthrow an oligarchy in his native city but refused to become its tyrant. His greatest contribution to science was his suggestion that the universe was made up of four fundamental substances (or "elements" as they came later to be called): earth, water, air and fire. This notion of the "four elements" was retained for over 2000 years after his time, so it was certainly a successful theory, although we now know it to have been quite wrong.

Empedocles was a Pythagorean who had a number of mystical notions. He had no objection to being looked upon as a prophet and miracle-worker. According to one tradition, he let it be known that, on a particular day, he would be taken up to

heaven and be made a god. On that day, he is supposed to
have jumped into the crater of Mount Etna in order that, by
disappearing mysteriously, he might be thought to have made
good his prediction. This was in 430 B.C. or thereabouts.

Hiero I died in 466 B.C. and the Syracusan tyranny came, at
least temporarily, to an end. There followed a half-century of
relative quiet. It was broken by uprisings among the native
peoples of Sicily, who won a number of successes against the
Greeks but were finally subdued.

VICTORY

Whereas the single battle of Himera had lifted from the western Greeks the cloud of Carthage, the single battle of Salamis
was not quite enough for the Greeks of Greece itself.

The Persian fleet had been destroyed, but the Persian army
remained. It had retired northward but when winter was over,
it moved forward into Boeotia. It was a smaller army, thus
easier to handle and more dangerous. It was led by Mardonius,
a capable general who had strongly urged the not-very-brilliant
Xerxes to leave and who now had a free hand, which was all the
worse for the Greeks.

Mardonius' first move was to send King Alexander I of Macedonia to Athens (now once again occupied by Athenians) in
an effort to persuade them to desert the Greek cause now that
they had rescued their own city. The Athenians refused and, in
their turn, tried to persuade the always slow-moving Spartans
into fast action.

By the time the Spartans managed to collect their army, Mardonius had raided Attica and burned Athens once more.

However, the Spartans were in earnest now. At the death of
Leonidas at Thermopylae, his infant son had inherited the kingship but was not old enough to lead an army. Pausanias (paw-

say'nee-as), a cousin of the king, acted as regent and general. Under his leadership, an army of 20,000 Peloponnesians moved northward, and of them, fully 5000 were Spartans. This was probably the largest detachment of Spartans to take part in a single campaign in all Greek history.

Contingents from other Greek cities joined them, including 8000 Athenians under Aristides, and the total Greek force may have amounted to 100,000 men. Against these, Mardonius had perhaps 150,000 Persians and their allies.

The two armies met at Plataea in August, 479 B.C., and the battle that followed was sharp and difficult. More than once, the Greeks (whose maneuvering before and during the battle was rather clumsy) seemed on the point of breaking. However, the Spartans and Athenians held steady and, as at Marathon, their heavier armor made them more than a match, man for man, for the Persians. At the height of the battle, Mardonius, leading a charge of 1000 men, was struck by a spear and killed and, with that, the heart went out of the Persians. They fled and those who survived, made their way to Asia.

Mainland Greece was now safe on land, as well as at sea. From that time forward, for 1000 years, when Greek fought Persian, it was always in Asia and never in Europe.

The victorious Greeks moved on Thebes which, throughout the Persian War, had proved always ready to side with Persia. It had saved itself from destruction as a result, but it had merely insured its burning by the Greeks themselves. The Theban oligarchs were exiled and a democracy was established.

Events were also progressing at sea. With much of the Persian fleet destroyed at Salamis, it would have been reasonable to expect the Greek fleet to follow up the victory with a strong movement toward Ionia. However, before that could be done, the slow-moving Spartans had to be persuaded to action and, as always, this took time.

The island of Samos was menaced by what was left of the Persian fleet and its pleas for help finally moved the Spartans.

The Greek fleet under Leotychidas (lee"oh-tik'ih-das), one of the Spartan kings, sailed eastward. The Persians were by no means willing to undertake another sea battle, however. They therefore retired toward Cape Mycale (mik'uh-lee), a projection of the Ionian coast just east of Samos. There they beached their ships and waited on land for the Greeks.

The Greeks landed, too, and assaulted the Persian camp, forcing a Persian retreat. As soon as the tide of battle seemed to favor the Greeks, the various Ionian contingents, whom the Persians had forced into battle along with themselves, revolted. They turned their arms against those who had been their masters, and this decided the issue. The Persians fled and, as a result of the Battle of Mycale, the Greek cities of the Asia Minor coast regained the independence they had lost a century earlier to Alyattes of Lydia.

Later tradition would have it that the Battle of Mycale was fought and won on the very day of the Battle of Plataea. This is not likely, however; the Battle of Mycale was probably fought a few days later.

The fleet went on, under Athenian direction (for Athens was, as always, worried about her lifeline to the grain-growing areas of the Black Sea) to clear out the region of the Hellespont and Bosporus in 478 B.C. and the Persian War was over. The net result of twenty years of fighting, starting with the Ionian revolt, was that almost the entire Aegean area was free and a Greek lake once more.

The Persian War was made forever famous not merely through its own importance, but through the man who wrote about it. As the Trojan War found a Homer, so the Persian War found a Herodotus (hee-rod'oh-tus). Herodotus was born in Halicarnassus (hal"ee-kahr-nas'us), a city on the Asia Minor coast south of Ionia, in 484 B.C. During his younger years, he traveled all over the ancient world, observing everything with sharp eyes, and listening to all the tales told him by the priests of Egypt and Babylonia. (Sometimes he believed a little too much of the tall stories they fed the eager Greek stranger.)

About 430 B.C. he wrote a history of the Persian War. It was intended for an Athenian audience and it was therefore heavily pro-Athens. He was awarded a huge money prize by the Athenians but this was not entirely in reward for praise. His work was fascinating enough to be copied over and over, so that it managed to survive, in full, through disasters that later destroyed most other works of Greek literature.

Since Herodotus is the earliest Greek writer whose work exists in detail and since his chief concern is with the Persian Wars, the history of Greece prior to 500 B.C. is known only sketchily. Fortunately, in an attempt to explain the background of the war, Herodotus gives the earlier history not only of Greece but also of the various nations included in the Persian Empire. He skips over this earlier history rather lightly, but most of what we do know of events prior to 500 B.C. also comes from Herodotus and we can only be grateful that he decided to discuss early history at all.

9

THE GOLDEN AGE

THE TROUBLES OF SPARTA

The Persian War left Sparta and Athens the two most powerful cities in Greece. One might have expected that Sparta would be jealous of Athens' rise to power and would do her best to prevent it.

Sparta was jealous indeed, but two factors kept her from opposing Athens effectively. At first, Athens applied her new-found strength to conquests at sea rather than in Greece itself. Sparta, always preferring inaction to action and always uncomfortable at sea, anyway, was willing to let that go and confined herself to keeping her land supremacy.

Secondly, in the years immediately following the Persian War, Sparta underwent several disasters.

For one thing, Pausanias behaved badly. He was the hero of Greece after the battle of Plataea and he went on to conquer Byzantium in 477 B.C. However, this went to his head. It often happened that a Spartan, once away from the rigid virtue and discipline of Sparta, went to the other extreme. Abroad, he would revel in luxury and become avaricious for money. This happened to Pausanias, who took to wearing elaborate Persian costumes and to treating his fellow-Greeks haughtily, as though he were an oriental monarch himself.

Soon he began negotiating with Xerxes in an attempt to gain greater power with Persian help (or at least he was suspected of this). He was recalled to Sparta by the ephors, who were jealous of his success in any case, and tried for treason but was acquitted on the grounds of insufficient evidence.

He was no longer allowed to lead Spartan armies, however, so he went off on private expeditions to the Hellespont where he was defeated by the Athenians and where he continued dealing with the Persians. He was called back to Sparta a second time and there he committed what, to Spartans, was the most unforgivable sin of all. He tried to organize a revolt of the helots.

The plot was discovered and Pausanias fled for safety to a temple. He could not be taken from the temple by force so he was kept there without food until he was nearly dead of starvation; then he was removed since it would have been sacrilege to allow him to die on sacred ground. He died outside. This was about 471 B.C.

Meanwhile, Leotychidas, the leader of the Greek fleet at the Battle of Mycale, had been convicted in 476 B.C. of accepting bribes and had been banished.

All this caused Sparta to lose considerable prestige. The other Greek city-states could not help but feel that if the Spartan heroes of Plataea and of Mycale could be traitorous and corrupt, then no Spartan could be trusted. Athens, on the other hand, bold and resolute, never hanging back as the slow-moving Spartans did, and always in the forefront of resistance against Persia, was all the more admirable in contrast.

As a result, Argos, finally recovered from her defeats at the hands of Cleomenes I, was encouraged to attempt once again to withstand the Spartan overlordship in the Peloponnesus. She won initial successes, taking Mycenae and Tiryns (miserable little villages now, with nothing left of their ancient glories) and other cities joined her. Even Tegea, usually solidly pro-Spartan, entered into allience with Argos. Sparta, far from being able to counter Athens' rise to power everywhere in the Greek world was suddenly forced to fight for leadership in the very Peloponnesus where she had considered herself safely supreme for a century.

Fortunately for Sparta, a young king, a worthy successor of Cleomenes I, was on the throne. This was Archidamus II (ahr″kih-day′mus) who became king on the banishment of his grandfather, Leotychidas. Archidamus defeated Argos and her allies at Tegea in 473 B.C. Argos, having had enough, retired from the war, but the Arcadian allies, Tegea at their head, continued resistance. In 469 B.C. a second battle ended that and Sparta was securely master in the Peloponnesus again.

But there was worse in store for her. The severest blow of all was struck by an enemy even Sparta could not fight. In 464 B.C., an earthquake shook the city of Sparta to pieces, and, for a moment, the Spartans were dazed and thunderstruck.

At this moment, the helots seized their chance. Eight years before, Pausanias had given them cause to hope that two centuries of martyrdom might be brought to an end, but that plot had been foiled at the last minute. Now the Spartan masters were helpless for the moment; the time had come.

The helots hastily organized themselves and tried to fight the Spartans. Once the Spartans had caught their breath, however, the helots didn't have a chance. As their ancestors had done two centuries before, the helots retreated to Mount Ithome and fortified themselves there. They held out for five years in

what is sometimes called the "Third Messenian War." The fact
that it took the Spartans so long to subdue their own slaves
further hurt their prestige.

In 459 B.C. the helots were finally forced to surrender, but
only on condition that they not be killed or forced to return to
slavery. The Spartans agreed to let them leave Sparta, and
Athenian ships took them to Naupactus (noh-pak'tus), a naval station that had recently been founded by Athens on the
northern shore of the Gulf of Corinth.

THE CONFEDERACY OF DELOS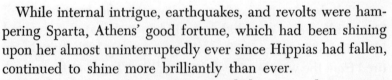

While internal intrigue, earthquakes, and revolts were hampering Sparta, Athens' good fortune, which had been shining
upon her almost uninterruptedly ever since Hippias had fallen,
continued to shine more brilliantly than ever.

The freed cities of Asia Minor needed continued protection
against any attempt by Persia to re-establish its overlordship.
Such protection could come only from the Athenian fleet. In
478 B.C., therefore, soon after the Battle of Mycale, the cities of
the Asia Minor coast and the islands of the Aegean Sea began
to join with Athens in an alliance designed to present a united
front against Persia.

Each town was supposed to contribute ships to a united fleet
or money to a central treasury. The number of ships contributed or the sum of money paid was adjusted by Aristides
the Just according to the size and prosperity of the individual
cities. And, tradition has it, he did the job so well that no city
felt itself taxed too much or its neighbors taxed to little. (This
is the last tale told of Aristides' justness, but even the circumstances surrounding his death gave further evidence. Far from
using his power to enrich himself, the estate he left at his death

in 468 B.C. was not even large enough to pay his funeral expenses.)

The central treasury of the alliance was located at Delos, a hundred miles southeast of Athens. Delos is a tiny island, not much larger than Manhattan's Central Park, but because of the location of the treasury there, the grouping of cities under Athenian leadership came to be called the "Confederacy of Delos."

The weak point of the confederacy was Athens itself. The fleet could protect the islands and the Asia Minor coast, but what good would that do if an enemy could march into Attica and burn Athens itself? Persia had done so twice and Sparta might do it in the future.

Themistocles, whose great prestige after the Battle of Salamis kept him in power in Athens, decided on a daring new stroke of policy. The "wooden walls" of the Delphic prophecy had saved Athens in the form of ships, in accordance with his own interpretation of the oracle. Now it was time to use Aristides' interpretation and build actual walls — not only about the Acropolis, but around the whole city.

In case of invasion, then, though Attica might be devastated the population could retreat into the city and fight back from behind the walls.

The Spartans naturally objected to such a course of action, considering it an unfriendly act. Sparta itself had no walls and she suggested that all city walls in Greece be destroyed. (There is a story that someone visiting Sparta once asked why it had no walls. The answer came quickly, "The Spartan soldiers are Sparta's walls." True enough! And if all fortifications were destroyed, the Spartan soldier would have been absolute master in Greece.)

However, the Spartans, as always, acted slowly; and the Athenians, as always, acted quickly. While the Spartans were objecting, and while Themistocles was keeping them busy talking, the Athenians were building. By the time the Spartans were ready to act, the walls were high enough to make such action too late.

Along with Athens, the seaport Piraeus, first established by the far-seeing Themistocles even before Marathon, was fortified.

But despite all his successes, Themistocles was losing popularity. He lacked the absolute honesty of Aristides and as he grew wealthier, he was suspected of taking bribes. He also showed an arrogant pride in his own abilities and triumphs that was fully justified but that displeased the Athenians anyway.

His great postwar opponent was Cimon (sigh'mon) the son of Miltiades, the hero of Marathon. Cimon, like his father and like Aristides, did not trust the democracy and was a conservative influence at Athens. Nevertheless he was enormously popular in democratic Athens.

For one thing, he paid the huge fine that had been imposed on his father the year after Marathon (see page 105). He also used his wealth to establish parks and buildings for public use. Even more than that, he was a capable military leader who led Athenian forces to victory upon victory.

Cimon had served under Aristides during the Persian War and in 477 B.C. he had taken over leadership of the Athenian fleet. Almost at once he was able to take Byzantium from Pausanias of Sparta and thus help safeguard Athens' lifeline to the Black Sea.

Cimon threw his own popularity into the scale against Themistocles and in an ostracism vote in 472 B.C. Themistocles (like Aristides exactly ten years earlier) was banished. Themistocles was less fortunate than Aristides, though, for he was never able to return to Athens.

He went to Aegina first and there engaged in intrigues against Sparta. He may even have joined in Pausanias' plot to bring about a helot rebellion. In any case, Athens eventually declared him a traitor and he was forced to flee Greece altogether.

He managed to reach Persian territory in Asia Minor and there he was treated with great kindness. Themistocles reminded the Persians that just before the battle of Salamis, he had tried to arrange matters so that the Greek fleet was trapped. The Persians apparently believed that Themistocles had honestly tried to trap the Greeks; just as the Greeks believed Themistocles had honestly tried to trap the Persians. (What had been Themistocles' *real* motive? No one will ever know. It is very likely that the shrewd Athenian had calculated that whichever way the battle went, he himself would win.)

Themistocles died in Magnesia in 449 B.C. He left behind a saved Greece, a liberated Asia Minor coast and a fortified Athens. Not bad for twenty years of political power.

After Themistocles' ostracism, Cimon was dominant in Athens. Where Themistocles favored a sharp anti-Spartan policy, Cimon was strongly pro-Spartan. He believed that Athens should maintain its wartime alliance with Sparta and turn all its strength against Persia.

He was also a strong imperialist; that is, he wanted Athenian influence spread over as wide an area as possible. Thus, after conquering Byzantium, he used his fleet to make sure that the Greek towns along the north Aegean coast joined the Confederacy of Delos.

Nor was Cimon prepared to allow any member of the confederacy to leave it. About 469 B.C. the island of Naxos had decided Persia had been taken care of and it was now safe to leave the confederacy and go her own way, using her ships for herself instead of contributing them to the Athenian fleet.

Cimon thought otherwise. The confederacy was no voluntary association in his eyes, but a union under Athenian domination. He attacked Naxos and took it, destroying its fortification and confiscating its fleet. The island was forced to pay tribute thereafter instead of building ships for the common fleet.

However, opposition to Cimon was growing at home. The democrats were displeased with Cimon's aristocratic and pro-Spartan tendencies and they found a leader in Ephialtes (ef"ee-al'teez). Ephialtes' chief target was the Areopagus, last stronghold of the conservatives. However, as long as Cimon was victorious, Ephialtes could do nothing. He accused Cimon of having taken a bribe from Alexander I of Macedonia, but Cimon was triumphantly acquitted. Obviously, the democrats would have to wait for Cimon to endure a defeat before they could make headway against him.

Then came 464 B.C. and the terrible disaster of earthquake and helot revolt that laid Sparta temporarily low. That gave occasion for a new dispute. To Ephialtes, this seemed a god-sent opportunity for Athens. Why not help the helots and cripple Sparta permanently?

Cimon fought strenuously against this. He reminded the Athenians of Spartan dead at Thermopylae, of her deeds at Plataea. Greece, Cimon said, was led by Sparta and Athens who were like two oxen pulling a common load. If one were destroyed, all of Greece would be lamed.

Cimon's arguments and his popularity won out. In 462 B.C. an Athenian army was sent to help the Spartans beat down the poor helots who were fighting against the most brutalized slavery in Greece. The Athenian soldiers could not have been comfortable at the task.

It was the Spartans themselves, however, who destroyed Cimon, their best friend in Athens, out of blind and sullen jealousy. They couldn't bear to see Athenians come patronizingly to help them against their own slaves. "We don't need you," muttered the Spartans savagely and ordered the Athenians to return to Athens.

It was a terrible insult, one that was more than the Athenians could bear. Cimon had led them into this humiliation and they turned upon him. An ostracism vote was arranged and in 461 B.C. Cimon was banished and Ephialtes came to power. He at once weakened the Areopagus, restricting its powers to the judging of murder cases and nothing more. The power of the popular assembly was correspondingly increased.

Ephialtes did not remain in power long for, shortly after Cimon's ostracism, the democratic leader was assassinated. This, however, proved to be of no service to the conservatives; for into Ephialtes' place stepped an even more capable democrat, Pericles (pehr'ih-kleez).

Pericles was born in 490 B.C., the year of Marathon. His father had led an Athenian squadron at the Battle of Mycale, while his mother was a niece of Cleisthenes (see page 81) so that on his mother's side, Pericles was a member of the Alcmaeonidae. He was well educated and among his teachers was Zeno of Elea (see page 117).

Pericles was to remain in power to the day of his death thirty years later, despite all his enemies could do. During this period, Athens reached the height of its civilization and experienced a "golden age."

Pericles continued to expand democracy at home. He started the custom of paying officials so that even the poorest could afford to serve the city. He also labored to strengthen the city. Even though Athens and Piraeus were both fortified, there remained a five-mile gap between the cities. Food and supplies might reach Piraeus from overseas but how was that to reach a besieged Athens five miles distant. The solution was to build walls from Piraeus to Athens, the "Long Walls," to form a protected corridor across which supplies and men could move in safety. In this way, Athens plus Piraeus could be converted into a kind of island in the midst of land. The Long Walls were completed in 458 B.C.

Pericles made use of the common treasury of the Confederacy of Delos not merely to strengthen Athens but also to beautify it. This seems like misappropriation of funds and is hard to justify. Still, people have argued that the confederation was secure against Persia so that Athens was fulfilling its part of the bargain. Then, too, the new beauty of Athens was the glory not only of Athens but of all Greece and by making Athens more glorious in men's eyes, its reputation was enhanced, and it could more easily use its reputation to protect the confederacy.

In particular, Pericles commissioned the architect Ictinus (ik-tigh'nus) to crown the Acropolis with a temple to Athene Polias ("Athene of the city"). The sculptor was Phidias (fid'ee-as). It came to be known as the Parthenon (pahr'thih-non). It was begun in 447 B.C. and was not completely finished until 432 B.C.

Phidias, born about 500 B.C., is generally accepted as the greatest of all Greek sculptors and the Parthenon is his greatest work. It is perhaps the most perfect structure ever built, and the most famous. It has been in ruins for many years now (see page 297), but the rectangle of pillars in the Dorian mode that rise on the Acropolis still symbolizes all that was glorious and beautiful in ancient Greece.

In 436 B.C., Phidias supplied the Parthenon with a large wooden statue of Athena, covered with ivory for bare skin and gold for the costume. Phidias also carved the statue of Zeus at Olympia, where it overlooked the stadium in which the Olympian games were held, and this was listed by the later Greeks among their Seven Wonders of the World.

Like so many of the great men of ancient Greece, Phidias came to an unhappy end. The aristocrats of Athens, always the enemies of Pericles but never able to dislodge him from the affection of the Athenian people, attacked as many of his friends as they dared. They charged Phidias on two different occasions of wrong-doing, of misappropriating some of the funds entrusted to him, and of sacrilege because he included among the figures on Athena's shield (they said) portraits of himself and Pericles. Phidias died in prison while the second trial was under way.

The century after the Persian War was the time of three great tragedians; the most important literary figures, perhaps, between the time of Homer and that of Shakespeare.

The first was Aeschylus (es'kih-lus). Born in 525 B.C., he fought at Marathon and was also present at the battles of Salamis and Plataea. He advanced the art of the drama past the beginning made by Thespis (see page 80). Aeschylus reduced the chorus from fifty to fifteen members and introduced a second actor. This made dialogue possible for the first time. He also first made use of costumes, high shoes, masks and other devices to make the actors and their message more visible to the audience.

Between 499 B.C. and 458 B.C., Aeschylus wrote over ninety plays. In the annual competitions in Athens at the festival in honor of Dionysus, he won first prize thirteen times. However, only seven of his plays survive today.

He visited Sicily on several occasions, and ended his life there, dying in Gela (jee'luh), a city on Sicily's southern coast, in 456 B.C., shortly after Pericles came to power. There is a legend that he was killed by an eagle trying to crack the shell of a tortoise it was carrying; it dropped the tortoise on Aeschylus' bald head, thinking it was a rock. This is a famous story, but is undoubtedly pure fiction.

Sophocles (sof'oh-kleez), the second of the big three, was born in 495 B.C. and lived to be ninety years old. He added a third actor to the tragedy and, in 468 B.C., managed to defeat Aeschylus and win the annual drama competition. He went on to win some eighteen or twenty times altogether. He wrote over a hundred plays, but of these, also, only seven survive. He remained active to the very end, for as his ninetieth year approached, his son tried to have the courts declare him incompetent to manage his own affairs. In defense, Sophocles read, in open court, passages from *Oedipus in Colonus* the play on which he was then working. He won his case easily.

Finally, there was Euripides (yoo-rip'ih-deez), born about 484 B.C. He was the most human of the three. Where the characters in Aeschylus and Sophocles talked in stately and lofty fashion, with only the noblest passions and motives investigated, Euripides brought the plays down to the people. He was interested in all the odd angles of human psychology and his characters had human failings and spoke in everyday fashion.

This made him unpopular with the leading critics so that he won the annual drama competition only four times (plus a fifth after his death). The lack of appreciation which he experienced during his life is supposed to have embittered him. He took to living alone and shunning society and was supposed to be a woman-hater. Late in life, he left Athens to answer an invitation from Macedonia and died abroad.

His popularity grew after death, however. Of the ninety-two plays he wrote, fully eighteen have survived. One of them, *Medea,* was produced on Broadway in recent years, and later appeared on television. It was a great success, for genius does not age.

A fourth dramatist was not a tragedian but was the great comic writer of the golden age. This was Aristophanes (ar"is-tof'uh-neez), who was born about 448 B.C. His comedies, while full of slapstick, were not merely laugh-producers. His weapon was biting wit and sharp satire against the weaknesses of the time, and against individuals of whom he disapproved, such as Euripides.

He was descended of a landowning family and was conservative in temper. He spared no effort to make fun of the democrats. He could do so because the very democracy he attacked was so absolute that he could say anything he wanted, including remarks that today would be excluded from even our own stage as being too bad-mannered to be endured. Of his forty to fifty comedies, eleven still survive.

Ionian science was dying in those days, but a few final sparks still lit the Greek heavens, both inside and outside Athens.

Anaxagoras (an"ak-sag'oh-ras) was born about 500 B.C. in Clazomenae (kla-zom'ih-nee), one of the twelve Ionian cities. In middle life, he emigrated to Athens, bringing with him the scientific traditions of Ionia. He became a great friend of men such as Pericles and Euripides.

Anaxagoras believed the heavenly bodies to be no more divine than the earth was; that they were formed of the same materials and through the same causes. The stars and planets, he said, were flaming rocks and the sun, in particular, he believed to be a white-hot rock about the size of the Peloponnesus.

Anaxagoras taught in Athens for thirty years, but he was not allowed to end his days in peace. Because he was a friend of Pericles, he was fair game for the conservative enemies of the Athenian leader. It was easy to show that Anaxagoras' views were against the Olympian religion. (If the sun were a flaming rock, what became of Helios, the god of the sun?)

Pericles managed, with difficulty, to have Anaxagoras acquitted, but the philosopher felt it would be unsafe to remain in Athens. In 434 B.C. he retired to Lampsachus (lamp'suhkus) on the Hellespont and there in 428 B.C., he died.

The last flicker of Ionian science came with Leucippus (lyoo-sip'us) of Miletus, who lived about 450 B.C. and who is supposed to have first suggested that matter was not composed of substances that could be divided and sub-divided indefinitely, but consisted of tiny particles that, once reached, could be divided no further.

This view was carried further by one of his disciples, Democritus (dee-mok'rih-tus), born in the town of Abdera about

470 B.C. Abdera had been founded seventy years earlier by Ionian refugees fleeing from Cyrus of Persia (see page 93) so Democritus may well be considered an Ionian.

He termed the ultimate particles of Leucippus "atoms." His views on such atoms were quite similar in many respects to modern beliefs on this subject, but they did not win acceptance among the Greek philosophers generally.

The island of Cos, off the Asia Minor coast near the city of Halicarnassus, was a Dorian island and therefore cannot be considered a part of Ionia. Nevertheless, some of the Ionian spirit drifted in its direction. About 460 B.C., Hippocrates (hih-pok'ruh-teez) was born there, and eventually founded the first rational theory of medicine, one that did not depend on gods and demons. It is for this reason that he is often called "the father of medicine."

Numerous writings (called the "Hippocratic collection") have been attributed to him, but it is more than doubtful that these are really his. They are rather the collected works of several generations of his school, and were attributed to him by the later physicians in order to gain them more attention.

Hippocratic ethics are reflected in the "Hippocratic Oath," originated by later members of his school, and still taken by medical students today, upon the completion of their course of training.

A new type of learned man arose in Athens, during the time of Pericles, who professed to be able to teach those qualities which best fitted men for public life. They were "sophists," from a Greek word meaning "to teach."

An important function of any man in public life in those days was that of presenting arguments for or against some proposed law, or some person who was on trial. Many sophists openly claimed they could (for a fee) teach people to argue on either side of any question and to make the weaker side seem better by clever argument. This is just the opposite of the dialectic developed by Zeno (see page 118) and is not exactly an honorable way of using one's learning.

The greatest and most popular of the sophists was Protagoras (proh-tag'oh-ras) who, like Democritus, was born in Abdera. He was the first to analyze the Greek language carefully and to work out the rules of grammar. Since he was a friend of Pericles, he drew down upon himself the enmity of the conservatives. In 411 B.C., long after Pericles' death and when he himself was about seventy years old, Protagoras was accused of atheism since he questioned, in public, whether the gods really existed or not. He was banished from Athens and while on his way to Sicily was lost at sea.

THE TROUBLES OF ATHENS

If Sparta was sometimes badly hampered by her tendency to do nothing, when something had to be done, Athens made trouble for herself by trying to do everything at once.

During Pericles' first years, Athens seemed to be driven by demons, as she struck everywhere. She crushed Aegina, took part in a quarrel between Corinth and Megara in 458 B.C., defeated Corinth (and made a deadly enemy of her) and took Megara under her protection. She allied herself with Argos as an open gesture of enmity to Sparta. And on top of that she was feverishly building the Long Walls.

All this Sparta had to endure because the helot revolt occupied her. However, in 457 B.C., with the worst of the aftermath of the helot revolt done with, Sparta had recovered and could once again assert her accustomed mastery. Athens decided she was not ready to fight Sparta on land and so Cimon (Sparta's old friend) was recalled in the hope that he might arrange a truce.

The truce was all the more important as a still heavier blow struck Athens from overseas. In 460 B.C. she engaged in a venture even more foolish than rushing to the aid of Ionia a generation earlier (see page 98).

This second venture began with the death of Xerxes who was assassinated in 464 B.C. In the confusion that followed it was some time before Xerxes' son, Artaxerxes I (ahr"tagzurk'seez) was secure on his throne.

During this unsettled period, Egypt once more revolted as it had revolted after the death of Darius. Egypt appealed for help to Athens, as Ionia had once done, and once again Athens responded. Athens was a far stronger city in 460 B.C. than in 500 B.C. and she sent a correspondingly bigger fleet. Instead of a mere twenty ships, she sent two hundred according to some (possibly exaggerated) accounts.

As on the earlier occasion, the Athenians had begun by taking Sardis, so now they began by taking the Egyptian city of Memphis. However, the Persians fought back vigorously and the Athenians, in a strange, distant land, surrounded by a barbarian population rather than by their own people, fell back. Little by little, their situation grew worse and by 454 B.C. the entire Athenian army, together with such reinforcements as had been sent from time to time, was lost.

The defeat was disastrous. The men and ships were more than Athens could afford to lose considering her attempt to fight everywhere at once. Besides, Athens' confidence in herself was seriously shaken. Not only Sparta and Persia could encounter disaster, it seems, but even Athens.

So great was Athens' shock over the Egyptian defeat that she no longer trusted the island of Delos with the treasury of the confederacy. She brought the money to Athens itself and with that, she assumed open domination over the cities of the confederacy. In fact, one can speak of an "Athenian Empire" from this point on.

The Athenian Empire looked well on the map. Boeotia and

Megara were under the control of Athens; Phocis and Argos were in alliance with her. Even some towns in Achaea in the Peloponnesus had allied themselves with her. This, together with her control of Naupactus on the northern shore of the Gulf of Corinth, made the Gulf almost an Athenian lake, as the Aegean Sea itself was.

But meanwhile the Persian forces, having pacified Egypt, moved on to the island of Cyprus, which had also revolted. Again, an Athenian fleet was sent to aid rebels against Persia, this time under Cimon. With Cimon in charge the Persians were defeated, but Cimon died in 450 B.C. in mid-campaign and the Athenians made peace.

With peace established all about, the Athenian Empire was at the peak of its power, but troubles began almost at once. In a way, it was Athens' fault again. She was a sea-power and her attempts to establish control over land as well only served to weaken her.

In 447 B.C., for instance, Boeotia rose against Athenian domination. Had Boeotia been an island, the Athenian fleet would have taken care of the matter. But Boeotia was a land power and the Boeotians were hard fighters when they fought for themselves. Athens sent an army into Boeotia and it was met by the Boeotians at Coronea (kor"oh-nee'uh) some twenty miles west of Thebes.

The Athenians were completely defeated and Thebes gained control of all Boeotia again, as a result. She cast down all the democracies which Athens had caused to be established and set up oligarchies instead.

The defeat set off a series of reverses. Only two years before, the Phocians had seized Delphi, and Sparta had sent an expedition to defeat the Phocians (the "Second Sacred War"). The Phocians had been defeated, of course, but after Spartan forces had departed, Athens had taken sides with Phocis and helped her recover. Nevertheless, with Boeotia out of Athenian

control, Phocis, immediately to the west of Boeotia, considered
its own interests and promptly abandoned its alliance with
Athens.

Then both Euboea and Megara revolted. Pericles led an
Athenian force to Euboea which was, after all, an island, and
held it to the Athenian alliance. Megara, however, which was
not an island, received help from the Peloponnesus and was
permanently lost to Athens. The brief Athenian experiment in
establishing power on the Greek mainland as well as at sea
thus came to an inglorious end and in 446 B.C. Athens signed a
thirty-year truce with Sparta on that basis.

Pericles tried to balance these numerous blows to Athenian
influence by expanding her power overseas. He sent Athenian
colonists to various islands in the northern Aegean and to the
Thracian Chersonese (where Miltiades had once ruled). Athenian ships penetrated the Black Sea (Pericles himself going on
one such expedition) and established relations with the Greek
cities of the coastal areas.

Athens even founded new cities, as the Greeks had not been
doing for more than a century, including Amphipolis (am-
fip'oh-lis) on the northern Aegean coast just east of the Chalcidice and Thurii (thyoor'ee-igh) in Italy, on the site where
Sybaris had stood a century before.

Nevertheless, Athens, and all of Greece, was seated at the lip
of a volcano. Not only did the various city-states fight among
themselves, but within each city-state there was constant
fighting between oligarchs and democrats. Whenever either
side won, the other side was exiled and waited in neighboring
cities for a chance to return.

Even inside the Athenian Empire itself, this conflict was to
be seen. The island of Samos and the city of Miletus got into
a dispute in 440 B.C. over which was to have control of the city
of Priene. The dispute was put up to Athens, which sided with
Miletus. To prevent trouble from the discontented loser,

Athens then threw out the oligarchs who controlled Samos and installed democrats.

Samos at once revolted and restored its oligarchs. It took the Athenians (with Pericles in personal command) a year before they could restore order. Revolts elsewhere were also beaten down, but they kept Athens off balance.

Every little quarrel in Greece pulled Sparta in on one side and Athens in on the other. Sooner or later, there was bound to be an explosion!

10

THE PELOPONNESIAN WAR

THE BEGINNING OF THE WAR

The explosion came on the island of Corcyra, which was having a bitter civil war between its oligarchs and democrats. In 435 B.C., the oligarchs turned for help to Corinth, the mother-city, which was itself an oligarchy. Corinth was only too glad to help. She sent a fleet which, however, was promptly defeated by the Corcyrean democrats.

Corinth, furious, prepared a much larger expeditionary force. The democrats of the island naturally appealed to Athens, the great helper of democrats everywhere. Athens sent ten ships. This was not entirely because of love of democracy alone. Athens had a new interest in the west now that she had founded Thurii in southern Italy, and a friendly Corcyra (which was on the sea-route to Italy) would be most useful.

By 433 B.C., the fleets of Corcyra and Corinth were in position again. This time Corinth had 150 ships (twice as many as she had sent the first time) and she was gradually beating the Corcyreans back, when the Athenian ships which had been watching the battle came swooping in on the side of the Corcyreans. That swung just enough weight to alter the course of the battle, and when twenty more Athenian ships made their appearance over the horizon, the Corinthians rowed off, defeated again.

Corinth was beside herself with rage. She had plenty of ground for enmity against Athens. Athens was a competing sea-power which in the past generation had reduced Corinth to second-class status, and Corinth had the bitterness of remembering that she had saved Athens herself when Cleomenes I might have nipped her in the bud (see page 83). Athens had defeated Corinth on land by siding with Megara twenty years before and now she had defeated her on sea by siding with Corcyra. It was the last straw.

In revenge, Corinth used her influence on the city of Potidaea (pot"ih-dee'uh) in the Chalcidice (which she had founded two centuries before) and instigated a revolt of that city against Athens. However, the Athenians swung into action and although Potidaea and other areas of the Chalcidice kept matters hot for a while, it didn't look as though Athens would be in major trouble.

In despair, Corinth beseeched Sparta, early and late, to take action. In this she was opposed by Sparta's able king, Archidamus II, who had come to power in the days before the earthquake forty years before. He was a friend of Pericles and had consistently done his best to keep the peace.

However, Athens herself cut the ground from under Archidamus. Pericles decided to take a strong line and show Athenian power. He declared a trade embargo against Megara, a particularly vulnerable member of the Spartan team. No Megarian trader could deal at any port controlled by Athens —

which meant they could deal practically nowhere. Now that city-states dealt in industry and specialized farming, trade was essential. Only by trade could food be brought into the city. With her trade choked off, Megara was soon starving.

Unfortunately, this frightened Sparta in the wrong way. With their own eyes, the dull Spartans could see the frightening effects of sea-power and they realized that there was no safety even in land armies as long as Athens controlled the sea — unless she were crushed before she got even stronger. In 431 B.C., therefore, the ephors overrode Archidamus and declared that Athens had broken the Thirty Years Truce (which was then only fourteen years old) and the general war between Athens and her allies versus Sparta and her allies began.

This war, which was to damage all of Greece beyond repair and put an end to its golden age, is best known through the history written by Thucydides (thyoo-sid'ih-deez). He was an Athenian general in the war who was unjustly sent into exile in 423 B.C. He used that exile to write a history which, for more than 2000 years, has been considered a perfect example of impartial writing. As nearly as we can tell now, he did not try to slant his reports in favor of Athens because it was his city, or against Athens because it had treated him unjustly. Furthermore, he was a complete rationalist, and never brought in the gods, or omens, or superstitious reasoning of any kind (as Herodotus constantly did).

Since the war is viewed from the Athenian side generally, Thucydides being best acquainted with the internal affairs of Athens, and since the Athenian enemies were the Peloponnesians, Sparta, and Corinth, the war has come to be called the "Peloponnesian War."

Pericles had expected the war and had already worked out his strategy. He saw that it would be useless to attempt to fight the Spartans in open battle. That would lead to a certain defeat. Instead, he had all the Athenians retire into the "island" formed by the Long Walls about Athens and Piraeus. Whatever the Spartans might do outside, those inside were safe — at least from human enemies.

The Spartans under Archidamus marched into empty Attica and did what damage they could, destroying homes and farms. The grim Athenians did nothing. There was no danger of starvation as long as Athens' fleet controlled the sea and brought in food. Meanwhile, those same ships could ruin the trade of the enemy cities and conduct raids on their coasts. Before long, Pericles felt sure, the Spartans would get tired of useless maneuvering among ruined farms and would agree to peace on reasonable terms.

The first year saw Pericles' plans working out. Athenian ships raided boldly and in return, except for ravaging Attica, the Peloponnesians had accomplished little. With the coming of winter, the Spartans were forced to leave Attica, and the Athenians made ready for more of the same the next year, and for as many years afterward as the Spartans had the spirit to continue.

At the end of the first year, there was a public funeral in Athens for those who had died in the war and Pericles delivered a funeral oration. As reported in Thucydides it is one of the great speeches of history; a hymn to democracy and freedom.

Pericles praised democracy for leaving each man free to behave as he chooses, for considering men equal and giving the poor man a chance to govern if it is considered he can help the city, for leaving their city free to foreigners and hiding nothing, for believing in the good things of life, in festivals and joy and refinement, for not training themselves to war as the Spartans did and yet fighting just as bravely when war came.

"Our city, considered as a whole," he said, "is the schoolmistress of Greece." And indeed not Greece only, but all the world ever since, has been able to learn from Athens of the golden age.

But Pericles' speech was the last of the golden age. An en-

emy that was not human — the only one for which Pericles'
plans had made no provision — was about to make its appearance.

In 430 B.C., the Spartan army invaded Attica again, and once
more the Athenians crowded inside the Long Walls. This time,
however, disease struck; a violent plague that leaped from man
to man and killed almost every time. The Athenians knew no
way of treating it and were helpless before it. Twenty per cent
of the population died and through all ancient history, the population of Athens was never again to reach the number it had
attained just before the plague.

Athens was plunged into despair and Pericles himself was
voted out of office and tried for misappropriating public
funds. There was no substitute for Pericles, however, and he
was reinstated. The plague had almost run its course, but it had
one serious blow remaining. Pericles caught the disease and
died. (Archidamus of Sparta did not long survive, either, dying
in 427 B.C.)

SPHACTERIA AND AMPHIPOLIS

With Pericles gone, two parties rose in Athens. One was
fiercely democratic, preaching a continuation of the war. Its
leader was Cleon (klee'on). He had been opposed to Pericles
in recent years, believing Pericles to be insufficiently forceful
in his policies. The conservatives, favoring peace, were led by
Nicias (nish'ee-us).

Cleon won control and for several years carried on the war
in energetic fashion, but without quite the steady, far-seeing
policy of Pericles. (The comic poet, Aristophanes, was of the
peace party and wrote a number of plays that poked merciless
fun at Cleon.)

Athens continued its policy of naval raids upon the enemy.

Successes at sea made up for the fact that Sparta, after a two-year siege, took Plataea in 427 B.C. and wiped out its population, loyal allies of Athens since before the days of Marathon.

In 425 B.C. the Athenian admiral Demosthenes (dee-mos'thih-neez) won his greatest victory when he seized and fortified the promontory of Pylos where once a Mycenean city had stood, on the western coast of Messenia, in the heart of Spartan territory.

Sparta could not take this without reacting. She sent a force of men to Pylos. They took up positions on Sphacteria (sfak-tee'ree-uh), an island in the harbor, and laid seige to the Athenians. However, the Athenian fleet, momentarily absent, returned and laid siege to the Spartan besiegers.

The besieged Spartans included several hundred full Spartiate citizens and the Spartan ephors were terribly concerned. The number of Spartan citizens with full rights at the public tables had been dropping steadily and they were now less than 5000 in number. A sizable percentage of the citizen population was thus trapped on Sphacteria and Sparta could not afford to lose them.

Sparta decided to ask for peace. In exchange for the trapped Spartans, she was prepared to offer generous terms. If Pericles had been alive, it is very probable that he would have accepted, but Cleon was not quite statesman enough for that. He could not resist squeezing a little harder. He demanded a return of the land areas lost twenty years earlier: Megara, Achaea and so on. The Spartans felt themselves insulted and returned to Sparta in anger. The war continued.

Almost at once, it began to seem that Cleon had badly overplayed his hand. Trapping the Spartans was one thing; capturing them another. Sphacteria was heavily wooded and going into the bush after a Spartan was much like reaching a hand into a lion's cage. The siege dragged on uselessly and many Athenians came to regret Cleon's failure to make peace when he might have had it.

Cleon covered up by furious speeches to the effect that the Athenian generals at Pylos were cowards. He, himself, he said, could do better, if he were only there.

Nicias then made the only shrewd move of his life. He promptly rose to ask for a vote on a resolution to send Cleon to Pylos and the vote passed. Cleon was neatly trapped; he had to go.

Cleon played in incredible luck, however. Just before he arrived, an accidental fire on Sphacteria had burned down its trees. Cleon headed a vigorous attack and the Spartans, fouled with smoke and ashes and worn out with the siege, were defeated. Wonder of wonders, 120 full Spartan citizens *surrendered!* (Leonidas must have turned in his grave.)

Cleon brought his Spartan prisoners home in triumph. They served as hostages against renewed invasions of Attica, and for a number of summers the Athenians were free of Spartan occupation of their homes.

This victory drove Athens onward to redoubled energy, and in 424 B.C. Nicias took the Spartan island of Cythera. Furthermore, Cleon felt it was time to strike openly for the land empire that Pericles had lost and that the Spartans would not give up in exchange for the prisoners of Sphacteria.

The Athenians struck southwest and captured Nisaea (nigh-see'uh), the port city of Megara. Megara itself might have fallen and that might have been the last straw driving the Spartans to take any peace they could get, were it not for the rise of a new war-leader in Sparta.

This was Brasidas (bras'ih-das) a most un-Spartan Spartan who was lively, eloquent, intelligent and charming, as well as brave. In the first year of the war he had fought off a raiding party in Messenia and later he had fought ably at Sphacteria where, however, a wound had taken him out of action.

Now, in 424 B.C. he took leadership in the war. Driving into the isthmus, he forced Athens to shy away from Megara and brought them to a standstill there. He then dashed northward through Thessaly and Macedonia to the Chalcidice, a very valuable Athenian stronghold.

The Athenians did not at once recognize the danger. They were intent on invading Boeotia. However, they were badly defeated by the Thebans at Delium (dee'leeum) on the coast just opposite Euboea and they gave up all attempts to make themselves a land power.

Now they had time to become aware of what was going on in the Chalcidice. Brasidas, through his tact and diplomacy (almost nonexistent among Spartans generally), together with some help from Perdiccas of Macedonia, persuaded town after town to revolt. Finally, he advanced on Amphipolis itself.

Amphipolis had been founded by Athens only thirteen years before (see page 140) and Athens felt a strong attachment to the city. Thucydides the historian was in charge of the defenses of Amphipolis, but he was not on the spot. He hastened back as soon as news of the siege reached him, but he wasn't in time. Amphipolis had surrendered speedily on being offered extremely generous terms. Thucydides was scarcely to be blamed for Brasidas' skill as a negotiator, but the furious Athenians needed someone to blame and Thucydides was exiled. (And a good thing, too, for otherwise we might not have had his history.)

Now it was Athens' turn to be willing to consider peace and they succeeded in gaining a year's truce. However, Brasidas played the part of a Spartan Cleon. He felt that the war might as well continue to complete Spartan victory. He therefore continued his operations, much to the exasperation of the Athenians and the truce fell through.

The Athenians turned to Cleon. He had been the great general who had taken Sphacteria and captured 120 Spartans. Could he not do something about Brasidas?

In 422 B.C. Cleon was forced to lead an army to the north. He won some successes, but when he tried to attack Amphipolis, the superior ability of Brasidas made itself clearly evident. He outmaneuvered Cleon and won a victory. During the battle Cleon was killed, but in a way, Cleon's luck still held, for Brasidas was killed also.

The war leaders on both sides had thus died and the way was finally open for peace. Sparta wanted the captured Spartans back and she wanted her hands free for trouble she expected (once again) from Argos. As for Athens, her wild career of fighting here, there, and everywhere, had left her virtually without funds. She had borrowed temple treasures with a liberal hand and even so had to nearly double the tribute being taken from the cities of the Athenian Empire. Both sides were simply sick of fighting.

In 421 B.C., then, the "Peace of Nicias" (after the chief Athenian negotiator) was agreed to. The Spartan prisoners were returned and the situation was placed very much where it had been when the war had begun ten years earlier, except that Amphipolis was allowed to remain independent. (Indeed, Athens was never to regain that town.) Ten years' blood and suffering had bought very little for either Athens or Sparta and had sent all of Greece a good way down the road to ruin.

THE SICILIAN EXPEDITION

The Peace of Nicias was supposed to last for fifty years, but actually, it never even started. The cities of Corinth and Thebes, as well as others, refused to be bound by it. They wanted the destruction of Athens and nothing less. The rescue of Spartan captives was nothing to them.

Then, too, Athens was angered at the fact that Amphipolis was not returned to them and therefore refused to return Pylos and the island of Cythera to Sparta.

What's more, a new war-leader had arisen in Athens. This

was Alcibiades (al"sih-bigh'uh-deez). His mother had been Pericles' cousin and he was of the family of the Alcmaeonidae. He was the last of that family to be important in Athenian history. He was rich, handsome, intelligent and charming but completely without morals. He was anxious to perform great feats and for that he needed war. For his own desires, he had no hesitation in pushing Athens back into a war she neither needed nor wanted.

In fact, he was to do more than any other individual to ruin Athens and in him the "curse of the Alcmaeonidae" over the sacred oath that had been broken two centuries before (see page 73) was fulfilled. Since the Alcmaeonidae were not kept in exile, the curse fell on all Athens because of Alcibiades.

The young man had his chance in the Peloponnesus, where once again Argos was going to try to measure strength with Sparta. Despite Brasidas, Sparta's reputation had gone downhill because of the surrender on Sphacteria and Alcibiades had little trouble in engineering an alliance against Sparta among Argos, Elis and the Arcadian town of Mantinea. He promised to bring an Athenian force to their aid.

Unfortunately, Nicias was opposed to the Peloponnesian adventure and Athens fell between two stools. She did not send a large force that would help the Argives and their allies defeat Sparta. Neither did she remain neutral and stay out of trouble. Instead, she sent an inadequate force under Alcibiades.

The Spartans were under Agis II (ay'gis), who had succeeded his father Archidamus II in 427 B.C. They were now fighting once more in their familiar Peloponnesus, against their old enemies whom they had beaten so often before. Near Mantinea, Sparta defeated the allies in a decisive battle in 418 B.C. The situation in the Peloponnesus was restored to its previous status, with Sparta firmly in control. The only change was that Sparta and Athens were back at war.

There was considerable anger, in Athens, against Nicias, sparked by the more radical democrats who, since Cleon's

death, were led by Hyperbolus (high-per'boh-lus). They felt
that Nicias' opposition had kept Athens from making effective
use of the alliance against Sparta. Hyperbolus called for an
ostracism vote, certain that the followers of Alcibiades would
join his and that Nicias would be banished. The war would
then proceed more vigorously.

However, the followers of Nicias and Alcibiades came to an
agreement of their own. Both voted against Hyperbolus who,
to his astonishment, found himself ostracized. This made a
mockery of the whole system of ostracism, however, and no
ostracism-vote was ever held in Athens again. The device had
lasted nearly a century and had performed its service. Now it
was done.

However, Athens had had a chance to catch her breath again
in the two years of near-peace that had followed the Peace of
Nicias. Money had come in and her self-confidence had been
regained. She was ready to listen to Alcibiades' schemes.

Twice before, Athenian over-confidence had sent her into
grandiose efforts beyond her strength and twice before these
had ended in disaster. The first had been the force to help the
Ionian revolt in 499 B.C.; the second, the force to help the Egyptian revolt in 460 B.C. The first disaster had been retrieved and
turned into victory and the second disaster had been at least
survived.

The third effort, now at hand, was to be far the worst of the
three, and it involved Sicily, where Athens felt there was excit-
ing fruit, ripe for the gathering. Opposed to Athens was Syracuse.

The last thing Syracuse wanted was outside interference in
Sicily. She was herself the most powerful city there and interference was bound to hurt her most. She could not control the
squabbling of the other Sicilian cities, however. In 416 B.C.,
Segesta (see-jes'tuh) in western Sicily was at war with the
neighboring city of Selinus (see-ligh'nus) and called on Athens
for help. Alcibiades heard the call.

The rich Greek cities of Sicily and Italy seemed like pure gold to Alcibiades. By a bold and unexpected stroke in the west (so he felt) an area of untold wealth could fall into the Athenian grasp. With Sicilian men and money at her disposal, Athens (with Alcibiades at her head) could sweep up all the counters in the Peloponnesian war without trouble. Who would dare oppose her?

The logical point of attack was Syracuse. She was a Corinthian colony, originally, and Corinth was Athens' most implacable enemy, the city which had started the disastrous war. Syracuse was also the traditional home of tyranny and of Sicilian isolation, and therefore a proper target for democratic and imperial Athens. Finally, Syracuse was the strongest city in the west and if she fell, all else would follow.

The conservative peace party, under Nicias, opposed the wild scheme but Alcibiades managed to catch the imagination of the Athenian people and they voted for the expedition. In 415 B.C. a grand fleet was ready to sail and the people were as happy about it as though it were one grand holiday.

But now the Athenians began a series of mistakes. Granted that the Sicilian expedition was foolish, still Alcibiades was the one man daring enough and able enough to carry it off. If Athens were going to attempt the project, it should have left the leadership to him. It did not do so, but placed the leadership in several men, one of them being Nicias.

Since Nicias was against the project from the start, how much energy could he bring to it? He was simply the worst man to choose, mediocre, indecisive, superstitious and not very intelligent. (He was as un-Athenian an Athenian as Brasidas had been un-Spartan a Spartan.)

Worse still was to take place. Just before the fleet set out, certain religious statues in Athens were found mutilated during the night. The Athenians were horrified, for this seemed an awful omen.

Alcibiades was already under suspicion for having poked

fun at the Eleusinian mysteries and the peace party promptly accused Alcibiades of the mutilation as well. Alcibiades stoutly maintained his innocence, and certainly even Alcibiades would not have been so wild as to do such a thing at the very moment of the start of his great adventure. It seems much more likely that the peace party had carried through the mutilations themselves in order to frame Alcibiades. However, this is one of the mysteries of history. No one will ever know the truth.

Again, the Athenians chose the worst possible course of action. They might have held Alcibiades for trial at once and kept the fleet from sailing until the matter was decided one way or the other. Or they might have let Alcibiades take the fleet to Sicily and postponed the trial for the day when the campaign was over. What they actually did, however, was to let the fleet sail with Alcibiades and then send a messenger to recall him for trial.

Alcibiades could come to only one conclusion. In his absence, his enemies had seized control. Returning for trial would be suicide and he was not the kind to sacrifice himself for the good of the city. He saved his own skin by slipping away out of reach of Athens and then deserted to the Spartans.

This left the thoroughly incompetent Nicias in chief command of the expedition.

The Athenians landed near Syracuse and won some victories to begin with, but Nicias was not the man to make the most of it. He could always think of reasons to delay, to backtrack. If circumstances forced him forward, he moved as slowly as possible. The Syracusans always had time to recover, to strike back.

Worse still, Alcibiades was in Sparta, intent on only one thing — vengeance against Athens. The Syracusan expedition had been his own brainchild, but now that it was taken out of his hands, he was ready to ruin it. Using all the force of his eloquence, he persuaded the slow-moving Spartans that they dared not allow the Athenians to take Syracuse and the rest of Sicily. They must join the fight on the side of Syracuse.

In consequence, Sparta sent a general named Gylippus (jih-lip'us) with a small force to Syracuse in 414 B.C. They came just in time, for Nicias was managing to win despite all the bumbling he could do. Slowly, he had been building a wall about the city in order to place it under strict siege and Syracuse was actually considering surrender. However, Nicias was working too slowly, as usual, so that when Gylippus arrived there was still a gap in the ring through which he could enter Syracuse. With the vigorous note he added to the defense, the heartened Syracusans drove Nicias back, and the wall was never completed.

That really ended any chance at victory, but at least there was still a chance to avoid catastrophe by a rapid withdrawal. Instead, Nicias sent for reinforcements and Athens compounded its error by sending good money after bad. In 413 B.C. a new expedition under Demosthenes (the general who had fortified Pylos a dozen years before) arrived. Demosthenes attempted an attack, which was beaten back.

Demosthenes was much more intelligent than Nicias and saw at once that the only thing to do was get out, and fast.

But Nicias was the commander; foolish, stupid Nicias. He had been slow to attack when attack might have won; now he was slow to retreat, when retreat was necessary. The blame of failure would rest on him, he knew, and he dared not face the anger of the Athenian people. So he procrastinated.

On August 24, 413 B.C., there was an eclipse of the moon. Nicias, full of superstition, forbade any movement until certain religious rites had been carried through. By the time those were finished, the Syracusan fleet had been brought up to block escape by sea and after the Athenians were defeated in two sea battles, they were trapped.

There was nothing left but to fight on land, in hopeless despairing battles that could not be won. Nicias fought bravely; there was that at least; but there was only one end. The Athenian army was killed or captured to the last man, and those who were captured were treated with abominable cruelty and they were not long in dying, either. Nicias and Demosthenes were both killed.

The catastrophe of the Sicilian campaign broke the spirit of Athens forever. She kept on fighting the Peloponnesian War bravely and in the following century she performed well on occasion — but never was she wildly self-confident again. Never again did she try to undertake great projects. Never again would she stand at Marathon or at Salamis and dare the enemy to do its worst. From now on, when showdowns came, Athens would flinch.

THE FALL OF ATHENS

Alcibiades did more to ruin Athens than merely to direct the Spartans into Sicily. His lively intelligence pointed out something to the Spartans that, to anyone but a Spartan, might have needed no pointing out. On a number of different occasions during the war, the Spartans had invaded Attica in the summer and left it in the winter, so that there had always been winter months in which Athens might relax and, to a degree, recover.

Alcibiades showed the Spartans that if they took and fortified a post at the Attic border, they could occupy it the year round. They would then keep Attica under control and force the Athenians to remain within the Long Walls not only part of the year but all the year.

In 413 B.C., the Spartans under Agis II took this advice, and the Athenians were penned in. They could not even make use of the silver mines at the southeastern tip of Attica, mines that had supplied them with wealth for seventy years.

The Athenians had a large sum of money which, in more

prosperous times, had been put to one side for use only in the extremest of emergencies. With the awful disaster in Sicily and with the Spartans permanently entrenched in Attica, the time had clearly come. The money was used to build a fleet to replace that lost in Sicily, and with it, they tried to fight the revolts that the Spartans were now stirring up all over the Aegean Sea.

By now Sparta had realized that the war would never be brought to a complete end until Athens was defeated at sea. Like it or not, Sparta would have to become a sea power. For ships and rowers, she needed ready money, and for money, she knew where to turn — Persia.

Artaxerxes, the Persian king, had kept the peace while he lived and had not interfered with the embattled Greeks. In 424 B.C., however, he died. Two of his sons were quickly assassinated and the third, Darius II, came to the throne. Once he had seated himself securely, he was ready to resume an aggressive policy toward Greece. He intended no actual warfare, to be sure (Persia had had enough of that) but made use of a more deadly method — money for the warring Greek cities to keep them fighting and ruining each other.

It was Sparta who was most eager for the money and in 412 B.C. she came to an understanding with Tissaphernes (tis″uh-fur′neez) and Pharnabazus (far″nuh-bay′zus) who were satraps of the southern and northern parts of Asia Minor respectively.

Athens nearly gave up. The last of her money was gone, defeat was piling upon defeat, her empire was in revolt, and Persia was lending her giant weight to Sparta. How much could one city bear?

The Athenian conservatives seized their opportunity, in this moment of despair, to set up an oligarchy in 411 B.C. It was called the "Four Hundred" because it consisted of about that many men. Undoubtedly the Four Hundred, pro-Sparta to begin with, would have asked for peace and submitted even to hard terms. However, they weren't given the chance.

The Athenian fleet, then at Samos, was heart and soul with the democracy. One of the captains, Thrasybulus, seized power and set up a democratic rule over the navy. For a while, then, there were two Athenian governments — the oligarchs at home and the democrats at sea. An oligarchic surrender to Sparta was worthless if the Four Hundred could not surrender the navy, and so Sparta did not treat with them. Moreover, the oligarchy did not have a firm grip on the government and in a matter of months were replaced by a more moderate oligarchy consistening of 5000 men.

Meanwhile, Alcibiades had re-entered the picture. The charming Alcibiades had been entirely too charming to the wife of Agis II, king of Sparta. Agis therefore detested the Athenian and took measures to destroy him. Once again, Alcibiades did not wait to be destroyed, but, in 412 B.C., left Sparta as hastily as, three years earlier, he had left Athens. He fled to the court of the Persian satrap, Tissaphernes.

When the fleet at Samos became an independent power, Alcibiades negotiated with them. Thrasybulus and the fleet could not afford the luxury of being too picky. Alcibiades was a capable man who might now have influence with the Persians. Thrasybulus invited him back into Athenian favor therefore and placed him in charge of the fleet.

Alcibiades quickly proved he had not lost his ability. He pursued the Spartan ships over the Aegean, beating them whenever he caught them and in 410 B.C. he severely damaged the Spartan fleet at Cyzicus on the southern shore of the Propontis. Despite all that Sparta and Persia could do, Athens remained supreme at sea. When the news of Cyzicus reached Athens, the democrats, who had been slowly eroding the oligarchic position, rose in joy and re-established the full democracy.

In 408 B.C. Alcibiades won further victories, freeing the entire area of the straits, including Byzantium, of rebels and enemies, so that Athens' lifeline remained secure. In 407 B.C., he

judged it was safe to return to Athens. He was greeted with
wild joy, made a full general, and placed in charge of the war
effort. Athens even felt it had a chance of winning, and Spartan peace offers were rejected.

But the chance of victory was an illusion. Athens had been
too badly damaged to win unless, just possibly, she could
bring herself to trust Alcibiades completely, and she couldn't
do that. It would never be possible to trust Alcibiades completely.

At this point, too, disaster loomed for Athens in the shape of
(of all things) a capable Spartan admiral named Lysander
(ligh-san'der). His early history is not known, but in 407 B.C.
when the Spartans had been able to rebuild their fleet after the
defeat at Cyzicus, it was Lysander who was in charge.

Then, too, Darius II of Persia had sent his younger son,
Cyrus, to Asia Minor to take charge of Persia's part in the war.
Cyrus, only a teen-ager at the time, was intelligent and
vigorous; the greatest hope of Persia since the time of Darius I,
a century before. (This Cyrus is usually known as "Cyrus the
Younger" to distinguish him from the Cyrus who founded the
Persian Empire.)

The young Persian was powerfully attracted to the Spartan
admiral, and Cyrus and Lysander, the first with money and the
second with military ability, formed a team against Athens that
was deadly. Lysander carefully avoided fighting Alcibiades but
waited. Eventually, Alcibiades had to leave the fleet in order to
go off on a business trip intending to raise money, since
Athens was virtually penniless.

Earnestly, he warned his subordinates to fight no battles till
he returned, but they could not resist the attempt to gain glory
by destroying a few more Spartan ships. They attacked Lysander off the shores of Ionia, and were badly defeated. Alcibiades returned too late and the damage was done.

It had not been his fault, but that did not matter. The exasperated Athenians could not help believing there had been

some agreement between Alcibiades and Lysander, and Alcibiades was removed from office. For the third time, he did not wait for trouble but left, this time for the Thracian Chersonese, where he had some property.

With still one more effort, Athens again built a fleet, melting down the gold and silver ornaments in the temples at the Acropolis in order to get the money. As a result, they were to gain one more sea victory made possible by the Spartan ephors, who, suspicious of success as always, had replaced Lysander at the head of the fleet.

In 406 B.C. the Spartans were defeated, but rough seas prevented the victorious Athenian fleet from rescuing the survivors of those of their own ships which had been sunk. Many Athenian lives were lost in consequence.

The lives of good fighting men were losses that could scarcely be endured in Athens at this point. Driven almost to madness by continuing disaster, the Athenians tried the admirals and, quite illegally, had them beheaded. One admiral, Conon (koh'non), had not been at the scene of the battle. He escaped execution and became admiral of the fleet.

Cyrus the Younger was not going to have his own plans disrupted by Spartan folly. He demanded that the Spartans restore Lysander to his post as admiral and this was done. It was Lysander versus Conon now, in the last round of the long war.

They maneuvered about each other and at last, in 405 B.C., came to grips at Aegospotami (ee"gos-pot'uh-mee) on the Thracian Chersonese. The Athenian fleet had chosen to anchor in a dangerous position, one in which they might be easily attacked and in which they would be helpless to defend themselves.

Alcibiades, still in exile, was living nearby. For the first time in his life, perhaps, he was moved to an unselfish act. He came riding down to shore to warn the Athenians that their position was a dangerous one. He urged them to alter their arrangements. He was told coldly that the fleet needed no advice from traitors and with a shrug of his shoulders, he turned and left Athens to its fate.

A few days later, Lysander attacked suddenly. Twenty ships, under Conon himself, managed to escape to distant Cyprus. All the rest of the Athenian fleet was taken without a fight and the sailors killed. The Battle of Aegospotami ended the Peloponnesian War. The Athenians had nothing more to throw into the fight; a whole generation of their young men had been slaughtered; their last fleet was gone; their last bit of money, down to even the temple ornaments, was spent; their final will to resist had worn out.

Lysander subdued the cities on the northern Aegean and along the straits, so that Athens' lifeline was cut. When the Spartan fleet appeared off the Piraeus in 404 B.C., Athens had to face the bitter truth at last and, in complete helplessness, surrendered.

Some of Sparta's allies suggested that Athens be completely destroyed and her people sold into slavery, but Sparta, at this last minute, remembered what Athens had done for Greece at Marathon and at Salamis, and allowed her to survive over the protests of the sullen Thebans. In April, 404 B.C., the Long Walls were pulled down and Athens was placed under an oligarchy.

That same year, Alcibiades, seeking protection in Persian territory against Spartan vengeance, was assassinated there, probably by Persian orders.

In that year, also, Thucydides the historian, returned from his long exile. When he died some years later, he had only reached 411 B.C. in his history.

11

SPARTA IN CONTROL

ATHENS AFTER AEGOSPOTAMI

Sparta was now supreme over Greece and remained supreme for a generation. This period is known as the Spartan hegemony (hee-jem'oh-nee) from a Greek word meaning "leadership." For a while, Lysander was, in turn, supreme in Sparta and the most powerful man in all Greece. He set up oligarchies everywhere.

The oligarchy was cruelest and at the same time weakest in Athens itself. There it fell under the rule of thirty men (called "the Thirty Tyrants") under the leadership of Critias (krish'-ee-as).

Critias was almost another Alcibiades, talented, intelligent, and vigorous. He had been involved, along with Alcibiades, in the suspicion of having mutilated the religious statues and was imprisoned for a while because of it (see page 153). He had worked hard at Samos to bring back Alcibiades but had been banished in 407 B.C. During his banishment, he lived in Thessaly and tried to establish democracies there. Nevertheless, when he returned to Athens after Aegospotami, he had despaired of democracy. Becoming an oligarch, he quickly found he could not retreat but was forced on into more and more violent action.

He seized power and started a reign of terror, driving important pro-democrats out of Athens and killing others. He killed even those of his own party whom he considered too soft. In the space of a few months, he showed the Athenians what freedom really was by depriving them of it altogether.

One of those who went into exile was Thrasybulus, the leader of the democratic fleet at Samos, seven years earlier. Now he performed a second service to democracy when he gathered some other exiles and, in a daring raid into Attica, seized Phyle (figh'lee), a fortress about eleven miles north of Athens.

Twice the oligarchs tried to dislodge the democrats from Phyle and, in the second battle, Critias was killed. Thrasybulus gained power over Piraeus, where the democrats were always stronger than in Athens itself.

The remaining oligarchs then appealed to Sparta, and Lysander made ready to move against Thrasybulus. What saved the democrats was internal Spartan politics. Lysander was not popular with the Spartan kings or ephors. He was too successful and he had grown arrogant. The Spartan king, Pausanias, with the agreement of the ephors, replaced Lysander with himself and (to spite Lysander) did not save the oligarchs at all, but agreed to allow the Athenian democracy to be restored in September, 403 B.C., thus playing the role of Cleomenes I a century earlier (see page 82).

The oligarchy had been a bloody, nightmarish experience; and though an amnesty was declared between the two parties, the restored democracy was bitter toward those who seemed in the least anti-democratic. It was this that tempted the Athenian democracy to a particularly unfortunate deed — the execution of Socrates (sok'ruh-teez).

Socrates, born in 469 B.C., was a plain man, poor in later life, who won over many Athenians, not by wealth and beauty, but by virtue and wisdom. He was a brave soldier and had fought in the Chalcidice. At the Battle of Delium, he saved the life of Alcibiades.

Socrates began life as a scientist. He is even reported to have studied under Anaxagoras (see page 135). However, the coming of the Peloponnesian War, with its follies and disasters, seems to have convinced him that man, not the universe, was man's enemy; and that it was far more important to study man than to study the universe. For the rest of his life, he considered man's beliefs and way of life. He discussed the meaning of virtue and of justice; he pondered where lay true wisdom and so on.

He gathered admiring disciples about himself and, rather than explain, he questioned. He asked those with whom he discussed matters to define their terms and explain what *they* believed justice or virtue or wisdom to be. Then, on further questioning, he revealed that matters were not so simple; that what was taken for granted was not so certain as was supposed; and that even the most accepted views deserved the closest and most critical examination. ("The unexamined life," he said, "is not worth living.") To Socrates, as to Zeno of Elea, dialectic was the thing. Argument was intended to discover truth, and not, as with many sophists, merely to make a self-serving point.

Socrates disarmed his opponents by pretending ignorance and asking to be instructed; then allowing his opponent to fall into deep traps as this instruction proceeded. There is a story that the Delphic oracle proclaimed Socrates the wisest of men, and that Socrates responded that if he were wiser than other men it was only because he alone, of all men, knew that he knew nothing. This pretense of ignorance is called "Socratic irony."

The most famous of Socrates' pupils was Aristocles (a-ris'-toh-kleez) usually known by his nickname, Plato (play'toh). Socrates never wrote down his philosophy, but Plato wrote a charming series of descriptions of the discussions Socrates held with others. These are Plato's "Dialogues."

Some of them are named for the person with whom Socrates is described as carrying on his discussion. There is the "Gorgias," for instance, in which Socrates talks with the sophist Gorgias of Leontini. In that discussion, Socrates calls for morality in government and describes Aristides the Just as the one great political leader of the Athenian democracy. In the "Protagoras," Socrates and the sophist Protagoras debate the nature of virtue and discuss whether it can be taught.

One of the more famous of the dialogues describes a general discussion at a drinking party. This is the "Symposium" ("drinking together") and the general discussion dealt with the nature of love. That form of love was praised most highly which had as its object a person of virtue and wisdom, rather than merely one of physical beauty. (We still speak of "Platonic love.")

Socrates' views did not please all Athenians. For one thing, he unsettled people by leading them on, then getting them tangled in their own words. Again, he seemed to question the old religion so that many Athenian conservatives thought he was impious and that he was corrupting the young men of Athens. Aristophanes, the conservative satirist (see page 134) wrote a play called "The Clouds" in 423 B.C. which made bitter fun of Socrates.

One might think that with Socrates so unpopular with the conservatives, he might be quite popular with the democrats. Unfortunately, he gave them cause for offense also, for he seemed to be pro-Spartan. Thus, Plato's longest dialogue, "The Republic," deals with Socrates' attempt to consider the question, "What is justice?" In the course of the discussion, Socrates describes his views of the ideal city and in some ways it seemed very much like Sparta and very little like a democracy.

Then, again, among his pupils were several who did Athens great harm. There was Alcibiades, for instance, who was one of the important characters in the "Symposium." Another of his pupils was Critias himself, the leader of the hated Thirty Tyrants.

One of Plato's dialogues is actually named "Critias" and in it and in one other, Critias is described as telling the tale of an island that long ago existed out in the Atlantic Ocean. It was highly civilized but was eventually destroyed by an earthquake and sank beneath the sea. Plato named the island "Atlantis."

It is certain that Plato meant the story merely as a piece of fiction out of which he could draw some moral about ideal cities. However, ever since, there have been people who have insisted on believing that there once really was an Atlantis and in making up all sorts of more or less foolish theories about it.

Socrates was finally brought before a five hundred–man Athenian jury in 399 B.C. and was accused of impiety and of corrupting the youth, though his real crime was that of being, or seeming to be, anti-democratic. Socrates would probably have been acquitted if he had not insisted on using his Socratic methods on the jury and annoying them into convicting him by a narrow majority of 281 to 220.

At the time, executions were carried out by having the convicted person drink hemlock, a poisonous plant extract that kills without pain. For religious reasons, there was a delay of thirty days before Socrates had to drink the hemlock. He might easily have escaped in that interval; his friends had it all arranged and even the democrats would have been content to look the other way. However, Socrates was seventy years old and ready to die, so he insisted on keeping to the principles of a lifetime and of adhering to the law, even when the law seemed unjust.

After Socrates' death, Plato, in pain and grief, left Athens, and stayed first in Megara, then in Sicily. He probably thought he would stay away from Athens forever, but if so, he discovered quickly enough that the world is hard and men are foolish in all cities.

He returned therefore in 387 B.C. and founded a school on grounds just outside Athens. The land had once belonged, according to tradition, to a man named Akademus. The grounds and the school were therefore called (in our spelling) the "Academy."

THE TEN THOUSAND

The end of the Peloponnesian War came just in time for the Persian prince, Cyrus the Younger. He had been helping the Spartans not entirely out of unselfish love of Lysander or Sparta but also because he had made certain plans of his own. He was going to need reliable Greek soldiers for those plans.

His father, Darius II, died in 404 B.C., the year of the surrender of Athens and Cyrus' older brother had succeeded to the throne as Artaxerxes II. Cyrus had no intention of allowing this situation to remain unchallenged. He began to gather soldiers for an attack on his brother in order to win the monarchy for himself. If he could collect enough hoplites he was sure he could defeat any army of Asians his brother could bring against him.

Cyrus had no difficulty in raising his army. Sparta had had profitable dealings with him and she felt it might be a good thing to have a pro-Spartan prince on the Persian throne. She therefore did nothing to prevent Cyrus from proceeding with his plans.

Then, too, Greece had been full of soldiers for a whole generation, now, and with the coming of peace many of them did not wish to return to a civilian life to which they were no longer accustomed or to a city that was ruined. They were glad to serve as soldiers to anyone who would pay them.

Cyrus hired more than 10,000 Greek soldiers (popularly referred to afterward as "The Ten Thousand") under the leadership of a Spartan general, Clearchus (klee-ahr'kus). One of the soldiers in the ranks was an Athenian named Xenophon (zen'oh-fun) who had been a devoted disciple of Socrates.

In the spring of 401 B.C., the Ten Thousand set forth, working their way across Asia Minor to the Gulf of Issus (is'us), which is the northeasternmost corner of the Mediterranean Sea. Cyrus had not told any of his Greeks (except Clearchus) of his intentions, lest they refuse to follow him. At Issus, however, even the dullest Greek soldier realized he was leaving the Greek world behind him and venturing into the unknown depths of Persia. Only by threats and wheedling and the promise of higher pay could they be persuaded to proceed.

But they did at last. They reached the Euphrates and marched southeastward along its banks for 500 miles and more till they reached the town of Cunaxa (kyoo-nak'suh) about eighty-seven miles northwest of Babylon in the summer of 401 B.C. There the loyal Persian forces under the leadership of Artaxerxes II were drawn up.

Cyrus had one objective — his brother's death. He knew that if his brother died, the royal troops would flee or accept him as king. He tried to argue Clearchus into so arranging the battle that the Greek soldiers would make straight for Artaxerxes in the Persian center. Clearchus refused. He was the typical Spartan, brave but stupid, and he insisted on fighting the battle according to orthodox procedure with the strongest forces on the extreme right.

The armies clashed and the Greeks plowed through their opponents. Cyrus saw the battle virtually won, but there was his brother — still alive and well protected by a bodyguard. The sight drove him mad, for the victory would do him no good if his brother lived to gather another army. Without thinking, he charged straight at his brother, and was mowed down and killed by the bodyguard.

The Greeks had won, but they were left without a paymaster and with no one to fight for.

Both they and the Persians were caught fast in a peculiar situation. The Greeks were 1100 miles from home and surrounded by a hostile Persian army. The Persians, on the other hand, stared uneasily at a body of more than 10,000 Greeks whom they dared not attack and whom they could not permit to be at complete liberty.

The satrap Tissaphernes had sided with Artaxerxes against Cyrus the Younger, but now he approached Clearchus, pretending to be the same friend of Sparta he had been during the closing years of the Peloponnesian War. He persuaded the Spartan general to come to his tent, along with four other Greek generals, in order (Tissaphernes said) to discuss the terms of an armistice. Poor Clearchus took the Persian at his word. He and the other generals came to the tent and there the Persian calmly ordered them to be killed.

Tissaphernes was sure that the Greeks, leaderless, would either surrender and possibly join the Persian army, or degenerate into a broken mob that could easily be wiped out.

Neither of these alternatives happened because the Athenian, Xenophon, now emerged to take over the leadership of the leaderless Ten Thousand. They did not return along the Euphrates by the route they had taken from the Aegean, for the Persians blocked that path. Instead, they marched northward along the Tigris, defending themselves skillfully against Persian attack and raids from primitive tribesmen.

They passed the mounds which were all that were left of Nineveh, proud capital of the once-mighty Assyrian Empire. It was only two centuries earlier that Assyria had been destroyed (see page 90) but so complete had been the job that its memory seemed to have vanished from the minds of men and the Ten Thousand had to ask what ruins these were which rose so forlornly beside their route.

For five months they marched, holding off Persians and tribesmen. Finally, in February, 400 B.C., the Ten Thousand, on topping a rise, found themselves looking down upon the Greek city of Trapezus (trap'ih-zus). Beyond it was the Black Sea.

To the Greeks, who were used to the sea, and for whom the thousands of miles of solid, unbroken land within the Persian Empire had been a fearful nightmare, the first sight of ocean water meant uncontrollable joy. They ran to the shore, crying, "Thalassa! Thalassa!" (The Sea! The Sea!)

His adventure done, Xenophon then returned to Athens but did not stay long. The execution of his old teacher Socrates filled him with additional hatred for the Athenian democracy. Like Plato, he left Athens, but unlike Plato, he never returned. He became a Spartan in all but name. He lived among Spartans and fought with them, even against Athens.

Eventually, he wrote the story of the Ten Thousand and called his book the *Anabasis* (uh-nab'uh-sis) or "Up-going" referring to the manner in which the Greek army went up-country from the sea into the depths of Asia. It has remained a classic of military history ever since.

Xenophon also wrote a continuation of the history of the Peloponnesian War from the point at which Thucydides' history had been brought to a halt by the historian's death. Xenophon was not the writer Thucydides was by any means and he was without Thucydides' impartiality. Nevertheless, his work is valuable for there is no other good contemporary description of those days.

SPARTA AND PERSIA

The adventure of the Ten Thousand was more than a mere adventure for, as it turned out, Cyrus the Younger had proved to be the Alcibiades of Persia. For the sake of personal ambition, he had revealed Persia's fatal weakness to the Greeks. It was not just that the Greeks had defeated the Persians at Cunaxa; Greeks had defeated Persians before. It was that a small band of Greeks, stranded a thousand miles inside Persia, could have marched virtually at will through its dominions and come safely out.

It dawned on all thinking Greeks that Persia was terribly weak for all its apparent strength. A determined Greek army with a good general at its head could achieve deeds almost without limits. Even the slow-moving Spartans could see this and could begin to dream of daring Eastern expeditions.

Thus, when Tissaphernes returned to Asia Minor and attacked the Greek cities in reprisal for Greek help to Cyrus the Younger, Sparta did not hesitate to send an army against him, which was joined by many of the Ten Thousand.

The Persians decided it was best to strike back by sea. They had an admiral at hand. The Athenian, Conon, having escaped from Aegospotami to Cyprus (see page 161), was ready for vengeance against the Spartans by any means. He was placed in command of a fleet of 300 Persian and Phoenician ships and went out to hunt for Spartans.

Meanwhile, however, a new king had arisen in Sparta. Agis II, the victor of the Battle of Mantinea (see page 151), died in 399 B.C. His son ordinarily would have become king in his place, but there was doubt that the young man was really his son. He was born at the time Alcibiades was in Sparta and Agis had strongly suspected that Alcibiades was the real father.

Agis also had a younger brother, Agesilaus (uh-jes"ih-lay'us), who now stepped forward, claiming that he was the rightful heir of the throne. This met with some opposition. Agesilaus had been lame from birth and was undersized besides. An old prophecy existed, warning Sparta to "beware a halting reign." Surely, if the king limped, that was a halting reign.

Not at all, said Agesilaus. A king who is not truly heir is what is really meant by a halting reign.

The argument was settled by Lysander. He had been kept inactive after his taste of power at the end of the Peloponnesian War and he wanted to make a comeback. He felt that Agesilaus, the little lame prince, so un-Spartan in appearance, would be easy to handle. His backing helped the lame prince become Agesilaus II of Sparta.

However, Lysander had mistaken his man. Agesilaus for all his small size and limp was a true Spartan and the man did not exist who could handle him. Lysander continued to be kept out of power.

Agesilaus thirsted for military glory and took to heart the lesson of the Ten Thousand. In 396 B.C. he made ready to cross the sea to Asia Minor. In his own mind, he was another Agamemnon (the Peloponnesian king who had invaded Asia 800 years before.) Agesilaus determined to imitate Agamemnon closely and to sacrifice at Aulis (aw'lis), a coastal town in Boeotia, before setting out, just as Agamemnon had done before *he* had set out.

The only trouble was that the Thebans, an unromantic lot, wanted none of it. No Spartan king was going to sacrifice on their territory. They came riding up and chased him off. Agesilaus, feeling he had been made to look ridiculous and that the failure to sacrifice might ruin his entire expedition, gained an implacable hatred for Thebes, which was to influence his future actions in important ways.

In Asia, Agesilaus found that the lesson taught by Xenophon had been a correct one. He was able to roam up and down Asia Minor, defeating the satraps Tissaphernes and Pharnabazus time and again. In particular, he defeated Tissaphernes at Sardis in 395 B.C. and since failure is often considered a crime, Tissaphernes was executed shortly after.

Nevertheless, although the Persians could not defeat Agesilaus in battle, they had learned a trick worth two of that. Ten years earlier they had paid Greek states to make war on Athens, now they sent emissaries to Greece who were laden with gold with which to buy anti-Spartan actions.

To be sure, Greek cities never needed much urging to fight each other and they might have done so without Persian money — but the money helped.

Corinth and Thebes were smarting because though they had been allies of Sparta all through the Peloponnesian War, it was Sparta that took to herself all the benefits of the victory.

Sparta, aware of the growing feeling against her, decided to stop trouble before it began, and sent a force against Thebes which seemed to her (because of the incident at Aulis) to be the very center of anti-Spartan feeling. Sparta's remaining king, Pausanias (Agesilaus was in Asia), advanced from the south, while Lysander himself led a force from the north. It was Lysander's return to action at last, but he was promptly killed in a skirmish and Pausanias was forced to retreat.

Athens had already joined with Thebes in alliance, and now Argos and Corinth promptly joined also. Sparta viewed with horror this sudden coalition against her, and called back Agesilaus from Asia. Of what use were distant victories when one's own house was in flames? Agesilaus didn't wish to leave, but Spartan dsicipline made it necessary. He collected his men, together with as many of the Ten Thousand as remained, including Xenophon himself, and in 394 B.C. marched back via the Hellespont, Thrace and Thessaly — Xerxes' old route of a century before.

On his way, bad news reached him. It seemed that the Persian fleet under Conon had caught the Spartans off Cnidus (nigh'dus), one of the Dorian cities on the southwestern coast of Asia Minor. The Spartan fleet was destroyed and Sparta's naval power was gone after having existed only ten years. Those ten years was all the naval power Sparta would ever have.

Agesilaus realized that without sea power he could scarcely

expect to continue with his plans of eastern conquest. However, he took the disappointment with Spartan stolidity and kept it from his men. He continued to march southward and at Coronea (where fifty years earlier the Boeotians had defeated Athens, see page 139) Agesilaus met the united anti-Spartan forces, Thebes at their head. Agesilaus needed no urging to fight the Thebans he hated, and though they fought well, Agesilaus defeated them. The victory was by too narrow a margin, however, for him to feel secure in Boeotia, and he passed on to Sparta.

But now Sparta was on the receiving end of a number of bitter blows. Her garrisons in Asia Minor could not be reinforced or supplied without a fleet and they had to give in to Pharnabazus and his Persians. Persian money sent Conon back to Athens and there in 393 B.C., the Long Walls were built up again, eleven years after they had been pulled down. Furthermore, in 392 B.C., Corinth and Argos combined to form a single city-state, obviously aimed at Sparta.

Sparta could see nothing ahead but continuous fighting with city after city and she wanted none of it. She was already the leader of Greece and had very little further to gain from continued fighting. In fact, she was very likely to have much to lose.

In 390 B.C., for instance, some 600 Spartan soldiers were passing near hostile Corinth. They felt secure enough for, ordinarily, no force was foolish enough to attack so many Spartan hoplites in a group.

Inside Corinth, however, was an Athenian general, Iphicrates (ih-fik'ruh-teez), who commanded a contingent of a new kind of fighting man. These were lightly armed and were called *peltasts* (pel'tasts) from the light shield or *pelta* which they carried. If these had fought hoplites in a straight match of weight against weight, they would undoubtedly have been crushed as the lightly armed Persians had been crushed time and time again. Iphicrates, however, made use of the virtue of light armor, not its defects. The light armor enabled the peltasts to move quickly and Iphicrates had carefully trained and drilled them to be maneuverable.

The peltasts swarmed out of Corinth. The surprised Spartan hoplites turned to face them and fought with their usual bravery. Their heavy armor weighed them down, however, and tired them, while the light peltasts attacked first here, then there, dodging out of the way of the hoplites' clumsy counterstrokes. In the end, the Spartan group was virtually destroyed.

All Greece was amazed. Spartans might be overwhelmed by superior forces as at Thermopylae or starved into surrender as at Sphacteria. But here at Corinth they were defeated in even fight. For the first time it dawned on Greeks ⟨and even on Spartans⟩ that Spartans could be defeated by superior strategy, if not by superior strength and bravery.

At any cost, Sparta realized, she must establish a peace that would freeze the situation as it was at this moment, while she was master, in order that she might remain master.

Such a peace could only be enforced through the influence of Persian ships and money. Sparta therefore entered into negotiations with Persia and in 387 B.C. they concluded the Peace of Antalcidas (an-tal'sih-das), named for the Spartan admiral who had been the chief representative of his city at the negotiations. Sparta had to agree to give all the Greek cities of Asia Minor back to Persia. The Greek victory over Xerxes, a century earlier, was therefore partially undone, and at a time when Persia was much weaker than in Xerxes' time. However, Persia had learned her lesson and her hand remained quite light. The Greek cities went much their own way as far as internal government was concerned.

By the peace, Persia guaranteed the liberty of all Greek cities. This meant, as far as the Spartans were concerned, that all unions between Greek cities (even when voluntary) had to be broken up since each separate city had to be "free." Thus Corinth and Argos had to break up their union, and the city of Mantinea in Arcadia was forced to break up into five villages.

In this way, Sparta made sure that the rest of Greece remained weak, while she herself, of course, never for one moment dreamed of giving freedom to any of the towns in Laconia or Messenia.

Agesilaus' main target was Thebes, which had humiliated him at Aulis. She was head of the Boeotian confederation and Agesilaus demanded that the confederation break up in order that the various towns be made free.

Thebes refused, but certain Theban oligarchs, very pro-Spartan in sympathy, seized the Cadmea (named for Cadmus, the city's legendary founder). The Cadmea was the city's central fortress, much as the Acropolis was Athens' central fort. The oligarchs turned the Cadmea over to Sparta which occupied it in 382 B.C. As long as Spartan troops were there, Thebes lay occupied and as humiliated as even Agesilaus could desire. For the moment Sparta was supreme and, in Greece at least, at the peak of her strength.

THE FALL OF SPARTA

But Agesilaus' hatred had led him astray. A free Thebes might possibly have been made pro-Sparta, but with Spartan troops on the Cadmea, Thebes became permanently hostile. She waited only for the day when those Spartan troops were driven off.

For four years, Thebes suffered under the Spartan yoke and then one Theban, Pelopidas (pee-lop'ih-das) took action. He had gone into exile in Athens when the Cadmea had been taken but now he returned to lead a conspiracy. In 378 B.C. he and a small party of men, dressed as women, joined a drinking party the Spartan commanders were giving. At the last minute, a Theban traitor sent a message to the Spartan general telling him of the trickery. The general, being told that the note was on urgent business said "Business tomorrow" and put the note away unread.

For him, there was no tomorrow. The "women" drew their knives and slaughtered the Spartans. In the confusion that followed, the Thebans stormed the Cadmea and the Spartans, confused by the sudden assassination, gave it up. (They probably need not have done so, and the Spartan commanders who had yielded were executed when they returned to Sparta, but that did not bring back the Cadmea.)

Thebes now allied herself once more with Athens against Sparta. This was a formidable combination, for Athens was gradually winning over the islands of the Aegean Sea and the cities of the north Aegean coast so that the old confederacy was being formed again, after thirty years. This time Athens, having learned her lesson, did not try to dominate her allies as she had done under Pericles.

Sparta could not allow Thebes and Athens to combine against her and war began. Thebes, however, was now in good hands. In past history, Thebans had not been remarkable for brains or charm or intelligence. Indeed, the agile Athenians had used "Boeotian" as an adjective meaning "stupid." Now not one, but two, amazing men suddenly appeared to head the Thebans.

One was Pelopidas who had spearheaded the conspiracy that had freed the city. The other was Pelopidas' best friend, the even more remarkable Epaminondas (ee-pam"ih-non'das). He organized a special group of Theban soldiers, pledged to fight to the death. These formed the "Sacred Band." With these as the spearhead of the Theban army, Epaminondas managed to hold off the Spartans.

Meanwhile, the Athenians were winning victories at sea. The Spartans had outfitted ships designed to intercept vessels carrying grain to Athens. Thus, it was hoped, the Athenian lifeline would be broken. At Naxos, however, in 376 B.C., the Spartan fleet was, in turn, intercepted by an Athenian fleet and was almost completely destroyed. Spartan ships disappeared from the sea permanently after that.

However, succeeding years saw the tide shift. Syracuse returned Sparta's help in the days of the Athenian invasion by sending ships now to help Sparta. Once again, matters faded into the usual stalemate and, in 371 B.C., all was ready for peace.

But once again Agesilaus' hatred for Thebes stepped in to ruin matters for Sparta, this time permanently. Agesilaus insisted that each city in Boeotia sign separately and would not make peace if Thebes insisted on signing for all. Consequently the peace was only between Sparta and Athens; Sparta and Thebes remained at war.

Now Agesilaus had what he wanted all along — Thebes in isolation and outnumbered so that she might be crushed. In 371 B.C., the Spartan army under Cleombrotus I (klee-om'broh-tus), the king who had succeeded Pausanias on the latter's death in 380 B.C., marched northward. Hardly anybody in Greece doubted that Thebes was doomed.

But Epaminondas was making his own plans. Ordinarily, the Greeks, when fighting a battle, drew out their men into a broad, shallow line, only eight ranks deep at most, so that even the men in the rear had a chance to fight against the enemy. In such a battle, the Spartans were practically certain to win, because soldier for soldier, the Spartans were better. And in this case, matters seemed doubly sure because the Spartans outnumbered the Thebans.

Epaminondas, however, divided his army into three parts. He left the center and right in the usual formation, but the left part (which would face the main striking force on the Spartan right) he formed into a column, fifty ranks deep. The men in the rear of that column did not have to fight. They were there merely as weight. This deep column of men, charging into the Spartan lines would, Epaminondas hoped, plow through the enemy like a log of wood used as a battering ram. The center and the right would be held back and would hit other portions of the Spartan line only after the enemy right had been reduced to confusion.

Epaminondas' column of men was referred to as the "Theban phalanx" (fay'lanks) from a Greek word meaning a "log of wood."

The two armies met at the village of Leuctra (lyook'truh) ten miles southwest of Thebes. The Spartans studied the queer Theban formation and deepened their own line to twelve ranks, but that was not enough. The Theban phalanx charged and all went exactly as Epaminondas had planned. The Spartan line shattered and the army crumbled in confusion. A thousand Spartans died, including Cleombrotus, the first Spartan king to die in action since Leonidas at Thermopylae a century earlier.

Thebes had gained a complete victory and the Spartan hegemony was ended once and for all. It had happened during the "halting reign" of Agesilaus as the oracle had warned. Never again was Sparta able to dominate Greece. From now on, it was all she could do to protect her own territory.

Sparta's Peloponnesian allies deserted her at once. The cities of Arcadia joined into an anti-Spartan league and, as the capital city of the league, they founded (at Epaminondas' suggestion) Megalopolis (meg"uh-lop'oh-lis), meaning "great city," in 370 B.C. It was located almost exactly in the center of the Peloponnesus, just north of the Spartan dominions.

Agesilaus led an army into Arcadia, but the Arcadians promptly appealed to Thebes. Now, for the first time, it was not a Spartan army that issued northward to punish this city or that, but a Theban army marching southward to punish Sparta.

And Sparta, to her own horror, found that she could scarcely resist. For many years, her way of life had been decaying and fewer and fewer full citizens walked her streets. Without knowing it, she had come more and more to depend on her reputation and her allies. With her reputation gone at Leuctra and her allies fallen away, there was nothing left but a small, nearly useless, army.

Epaminondas tore Messenia away from Sparta, reversing the great victories of three centuries before which had laid the foundation for Spartan greatness. Messenia was made independent and about the old fortress of Mount Ithome, where a century earlier the helots had lain beleaguered, the city of Messene (meh-see'nee) was founded in 369 B.C. Sparta was reduced to Laconia itself and was hemmed in by deadly enemies on all sides.

From outside the Peloponnesus, however, came aid that prevented Sparta's total destruction. Athens, uneasy lest Thebes grow too strong, threw her weight on Sparta's side. Syracuse also sent soldiers. With such help, Sparta, under Agesilaus' grim and undaunted leadership, managed to save Laconia itself despite two more invasions by Thebes. (Thebes, as will be described later, was at this time expending much effort on military expeditions to the north and could exert only partial strength against Sparta.)

In 362 B.C., Thebes determined to make an all-out attempt to settle affairs in the Peloponnesus once and for all. With Epaminondas himself at the head of the Theban forces, Thebes invaded the Peloponnesus for a fourth time. It had been Epaminondas' intention to take Sparta, but withered old Agesilaus (now nearly eighty years of age) was still Spartan enough to face the Thebans in readiness to die fighting for the city. Epaminondas decided not to chance the Spartans with their back to the wall.

Instead, further maneuverings brought a battle near the city of Mantinea. This time, Thebes was fighting the allied forces of Sparta and Athens, and once again Epaminondas set up his Theban phalanx. The Spartans had not learned how to counter it. Once again, the flying column came down and shattered them and once again Thebes won a complete victory.

And yet the victory was disastrous for Thebes, for in the moment when the enemy was flying, a chance spear-cast struck Epaminondas and killed him. Without Epaminondas (and with Pelopidas dead in the north, too) Thebes could not help but fall back from the first ranks.

Matters settled down to the status quo in the Peloponnesus and the stalemate continued. Agesilaus, fighting for Sparta in every way he could, was finally reduced to hiring himself out as a mercenary in order to collect money that would enable Sparta to re-enter the arena in her old way.

Egypt was once again rebelling against Persia. Agesilaus offered his services to her and landed in Egypt with a force of men. However, even Agesilaus could not fight old age forever and in 360 B.C., he died.

In his youth he had witnessed Athens at its Periclean height. He had seen Sparta beat Athens and reach the peak of power herself. He had seen her hurtled from that peak in one battle and he had fought ten years to keep her from utter destruction. And now he died on foreign soil in a vain effort to retrieve what could never be retrieved.

12

DECLINE

THE SILVER AGE

Under the stress of the continual and seriously destructive warfare among the city-states of Greece from 431 B.C. onward, Greek culture began to decline. The golden age of Pericles came to an end and what followed over the next century or so can, at best, be described as a "silver age."

Optimism was gone. After the Persian War, it had seemed as though improvement and growth would be continual. The ideal city seemed on the horizon. To Pericles it actually seemed as though Athens were already an ideal city. Philosophers concerned themselves intimately with politics and tried to work out methods whereby man might best be fitted into a good society.

The philosophers that followed the Peloponnesian War, however, abandoned politics and the city as something that had failed. They concerned themselves only with the personal lives of the individual; how a man might best ignore what now seemed to be an entirely bad world and how he might adjust himself to some inner code.

There was Antisthenes (an-tis'thih-neez), for instance, born in Athens about 444 B.C., who studied under Socrates and under Gorgias the sophist. Antisthenes came to believe that happiness lay not in involving one's self with society but in just the opposite, in as complete a withdrawal as possible. One must seek for complete independence in order not to care anything for the opinion of others and therefore not be at the mercy of such opinion. To be truly independent, one had to be careful to avoid involving one's self with possessions, for their loss or even the fear of their loss would bring unhappiness.

The most famous and extreme follower of Antisthenes was Diogenes (digh-ah'jih-neez), who was born in Sinope (sih-noh'pee) on the Black Sea coast of Asia Minor about 412 B.C.

Not only did Diogenes feel that ordinary pleasure was no true path to happiness, but that pain and hunger helped one achieve virtue. He did without as much as possible. He lived in a large tub in order to have the minimum of housing and to be exposed to all kinds of weather. Once used to this, one could dismiss it; weather and changes in weather would then no longer have power to annoy and distress and another source of unhappiness would be gone. He drank out of a wooden bowl until he saw a boy drink out of his cupped palms. At once Diogenes threw away the bowl as an unnecessary luxury.

Naturally, when one withdraws from the world to such an unusual extent, it is because one feels the world to be evil. Diogenes had a very low opinion of other men and there is a famous story of his wandering about the marketplace in day-

light with a lighted lamp in his hand. He was asked what he
was doing and he said he was searching for an honest man. He
clearly implied that there were no honest men, for even in
broad daylight none were visible, so that a lamp had to be
used to add light in a forlorn hope that this might help.

Philosophers like Diogenes were called *kynikos,* from the
Greek word *kyon* meaning "dog," because they seemed always
to be barking and snarling at mankind (at least according to
one story of the derivation of the word). In our spelling, the
word becomes "cynic." The word is still used today for someone who is certain that all actions are brought about through
bad or selfish motives.

Cynicism couldn't possibly be a popular philosophy, but a
more refined version was introduced by Zeno of Citium
(sish'ee-um), a city in Cyprus. (He may have been part
Phoenician and must not be confused with Zeno of Elea, see
page 117, who lived over a century earlier.) Zeno studied under Cynic philosophers at first, but then opened a school of his
own in Athens in 310 B.C.

He taught that a man should be superior to emotion; should
avoid joy and grief and thus be master of fortune, whether
good or bad. His only interest should be virtue and duty, and
by being king over himself, he could not be slave to any man.

He taught such doctrines in a school that possessed a porch
adorned with paintings. The Greeks referred to this school as
the "Stoa Poikile" (painted porch). The teachings, therefore,
came to be referred to, in our spelling, as "Stoicism." To be a
stoic, even today, is to be unemotional and indifferent to pleasure or pain.

A man might withdraw from society not only by teaching
himself to do without material goods, but also by abandoning
himself to a life of personal pleasure.

The author of a philosophy of this type was Aristippus
(ar"is-tip'us). He was born in Cyrene (sigh-ree'nee), a city on
the north African coast west of Egypt, about 435 B.C., came

to Athens for an education and studied under Socrates. He then taught that the only good was pleasure and that pleasure right now is better than preparing for possible pleasure later.

A milder version of this philosophy was originated by Epicurus (ep''ih-kyoo'rus) who was born in Samos about 342 B.C. of Athenian parents. He came to Athens in 306 B.C. and taught that pleasure was the chief good, but emphasized that pleasure only came from a life of moderation and virtue. He adopted the views on atoms that Democritus (see page 135) had held and it was his philosophy of "Epicureanism" that helped such atomist views persist into modern times. To this day, the term "epicurean" refers to someone who appreciates the good things in life.

Literature, too, seemed to abandon the city. The great Athenian tragedians, had dealt with the great and serious relationships among gods and men in order to illuminate the workings of society. Aristophanes had dealt with the immediate politics of the day.

Toward the end of his life, however, with Athens defeated, Aristophanes began to abandon politics and find refuge in fantasies. Tragedy virtually disappeared and comedy began to deal with trivial things. In the period of "New Comedy," the plots involved love and intrigue, clever slaves, beautiful women, and so on. The most capable practitioner of this new form of literature was Menander (mih-nan'der), born in Athens in 343 B.C. He wrote over a hundred plays of which only one, discovered in 1957, survives intact.

Athens of the silver age produced no sculptor quite as great as Phidias; no structure as magnificent as the Parthenon. It did produce Praxiteles (prak-sit'uh-leez) who may still be considered of the first magnitude, however. One statue, believed to be his work, still survives. It is that of the god Hermes, carrying the infant, Dionysus.

Only in mathematics and science did advance still continue. Eudoxus (yoo-dok'sus) was a pupil of Plato and had been

BLAIRSVILLE SENIOR HIGH SCHOOL
BLAIRSVILLE, PENNA.

born in Cnidus about 408 B.C. He was primarily a mathematician who introduced many geometric proofs that, nearly a
century later, found their way into the summarizing work of
Euclid (see page 266).

Eudoxus applied his geometry to the study of the heavens.
He was the first Greek to establish the fact that the year was
not exactly 365 days long, but was six hours longer. Although
Plato had maintained that the planets (Mercury, Venus, Mars,
Jupiter, Saturn, the sun and the moon) traveled about the
heavens in perfect circles, Eudoxus' observations convinced
him they did not, at least in appearance.

He was the first to begin an effort to "save the appearances";
that is, to explain how motion in perfect circles, as required by
Plato's philosophy, could produce the uneven motions actually
observed. Eudoxus supposed that each planet was embedded
in a sphere that turned evenly, but with its poles embedded in
a second sphere, the poles of which were embedded in a third
and so on. Each sphere moved evenly, but the combination of
motions produced an apparent uneven motion of the planet
itself.

Eudoxus required a total number of twenty-six spheres in
order to account for the motions of the planets. Closer observations, however, showed that the accounting wasn't perfect. Callippus (kuh-lip"us) of Cyzicus, a pupil of Eudoxus,
was forced to add eight more spheres, making thirty-four in all.
In this way, the notion of the "heavenly spheres" was introduced; a notion that was to last for 2000 years before modern
astronomers laid it finally to rest.

Nevertheless, some Greek astronomers were on the right
road even then. There is the case of Heraclides (her"uh-
kligh'deez) born in Heraclea Pontica (her"uh-klee'uh
pon'tih-kuh) on the Black Sea coast of Asia Minor in 390 B.C.
(and therefore often referred to as "Heraclides Ponticus"). He
was a student of Plato and he pointed out that it was not necessary to assume that the earth remained motionless while the

entire vault of the heavens revolved about it every twenty-four hours. The same effect would be produced if the heavens were motionless and the earth rotated on an axis. He was the first man we know of who maintained the rotation of the earth.

Heraclides also maintained that the motions of Mercury and Venus could be far more easily explained if they were not assumed to have spheres of their own as Eudoxus had suggested. Instead, they could be viewed as circling the sun.

Heraclides' notions were carried further by Aristarchus (ar″is-tahr′kus) born in Samos about 320 B.C. He measured the comparative distance of the moon and sun from the earth. His theory was correct, but because his actual observations were faulty (the Greeks did not have adequate instruments with which to study the sky) he concluded that the sun was about twenty times as distant as the moon, whereas in actual fact it is about 400 times as distant. Even so, he concluded that the sun must be seven times as large as the earth in diameter. (It is actually a hundred times as large, but Aristarchus had made a great advance over Anaxagoras, see page 135).

Since the sun is larger than the earth, it seemed unreasonable to Aristarchus to believe that the sun revolved about the earth. He suggested, therefore, that the earth and all the planets revolved about the sun. For a moment, it seemed as though modern concepts of astronomy might come to birth. Unfortunately, the moment passed. The notion that the vast and solid earth might be flying through the heavens was simply too much for the philosophers of the time to swallow and astronomy had to wait 2000 years more to find the right path.

SYRACUSE AT ITS HEIGHT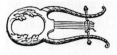

But while Greek culture was declining, it was also spreading outward. Every city, as far as it was able, began to imitate

Athens. What's more, regions on the outskirts of the Greek world, that were outside the mainstream of Greek development or were even barbarian, began to adopt Greek culture and Greek military methods.

This introduced a serious change in the world. The city-states were safe as long as they were surrounded by primitive tribesmen and by oriental kingdoms such as those of Egypt and Persia which lacked the intense efficiency and energy of the Greeks.

However, once outlying regions became Greek and efficient, they also became dangerous, for they had far larger areas and far greater resources than did the tiny city-states of Greece itself. In the century that followed the Peloponnesian War, the city-state gradually came to be outmoded as a political unit. The future was going to belong to large kingdoms. The Greeks never really recognized this and never succeeded in matching the strength of the surrounding regions by themselves uniting into something larger than the city-state.

Instead, the city-states kept fighting among themselves, completely oblivious to the fact that the world was changing and that, on the horizon, there were beginning to appear new powers that dwarfed them.

The first of these "powers on the outskirts" arose in an area that was actually Greek, but was outside Greece itself. It arose in Sicily where the barbarian danger had become acute again.

After the failure of the Athenian expedition against Syracuse (see page 155), Carthage had felt it would be a good time to strike again. For three years, the Carthaginians won battles against the disunited Greeks, who got no help from a Greece then involved in the final stages of the Peloponnesian War.

Then, in 405 B.C., a citizen of Syracuse, Dionysius (digh"oh-nish'ee-us) denounced the Syracusan generals as traitors. New generals were appointed, of whom Dionysius himself was one. Gradually and shrewdly, Dionysius courted

the common people and increased his powers (as Pisistratus
had done in Athens a century earlier) until he was tyrant over
Syracuse as Dionysius I.

Dionysius began by making peace with the Carthaginians
and utilizing the time so gained in reorganizing Syracuse. Then
he established mastery over neighboring Greek cities and in
398 B.C. was ready to take on Carthage anew. In the next
fifteen years, he fought three wars with them and eventually
had five-sixths of the island under his control. By 383 B.C. the
Carthaginians retained only the western tip of the island. This
was the point of maximum power for the Sicilian Greeks.

Meanwhile, in 390 B.C., Dionysius had turned his attention to
Italy itself and had won control of the toe of the Italian boot.
His influence extended more loosely over many of the Greek
cities on the eastern shores of the peninsula. He even extended
his power across the Adriatic into Epirus (ee-pigh'rus), a
tribal area northwest of Greece that was slowly being penetrated by Greek culture.

In part, Dionysius' successes in warfare arose from the
manner in which he adapted new inventions. His engineers
were the first to develop devices for throwing large stones, or
shooting huge bolts. These "catapults" became increasingly important in later warfare, down to the invention of gunpowder
sixteen centuries later.

Dionysius kept his power through eternal vigilance. For instance, there is a story that he had a bell-shaped chamber opening into the state prison, with the narrow end connecting to his
room. In this way, he could secretly listen to conversations in
the prison and learn if any conspiracies were brewing. This has
been called the "ear of Dionysius."

He had to be so much on his guard (as was true for all
Greek tyrants) that through all his years in power he could
never relax. This is made most dramatically clear in connection
with a famous story told about a Syracusan courtier named

Damocles (dam'oh-kleez) who openly envied Dionysius' power and good fortune.

Dionysius asked him if he would like to be tyrant for a night. Damocles agreed joyfully and that night sat down in the seat of honor at a glorious banquet. Almost at once he noted people staring at a point over his head. He looked up and there was a naked sword, point downward, just above him. It was attached to the ceiling by a single hair.

Bitterly, Dionysius explained that his own life was always under this sort of threat and that if Damocles was to be tyrant for a night, he would have to endure the threat throughout the banquet. Since then, any great danger which constantly threatens and which may fall at any time is called a "sword of Damocles."

Another famous story of Dionysius' reign concerns a man named Pythias (pith'ee-as) who was convicted of conspiracy against the tyrant and was condemned to death by hanging. Pythias needed time to arrange his affairs and a good friend of his, Damon, offered to remain as hostage in Pythias' place, while Pythias left for home. If Pythias did not return by the time set for execution, Damon agreed to be hanged in his place.

The day of the hanging came and no Pythias! However, even as the noose was placed about Damon's neck, Pythias' voice rang out from the distance. He had been unavoidably detained and was now charging in at a desperate mad gallop in order that he himself, and not his friend, might hang. The hardened old tyrant was so affected by this that (the story goes) he pardoned Pythias and said that he only wished he himself were worthy of the friendship of men such as these.

Ever since, the phrase "Damon and Pythias" has been used to express loving and inseparable friendship.

In the end, Dionysius died in peace, in 367 B.C., after having ruled successfully for thirty-eight years. While he lived he was the most powerful man in the Greek-speaking world, although this power was largely unappreciated since it did not make itself felt in Greece itself.

It is odd that while historians usually focus on the struggles for mastery of Sparta, Thebes, Athens, Corinth and the rest in the decades after the Peloponnesian War, it was Syracuse that was actually strongest. This is something like the manner in which European nations struggled for mastery in the early twentieth century when it was the United States in the far west that was really strongest. In fact, Syracuse is sometimes called "the New York of Ancient Greece."

If Dionysius had had successors as capable as himself, Sicily might have come to lead a united Greece that would then have striven on equal terms with the non-Greek nations that were slowly coming to power.

However, this did not happen, Dionysius' successor was his son, Dionysius II or "Dionysius the Younger." He was a young man who was dominated by Dion (digh'on) who had been the elder Dionysius' brother-in-law.

Dion was an admirer of Plato, whom he had met when Plato visited Syracuse in 387 B.C. Plato had then offended Dionysius with his criticisms of tyranny. Dionysius (no one to trifle with) had Plato sold into slavery. However, the philosopher was quickly ransomed and brought to Athens. Dion followed him there and studied at the Academy.

Now that Dionysius was safely dead, Dion invited Plato to return to Syracuse and be tutor for the new tyrant. This Plato was glad to do, for he had said that there was to be no ideal state until "philosophers were kings or kings were philosophers." Here was his chance to make a king a philosopher.

Unfortunately, matters did not work out according to plan, either for Plato or Dion. Dionysius II grew restless under Plato's teaching and began to feel that Dion was just putting him to school in order to keep him out of the way while Dion ran Sicily. Dionysius turned on Dion, drove him out of the country and then discharged Plato.

Dion returned, seized power in 355 B.C. and kicked out the young Dionysius. Despite Dion's philosophy, he ruled as tyrannically as ever either Dionysius had done, but two years later, in 353 B.C., he was assassinated.

Eventually, Dionysius II was able to take advantage of the confusion that followed and placed himself back in power. Sicily found itself ruled still more tyrannically and less capably than ever. There were uprisings and civil wars and life became insupportable. Syracusan citizens, in 343 B.C., finally appealed to Corinth (the mother-city) for someone to help rid her of her tyrants.

It might have seemed a forlorn hope, but it turned out that Corinth had just the man for the job in Timoleon (tih-moh'lee-on), a sincere and idealistic democrat. He disapproved so strongly of tyranny that when his own brother made himself tyrant, Timoleon approved of his execution. His family, in indignation, drove him into exile for twenty years. He was nearly seventy when the call from Syracuse came, but he answered at once.

With 1200 men, Timoleon landed in Sicily and found a violent civil war in progress with the forces of Dionysius the Younger being hemmed in by his enemies. Timoleon accepted the surrender of Dionysius who retired to Corinth and passed the rest of his days in peace, running some sort of school. Timoleon then arranged for peace among the warring factions and made himself master of Syracuse.

He called back exiles, attracted new colonists from Greece, re-established a democracy, then overthrew the tyrannies that had grown up in other Sicilian towns. When Carthage tried to interfere, Timoleon defeated her in 338 B.C. He was everywhere successful and when he had completed his work, he resigned, for he wanted no power for himself. The next year, 337 B.C., he died.

But the brief promise of power under Dionysius I had died in the generation of disorder that had followed his death. History's moment had passed Syracuse by and Syracuse was not fated, after all, to save Greece — or even itself.

THE MOMENT OF THESSALY

While Dionysius ruled in Sicily, and Sparta drove onward to its fall, Thessaly, in northern Greece, had her brief moment of power.

In Mycenaean times, the land that later became Thessaly gave rise to Jason, the leader of the Argonauts, and Achilles, the hero of the *Iliad*. It was the largest plain in Greece, fertile and lovely. (The beautiful "vale of Tempe" [tem'pee], which was immortalized by Greek writers, is in Thessaly.)

Thessaly is the one place in mainland Greece where horses were practical for warfare. The legendary "centaurs," half man and half horse were supposed to have lived in Thessaly and this may represent what primitive Greeks thought they saw when they first encountered Thessalian horsemen.

If Thessaly could have been under some united government it might have ruled Greece. However, after the Dorian invasion it fell out of the main current of Greek history. Thessalian cavalry remained famous and useful as mercenaries (a detachment served as bodyguard to Pisistratus, the tyrant of Athens, for instance) but Thessaly itself was occupied by squabbling tribes which could not unite to make their force felt.

Then, in the days of Epaminondas, a new Jason arose in Thessaly. He was Jason of Pherae (fee'ree), a town of central Thessaly. By clever political maneuvering and skillful use of mercenary troops, Jason united Thessaly behind himself and in 371 B.C. was chosen general-in-chief of the Thessalian clans.

Since Sparta (now in the last days of her hegemony) opposed the formation of any unions in Greece larger than the city-state, Jason allied himself to Thebes.

Almost at once the Battle of Leuctra took place (see page 178) and Jason, at the head of his cavalry, came dashing southward to look at the battlefield a few days later (as once the Spartans had come northward to view Marathon). For a brief time, with Sparta smashed and Thebes confining herself to making sure that Sparta stayed smashed, Jason felt himself to be the most powerful man in mainland Greece. He dreamed of establishing leadership over Greece and leading the united city-states against Persia. He might possibly even have done this except that, in 370 B.C., he was assassinated.

His death threw Thessaly into confusion. The rule over Pherae passed to Jason's nephew, Alexander. However, Alexander of Pherae was a cruel man, without the charm of the short-lived Jason. He could not command the submission of the Thessalian tribes, as Jason had. To make matters worse, Macedonia, to the north of Thessaly, seized the opportunity to interfere.

Macedonia was gaining in prosperity. Its capital, Pella (pel'uh), about twenty miles inland from the northwestern corner of the Aegean Sea, served as refuge for a number of Greeks exiled from home for political reasons. The Athenian playwright, Euripides, spent the last years of his life at the Macedonian court.

Jason's assassination opened the way for Macedonia and when, in 369 B.C., Alexander II came to the throne, he took a strong line and attempted to establish an influence over Thessaly in turn.

For a short while, the two Alexanders, one of Macedonia and one of Pherae, struggled. Then the Thessalian cities, which wanted freedom from both, sent a plea for help to Thebes which had now become, thanks to Leuctra, dominant in Greece.

In response, Thebes sent an expedition northward under Pelopidas, who had initiated the days of Theban greatness with his conspiracy against the Spartan overlords (see page 176). Pelopidas signed a treaty with Alexander II but that was promptly overturned by the assassination of the Macedonian king in 368 B.C. by one of his nobles. The assassin promptly assumed the role of regent for Alexander's older son, Perdiccas III.

Pelopidas had to return to Thebes. To make sure that Macedonia would make no trouble, whatever further disorders it might get involved in, he took several hostages back to Thebes from among the Macedonian nobility. One of them was the new king's thirteen-year-old younger brother, Philip.

Pelopidas did not have much luck in his task of chastizing Alexander of Pherae. On a second expedition, he was captured by Alexander and kept imprisoned for several months before a Theban force under Epaminondas could force Alexander to release him.

In 364 B.C. Pelopidas headed a third expedition into Thessaly and met the army of Alexander at Cynoscephalae (sigh″nuh-sef′uh-lee), not far north of Pherae. There the Thebans won a victory, but Pelopidas died. The infuriated Thebans struck at Alexander with all their force and he was compelled to make a peace that confined him to the city of Pherae itself. He took to piracy for a living and finally, in 357 B.C., was assassinated. The Thessalian threat to Greece was over for good.

THE MOMENT OF CARIA

But another threat arose in the east. It was not Persia, for that giant, while still in existence, was far too tired to want any

trouble. Rather, it was from that section of interior Asia Minor
called Caria (kar'ee-uh). Carian tribes had, originally, controlled the Ionian coast before the time of the Greek settlements that followed the Dorian invasions (see page 19). Afterward, they were under the control first of Lydia, then of
Persia, and made no separate mark in history.

Not, at least, until the period after the fall of Sparta. Then,
with Persian rule weak, the Carians had a brief moment of
power. They were under their own chiefs who, nominally,
were Persian satraps but who were independent in actual fact.

The ablest and most powerful of these was Mausolus (maw-
soh'lus) who came to power in 377 B.C. He extended his control over the entire southwestern corner of Asia Minor and
moved his capital from an inland Carian city to the coastal
Greek city of Halicarnassus (the home city of Herodotus the
historian). Slowly, he began to build a navy and to try for
domination of the Aegean Sea from his new coastal base.

The Greek enemy he faced was Athens. Sparta was done and
after the death of Epaminondas in 362 B.C., Thebes retired into
her shell and would involve herself in no distant adventures.
That left Athens and her navy. Once again, she ruled the
Aegean Sea, won victories in the north and secured her lifeline.

In 357 B.C., however, Mausolus was beginning his forward
move. He intrigued with the larger Aegean islands and persuaded them to rise in revolt against their Athenian rulers.
Athens sent a fleet to subdue them but it was defeated, and the
Athenian admirals were retired in disgrace. The Athenian general Chares (kay'reez), however, went on to land in Asia Minor
in 355 B.C. and to fight successfully against Persian armies.
Once again, the weakness of Persia and the ease with which
their armies could be defeated by Greeks was demonstrated.

Despite Chares' victories, Athens decided not to try any
great adventures. The Syracusan disaster had cured her of such
attempts once and for all. She agreed to peace with Mausolus
and if the large Aegean islands wanted to be independent, very

well, let them be. Athens gave them up. She no longer had any desire for empire and provided her lifeline was safe, she would ask for no more.

Mausolus continued to move forward, of course, and in 353 B.C. annexed the large island of Rhodes, some fifty miles southeast of Halicarnassus. However, at the moment when he seemed to hover at the point of great deeds, he died, and, as in the case of Jason of Pherae, the threatening power vanished at once.

Mausolus' widow, Artemisia (ahr″teh-miz′ee-uh) was inconsolable at his death. She determined to raise a monument for him, and built a large tomb above the harbor at Halicarnassus. It contained not only the body of the dead king, but gigantic statues of him and of herself, with a carved chariot on top of the tomb and sculptured friezes all about.

It is a sign of the declining culture of the silver age that Greek tastes were beginning to run to the elaborate and showy. The simple Doric column had lost its popularity and somewhere about 430 B.C. the architect, Callimachus (ka-lim′uh-kus), had invented the much more ornate Corinthian column.

In place of the glorious Parthenon was the tomb of Mausolus (or the "Mausoleum," a word still used today for a large tomb) which was probably far too decorated to be truly beautiful. Nevertheless, when the Greeks chose the Seven Wonders of the World, they included the Mausoleum on the list but *not* the Parthenon.

Another showy "Wonder" of the time was in Ephesus. The patron goddess of the city was Artemis, and an elaborate temple (the "Artemision," or, in Latin spelling, "Artemisium") had been built in her honor. It had been begun in the time of Croesus and it was completed about 420 B.C. It was impressive enough to be one of the Seven Wonders of the World.

In October, 356 B.C., the Artemisium was destroyed by fire and it proved to be a case of deliberate arson. When the culprit was captured, he was asked why he had done this deed. He replied that he did it in order that his name might live in history. To defeat this desire, he was executed and it was ordered that his name be erased from all records and never be spoken.

However, the man had his wish after all, for his name survived, somehow, and is known. It is Herostratus (her"oh-stray'tus) and he will always be remembered as the man who deliberately burned down one of the Seven Wonders of the World.

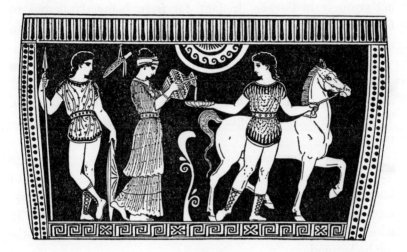

13

MACEDONIA

THE COMING OF PHILIP

The death of power-hungry men did not save the Greek city-states. As fast as one danger disappeared, another danger loomed. The real trouble was that the city-state was played out. The question was not whether Greece would fall under the domination of a kingdom of the new style; that was certain! The only question was: Which one?

In 365 B.C. no one would have thought of Macedonia as a danger. It had recently been dominated by Thessaly under Jason of Pherae, and more recently still it had undergone the upheaval of the assassination of its king, Alexander II. The young king, Perdiccas III, son of Alexander, was under the control of the assassin who was acting as regent.

Furthermore, Macedonia was surrounded by semi-civilized tribes who represented a constant danger. While she had to face outward against these tribes she had little opportunity to act strongly in Greece. In fact, far from being dangerous to Greece she acted as a useful buffer between Greek civilization and northern barbarism.

In 365 B.C., however, came the beginning of change. The young king, having carefully bided his time, had the regent assassinated in his turn and assumed sole rule of Macedonia. The next year, his younger brother, Philip, returned to Macedonia.

Philip had been taken to Thebes back in 367 B.C. (see page 195) as hostage. During his three years there, he learned to know Epaminondas. Philip, an exceedingly bright young man, took note of the Theban phalanx and of the new manner in which Epaminondas maneuvered his armies. Philip forgot nothing he learned.

His knowledge and abilities were to be badly needed, for Macedonia was in trouble. Its internal upsets were an open invitation to the surrounding tribes. In 359 B.C. Perdiccas was killed in a border skirmish. The kingdom found itself in the desperate position of being threatened with invasion from all sides and with only a boy king, Amyntas III (uh-min'tas), son of Perdiccas, on the throne.

Clearly, someone would have to act for the young king and his uncle Philip (only twenty-one himself) took over the regency. Philip had already insured the friendship of neighboring Epirus on the west (it had earlier been under the control of Dionysius I of Syracuse, but was now under native princes once more) by marrying Olympias (oh-lim'pee-as), the niece of the king of Epirus, in 359 B.C.

With incredible energy, Philip now began to strike out in all directions, and by 358 B.C., had put an end to border raids. He hurled himself first at the Paeonians (from the north) and then at the Illyrians (from the northeast) and drove them out of

Macedonia. (In a later campaign, he smashed at both again and ended their danger while he lived.)

With that done, and Epirus secure, Philip found himself in control of all the region north of Greece, from Thrace on the east to the Adriatic on the west.

He was now able to turn to face the Aegean and he promptly acquired valuable territory to the southeast in the Chalcidice. The strongest city of the peninsula was Olynthus (oh-lin'thus). It formed a confederacy of Chalcidian towns and stood in the way of Philip's ambitions.

Neither the Athenians nor the Olynthians regarded Philip with any concern at first. The Macedonians had never been more than nuisances before and each side felt perfectly safe in using Philip as a kind of tool against the other.

Philip found it perfectly easy to take advantage of the greed of each side and fool both. He kept the Athenians quiet by promising to turn over Olynthian territory to them, and Olynthus was calmed by his promises to deliver Potidaea, its neighbor and long-time rival, to them. Then, of course, whatever he took, he kept for himself and met all outraged cries of deception and fraud with bland calm. In particular, he took the city of Amphipolis in 358 B.C.

A few months later, he enlarged and strengthened a town about sixty miles northwest of Amphipolis and renamed the city Philippi (fih-lip'igh) after himself. Valuable gold mines were located nearby and these brought in handsome sums of money with which Philip could buy valuable allies among the Greeks.

In those early years, Philip was also busily engaged in reorganizing his troops. He already had cavalry, a traditional part of the Macedonian army, but what he needed were well-drilled foot-soldiers. He adopted the ideas of Iphicrates to build up contingents of light-armed peltasts and slingers.

More important still, he adopted the Theban phalanx and made crucial improvements. He wanted the phalanx to be more than a simple log of wood that could move only in the direction in which it was pointed. He made it less dense, therefore, and allowed it fewer rows, giving it room for maneuver this way and that. The men in the back rows rested their unusually long spears on the shoulders of the men in front, so that the "Macedonian phalanx" resembled a porcupine. By shifting the spears and turning, the porcupine could face the enemy in any direction.

In 356 B.C. Olympias gave birth to a son, who was named Alexander, and of whom much more will be said later. There is a story that he was born on the very day that the Artemisium in Ephesus had been burned down by Herostratus (see page 197), but this is probably a later invention.

By now Philip had proved his ability to the satisfaction of the nation. He had vast ambitions which he did not want to see interrupted by the coming of age of young Amyntas, particularly now that Philip had an heir of his own. In 356 B.C., therefore, Philip had Amyntas deposed and took over the kingship himself as Philip II.

THE ORATORS OF ATHENS

In the century following the Peloponnesian War, a new group of important men arose in Athens, the "orators." They spread their influence over Greece through the force of ideas which they presented persuasively and logically in their orations. (This indicates, after a fashion, how Athens was turning from deeds to words, from action to speech.)

One of the most famous, Isocrates (igh-sok'ruh-teez), was

born in 436 B.C. He had not the voice required to give his own orations effectively, but he wrote voluminously and was an effective teacher. Almost all the orators of the period were among his pupils.

Isocrates was one Greek (perhaps the only Greek) who had learned the correct lesson of the times; that the city-state was done. As early as 380 B.C. he began to preach one theme over and over again — Greeks must stop fighting among themselves. They must unite in a "pan-Hellenic" (all-Greek) league. If they needed some common enemy to hold them together, there was always the old enemy, Persia. Isocrates looked about for some strong leader who could lead the united Greek forces and, for a while, fixed hopefully on Dionysius I of Syracuse.

However, Isocrates, to the very end (and he lived for nearly a century) could get no one to listen to him. Greece had its heart set on suicide and suicide it was determined to commit.

But the greatest of all the Athenian orators and the one who stepped forward as the great opponent of Philip was Demosthenes. (He is not to be confused with the Athenian general of the same name who, during the Peloponnesian War, captured Pylos and died at Syracuse.)

Demosthenes the orator was born in 384 B.C., when Athens was just recovering from the Peloponnesian War. He had a hard childhood, since his father died while he was young and some relative then absconded with the family fortune.

Demosthenes was forced to struggle upward by his own exertions and many tales are told of the inhuman drive with which he urged himself onward to greatness. He was supposed to have shaved one side of his head so as to force himself to remain in isolation, studying. He copied all of Thucydides eight times in order to study good style. He had some sort of speech impediment, so he practiced speaking with pebbles in his mouth in order to force himself to enunciate clearly. He also shouted against the pounding of the surf on the shore so as to force himself to speak loudly. In the end, he made a great orator of himself; one of the greatest of all time.

Demosthenes' dream was that of an Athens that would serve as a shield for all Greece; one that would always come to the aid of any Greek town threatened by barbarians. To Demosthenes, Philip was a barbarian; and he watched in concern as the Macedonian took over the north Aegean shore bit by bit.

In 355 B.C., the situation in Greece itself began to play into Philip's hands. In that year, Phocis once again took Delphi in another of her repeated attempts to control the holy city that had once been part of her territory. This started the "Third Sacred War."

The Thebans marched against Phocis and defeated the Phocians in 354 B.C. but not conclusively. Once the Thebans were gone, Phocis, under capable leadership, expanded its influence again and even began to take control of sections of Thessaly to the north. For a brief moment, Phocis seemed on the point of gaining mastery over northern Greece.

However, the Thessalians appealed to Philip who had just succeeded in taking the last of the Athenian possessions in the north. On the pretense of protecting holy Delphi, he marched southward. The Phocians actually held their own for a while against him, but in 353 B.C. Philip defeated them and took over all of Thessaly. He was master of all the north (except for Olynthus) down to the Pass of Thermopylae. No barbarian had brought Greece to such a pass since the days of Xerxes.

Phocis itself was saved when Athens, Sparta and other Greek towns combined to help her, but, as usual, no combination could last long. Sparta was still trying to regain what she had lost twenty years before and prepared to attack Megalopolis in Arcadia. Athens turned to stop her and the united front against Philip was lost.

In 352 B.C. Philip turned on Thrace and advanced his influence to the very straits that were the lifeline of Athens.

This was the last straw. Mausolus was dead and there was

nothing to distract Athens. A blind man could see that Philip was infinitely more dangerous than ever Mausolus had been.

In 351 B.C., therefore, Demosthenes rose to deliver a major oration concerning the Macedonian danger. This is the "First Philippic" from the man against whom it was aimed and ever since that time, the term "philippic" has been used for any speech aimed squarely and violently at some particular individual.

Unfortunately, Athens was long past the time when she could indulge in a crusade. Demosthenes' stirring words could rouse only the most hollow response. There were even a number of Athenians who did not share Demosthenes' anti-Macedonian views. They saw in Philip, not a dangerous barbarian, but a borderland Greek who might be powerful enough to unite the city-states and lead them in a pan-Hellenic war against Persia. Isocrates was one of them. Then, too, there was Aeschines (es'kih-neez), an orator scarcely inferior to Demosthenes, who also remained a force for peace.

Philip, with a scant regard for the words of Demosthenes, now turned on what remained of the Chalcidice, on Olynthus itself. Olynthus, in panic, pleaded for Athenian help and Demosthenes made three speeches urging that such help be delivered. All Athens could do, however, was to send her general, Chares, at the head of a few mercenaries. It was completely inadequate. Philip brushed Chares to one side and took Olynthus in 348 B.C.

Athens could do nothing but ask for peace. Ten ambassadors were sent to Philip, to negotiate the terms; these included Demosthenes and Aeschines. Philip carefully delayed matters on one excuse or another and used the delay to extend his control over Thrace. Finally, he signed the peace which insured the Thracian Chersonese to Athens and in which Athens finally bowed to the inevitable (after eighty years) and gave up all claims to Amphipolis.

After the peace was signed, Philip calmly moved through the

Pass of Thermopylae to punish the Phocians who had now controlled Delphi for ten years. In combination with Thebes, he took Delphi from Phocis. In 346 B.C. it was Philip himself (not even a Greek as far as Demosthenes was concerned) who presided at the Pythian games, which Cleisthenes of Sicyon had set up over two centuries before on the occasion of the First Sacred War (see page 65).

THE FALL OF THEBES

Demosthenes allowed nothing to deflect him from his enmity to Philip and bent all his efforts to organizing a new and more successful war against Macedonia. Slowly, he gained power in the city over the pro-Macedonian faction and in 344 B.C. delivered a rousing "Second Philippic."

But Philip continued on his own path, occupying what was left of Thrace. In 341 B.C., he founded Philippopolis (fil"ih-pop'oh-lis) or "Philip's city" a hundred miles north of the Aegean. He had marched farther northward than had any civilized army since the time of Darius' invasion of Thrace a century and a half before.

In that year, Demosthenes delivered his "Third Philippic" and persuaded Greek cities on the Propontis, including Byzantium, to rise against Philip. He forced Athens to support Byzantium adequately and this meant renewed war between Athens and Macedonia. Philip now had his greatest failure for after a long siege he was forced to abandon his attempt to take Byzantium. His prestige fell and that of Demosthenes rose.

However, the town of Amphissa (am-fis'uh) in Phocis had been cultivating certain fields which had been part of Crisa two centuries before and which had been laid under a curse after the First Sacred War (see page 65). The priests who controlled Delphi now decided to take offense at this and the "Fourth Sacred War" was begun. Once again Philip was called in and soon his army stood on the shores of the Gulf of Corinth.

Demosthenes then won his greatest diplomatic victory. He persuaded Thebes to join in alliance with Athens against Philip. The Thebans, although they had done very little since the death of Epaminondas a quarter-century earlier, still hugged to themselves the memories of the Battles of Leuctra and Mantinea and considered themselves to be a major military power. Demosthenes believed this, too, and felt secure in the shadow of the Theban army.

Together, Thebes and Athens faced the power of Macedon at Chaeronea (ker"oh-nee'uh) in western Boeotia. The Theban Sacred Band which had never been defeated in battle since it had first been formed by Epaminondas a generation before, faced the Macedonian phalanx. It was the first really great test of the phalanx.

The result was disaster for the Greeks. The Athenians broke and ran. Among the runners was Demosthenes, who was not quite ready to die for his beliefs. (He was reproached after the battle for having run away, and he answered in a phrase that has now become famous. Slightly changed, it goes, "He who fights and runs away, lives to fight another day.")

The Thebans at Chaeronea fought more honorably. The Sacred Band broke and bled against the Macedonian phalanx, but they did not flee. They died, at last, to the final soldier, like the Spartans at Thermopylae, with their faces turned to the enemy. It was defeat but not disgrace for Thebes.

This was the end of the Theban hegemony and the beginning of a Macedonian hegemony that was to last for over a century.

It is reported that the old Isocrates died of a broken heart on hearing the news of Chaeronea, but this is unlikely. He had been pro-Philip all through, recognizing him as the man of the hour, and urging Philip to lead a united Greece against Persia (which is just what Philip was now planning to do). It is much more likely that Isocrates simply died of old age. He was, after all, ninety-eight years old at the time of Chaeronea.

Philip occupied Thebes and treated her harshly but left Athens untouched and won her submission by gentleness. This may have been the result of his admiration for Athens' past, but it may also have been his respect for the Athenian navy which was still intact and which could cause much trouble even if he occupied Attica.

Only the Peloponnesus remained and Philip now drove into it. He met with no resistance from anyone but Sparta. Sparta alone, in proud memory of her past, refused to submit. There is a story that Philip sent a message to Sparta which said, "If I enter Laconia, I will level Sparta to the ground." The defiant Spartan ephors are reported to have replied with a single word: "If!" It is the most famous laconism in history.

Philip may have felt astonished admiration at the pride of the helpless city. He may also have remembered Thermopylae and felt that Sparta could do him no harm, after all. At any rate, he left the Peloponnesus without attempting force on Sparta.

Philip was now in control of all Greece (except for isolated Sparta), and he called together a council of Greek cities. They met at Corinth in 337 B.C., as they had done a century and a half earlier to meet the Persian danger. This time, however, the tables were turned. They voted war against Persia, electing Philip as the commanding general. Advance Macedonian forces were even sent into Asia Minor to pave the way for the general attack.

At this point, however, domestic troubles interfered. Philip might defeat Demosthenes and rule all Greece, but in his family, there was someone stronger than himself; his Epirot wife, Olympias.

Philip had long since grown tired of Olympias, who was a fierce and difficult woman. In 337 B.C. he decided to divorce her and marry the young niece of one of his generals. Olympias left for her brother's kingdom of Epirus. She was furious and determined to get revenge by any means.

Philip went through with the wedding, however, and had a child by his new wife. Increasingly, there was the possibility that he might disinherit his son, Alexander, in favor of the new child, and the possibilities of an internal struggle that might upset all his plans loomed.

Philip decided to forestall trouble by winning over the king of Epirus (Olympias' brother) to his own side. Philip suggested a marriage between his daughter and her uncle the Epirot king. The offer was accepted and the wedding feast was gay and elaborate.

But in 336 B.C., at this marriage feast, Philip, the conqueror of Greece, at the height of his fame and at the point of stepping off into Asia, was assassinated! No one doubts that Olympias helped arrange the assassination, and many suspect that Alexander had a hand in it, too.

THE COMING OF ALEXANDER

With the death of Philip, the Greek cities rose joyously in the hope of recovering their freedom. They were fully confident they would do so.

After all, the Syracusan power had died with Dionysius; the Thessalian power with Jason; the Carian power with Mausolus.

Surely, the Macedonian power would vanish with Philip. Of course, Philip's son had succeeded to the throne as Alexander III, but he was only twenty years old ("a mere boy," Demosthenes called him with contempt) and not much attention was paid to him.

Unfortunately for Demosthenes, Alexander was no mere boy. Philip was one of the few very remarkable men in history to have an even more remarkable son. (In a way, this was unfortunate for Philip, for his great accomplishments were overshadowed by the still greater accomplishments of his son.)

Some famous stories are told about Alexander's youth. One of the most famous relates that as a teen-ager, he tamed a wild horse that no one else could manage. Alexander noticed that the horse was terrified of its own shadow; he therefore maneuvered the horse so as to have it face the sun. Once the shadow was behind it, the horse calmed down and could be handled with ease. The horse had a marking like an ox's head upon its forehead, so it was named Bucephalus (byoo-sef'uh-lus) or "ox-head." Alexander rode it through almost all his subsequent career and it is probably the most famous horse in history.

In 342 B.C., when Alexander was fourteen, he was placed by Philip under a Greek tutor. The tutor was Aristotle (ar'is-tot''ul) who, in later times, was to be considered the greatest of all the Greek thinkers.

Aristotle was born in 384 B.C. in the town of Stagira (stuh-jigh'ruh) in the Chalcidice. His father had served as physician to Amyntas II, father of Philip of Macedon. As a young man of seventeen, Aristotle had traveled to Athens to study under Plato, remaining at the Academy from 367 to 347 B.C. and leaving only after Plato's death.

When Alexander became king, Aristotle left for Athens and founded a school called the "Lykeion," or, in Latin spelling, Lyceum, in honor of a nearby temple to Apollo Lykeios ("Apollo, the Wolf-Killer").

Aristotle's lectures were collected into many volumes and

represent almost a one-man encyclopedia of the knowledge of the times, much of it representing the original thought, observation, and organizing ability of Aristotle himself. Nor was it confined entirely to science, for Aristotle dealt with ethics, with literary criticism, and with politics. Altogether the volumes attributed to him number about 400 and of these, some fifty have survived. (Aristotle lived at the time of the virtual death of the city-state, but his discussions of politics dealt with the city-state only. Although the greatest thinker of ancient times, he saw not one inch beyond it.)

Aristotle did not deal with mathematics, but he was the founder of a near-mathematical branch of thought — logic. He developed, in great and satisfying detail, the art of reasoning from premises to necessary conclusion.

His most successful scientific writings were those on biology. He was a careful and meticulous observer, who was fascinated with the task of classifying animal species. He was particularly interested in sea life and observed that the dolphin brought forth its young alive and in a manner similar to those of the beasts of the field. For this reason, he decided dolphins were not fish, and here he was fully 2000 years ahead of his time.

In physics, Aristotle was far less successful. He rejected the atomism of Democritus (see page 136) and the speculations of Heraclidus (see page 187). He went along with the heavenly spheres of Eudoxus (see page 186) and even added more of them, reaching a total of fifty-four. He also accepted the four elements of Empedocles (see page 118) and added a fifth, the "ether" which was supposed to make up the heavens.

How much of Aristotle's teachings were absorbed by Alexander is uncertain. He was Aristotle's student for a few years only and during those years, he was engaged in princely duties as well. When he was sixteen, he was already in charge of Macedonia while his father was engaged at the siege of Byzantium. While Philip was failing at the siege, Alexander was succeeding in fighting off some tribes who thought it safe

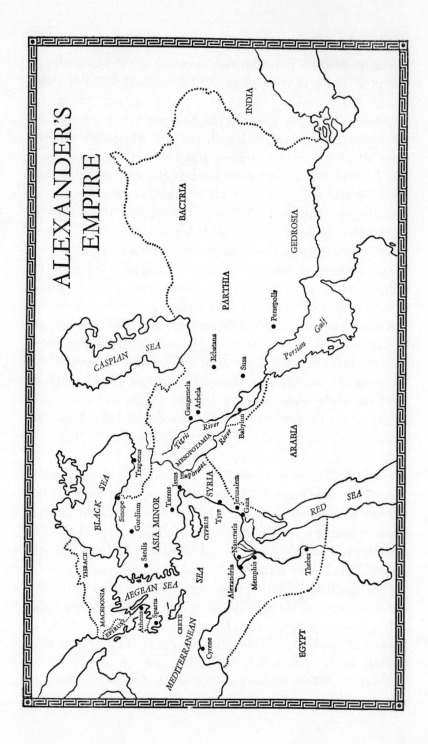

ALEXANDER'S
EMPIRE

INDIA

BACTRIA

GEDROSIA

PARTHIA

Persepolis

CASPIAN   SEA

Persian   Gulf

Ecbatana

Susa

Gangamela
Arbela

Babylon

ARABIA

Tigris   River

MESOPOTAMIA

Euphrates   River

Trapezus

BLACK   SEA

Issus

SYRIA

Jerusalem

RED   SEA

Sinope

Gordium

Tarsus

Tyre

Gaza

Sardis

ASIA MINOR

CYPRUS

Naucratis

THRACE

SEA

Alexandria

Memphis

Thebes

MACEDONIA

AEGEAN SEA

Athens

Sparta

EPIRUS

CRETE

EGYPT

MEDITERRANEAN

Cyrene

to march into Macedonia when only a boy was in charge. (They proved mistaken; they had the wrong boy.)

In 338 B.C., when Alexander was eighteen, he fought at Chaeronea, and ended the battle when he led the charge that finally crushed the Sacred Band and made his father supreme over Greece.

And now that he was king at twenty, he continued to act with extraordinary energy and without hesitating for a moment. Inside Macedonia he promptly arranged the execution of anyone who might dispute his right to the throne. This included Philip's second wife and infant son, as well as his cousin who had once sat on the throne as Aymntas III (see page 200).

Having done this, he dashed southward into Greece. The Greeks, their jubilation choking off as they suddenly realized that the young man was Philip all over again, and more, quieted down at once. At Corinth, Alexander was elected commanding general of the united Greek armies against Persia, in place of his father.

Outside Corinth, Alexander met Diogenes the Cynic, who was in his middle seventies at the time of the meeting. The Cynic was sunning himself outside his tub at the time of the meeting. Alexander is reported to have asked Diogenes if there was any favor he wanted to ask. Diogenes looked up at the youth who was the most powerful man in Greece and barked, "Yes! Stand out of my sun!" Alexander did so, and, recognizing the power of complete independence, said, "If I were not Alexander, I would wish to be Diogenes."

Having settled matters in Greece, Alexander raced back north in the spring of 335 B.C., where the barbarians again thought to take advantage of a boy king. Alexander smashed so quickly that they hardly had time to realize what was happening. A lightning stroke could have done it no more neatly.

However, while he was in the north, the news spread in Greece that he was dead. At once, Thebes was in revolt and laid siege to the Macedonian garrison at the Cadmea. Demosthenes supplied the Thebans with funds and persuaded Athens to ally itself with her.

But there was scarcely time to breathe before Alexander came dashing southward again at the first news. The armies met and for a while the Thebans fought with their accustomed valor, but no one could stand against Alexander and his phalanx. When the Thebans finally fled, they were pursued so closely that they and the Macedonians entered the city together.

Alexander felt that once and for all he must impress upon Greece that there were to be no revolts against him. He planned to be away in Persia and he wanted no wars at home to drag him back as half a century earlier they had dragged back Agesilaus (see page 173).

Consequently, he cold-bloodedly destroyed Thebes. He saved the temples of course, but pulled down every other building with the single exception of the home of the poet Pindar, whose verses Alexander admired and who had once written an ode for his ancestor, Alexander I.

The deed had its effect. Athens hastened to humble itself to the conqueror and once again, its past history saved the city. Alexander did not even press for the surrender of Demosthenes and the other leaders of the anti-Macedonian party.

He went on about his plans of conquest now, and earned, in full measure, the name, "Alexander the Great," by which he is invariably known in history. As long as he lived, Greece remained almost quiet out of fear of this extraordinary man.

THE FALL OF PERSIA

In Persia, affairs favored Alexander. Artaxerxes II, the victor at Cunaxa (see page 168), had died in 359 B.C., just as Philip was coming to power in Macedonia. He was succeeded by Artaxerxes III who in 343 B.C. with a last gasp of Persian strength crushed an Egypt that had once again risen in revolt.

In 338 B.C., however, Artaxerxes III was assassinated. His son, Arses (ahr'seez) succeeded and was in turn assassinated in 336 B.C. and was followed by a distant relative, Darius III. Persia, shaken by two successive assassinations found herself under a monarch who, though gentle, was weak and cowardly. He was certainly the last man to put up against the great Alexander.

In the spring of 334 B.C., Alexander placed his father's general, Antipater (an-tip'uh-ter), in charge of Macedonia and Greece and set off on his great adventure with another of his father's generals, Parmenio (pahr-mee'nee-oh), as second-in-command. Alexander crossed the Hellespont with 32,000 infantry and 5000 cavalry. He was twenty-two at the time and he never returned to Europe.

On the other side of the Hellespont, Alexander supervised a solemn sacrifice at the site of Troy. He, like Agesilaus before him, viewed himself as a Homeric hero reborn. He was a new Achilles, as Agesilaus had considered himself a new Agamemnon (see page 172.) Unlike his Spartan predecessor, Alexander was to prove his case.

The Greek mercenaries, fighting for Persia, were commanded by Memnon (mem'non) of Rhodes. He was a capable man and while it was doubtful that anyone could possibly have defeated Alexander, Memnon might have made a respectable fight of it. He had, in his time, fought with some success against Philip, and he understood the Macedonian army. He suggested that the Persians retreat inland and lure Alexander after them, while the Persian fleet descended on the Aegean Sea and cut his lines of communication and supply. His plan was also to encourage revolts in Greece where alone Alexander might find ships to fight on his side.

The local Persian satraps would not listen, however. They

felt Alexander was just another Greek who, like Agesilaus and Chares, would shuffle about a while and then leave. They were anxious to fight him on the spot and protect their provinces.

The forces met at the Granicus River (gruh-nigh′kus) near where Troy had once stood. Alexander sent forth his cavalry in a fast one-two punch that disorganized the Persians. Then he moved in his phalanx to grind up the hard-fighting Greek mercenaries. The Persians were utterly defeated.

Alexander sent rich spoils back to Greece with the inscription: "Alexander, son of Philip, and the Greeks except the Lacedemonians [Spartans] present these offerings out of the spoils of the foreigners inhabiting Asia." Sparta alone had not joined Alexander and Alexander, like Philip, did not try to force her into alliance.

There was no further Persian army in Asia Minor that dared resist him and Alexander proceeded to take all the cities.

The entire Aegean shore was his and yet Alexander was not completely safe. Memnon, still firm, despite defeats, was beginning to take over the Aegean Islands and was preparing a naval war in Alexander's rear. Fortunately for Alexander, Memnon died suddenly in early 333 B.C. while besieging Lesbos and the last possibility of intelligent resistance on the part of the Persians was gone.

Alexander next marched inland to Gordium, the capital of ancient Phrygia four centuries before. At Gordium, he was shown the Gordian knot (see page 86) and told the old prophecy that anyone who succeeded in untying it would conquer all Asia.

"Indeed?" he said. "Then thus do I untie it!" And, drawing his sword, he cut it through. Ever since then, the phrase "to cut the Gordian knot" has been applied to a direct and forceful solution to what had seemed a great difficulty.

Alexander moved southward to the Gulf of Issus where, seventy years earlier, the Ten Thousand had paused (see page 168). He had all of Asia Minor in his grip but so far he had fought only small forces. The battle at the Granicus had been but an appetizer.

Now, with Memnon dead, there was no one to counsel caution to the Persians. Darius felt that it was impossible to allow Alexander to march any farther, so he assembled a large army at Issus and prepared for battle.

The large Persian army outnumbered Alexander's small one many times, but numbers meant little here. The Macedonian phalanx could cut through mere numbers without trouble. Furthermore, Darius was at the battle himself and this was fatal, for he was an incredible coward. The Greek mercenaries were fighting well for him and even drove back the phalanx for a while, but when the push of the armies approached his own position and he felt himself to be in personal danger, Darius immediately fled, pell-mell. There is such a thing as intelligent retreat, but Darius' wild gallop off the field was simple desertion.

The battle was lost.

Darius, still trembling, sent ambassadors to offer Alexander all of Asia Minor and a large sum of money as well, if only he would call it quits. Parmenio, listening to the offer, said, "I would accept this, were I Alexander." And Alexander retorted, contemptuously, "And so would I, were I Parmenio."

Alexander demanded nothing less than complete and unconditional surrender of the entire Persian Empire and the war went on. He marched down the Syrian coast and the cities of Phoenicia surrendered, one by one. Only Tyre held out. She offered to accept Alexander's overlordship if she might be allowed to remain mistress of her internal affairs, but Alexander never accepted anything less than everything.

Tyre prepared for a siege and what followed was one of the most stubborn in history. Tyre held out for seven months with unbelievable tenacity and Alexander held on with equal tenacity. Finally, Tyre had to surrender and was treated with great severity by the exasperated Macedonians. Several more months were lost at Gaza (gah'zuh) a coastal city near Egypt which had once, seven centuries before, been one of the cities of the Biblical Philistines.

In 332 B.C., Alexander entered Egypt. After all the revolts against Persia, the Egyptians welcomed him as a liberator. They went over to his side at once and without a struggle. What was left of Persia was now cut off from the sea and what had been the Persian fleet was dead.

In 331 B.C., on the westernmost mouth of the Nile, the Macedonian monarch founded a city named for himself, Alexandria. It was to become one of the most renowned cities of the ancient world. While in Egypt, Alexander also traveled inland to a temple that had originally been dedicated to the Egyptian god, Amen. To the Greeks, this was "Ammon," with whom they identified their own Zeus, so that the temple was considered to be dedicated to "Zeus-Ammon." At this temple, Alexander allowed himself to be declared the son of Ammon (or Zeus) and there were undoubtedly many people who were ready to believe it.

But there still remained vast areas of Persia unconquered and large armies to fight and beat, so back into Asia went Alexander. Onward he drove, across the Euphrates and to the Tigris, where between the towns of Gaugamela (goh"guh-mee'luh) and Arbela (ahr-bee'luh), Darius had determined to make another stand. The Persian army was even greater than before, the ground had been chosen carefully, and all preparations had been made with thought and caution.

On October 1, 331 B.C., the Battle of Gaugamela was fought. The Persians relied on chariots with scythes attached to the wheels. These sharp knives, borne down upon the Macedonians with great speed, would (it was hoped) strike terror. However, the Macedonian cavalry attacked the chariots as they charged and few of them even reached the phalanx.

The phalanx cut into the enemy forces easily, as always. For a while, Darius maneuvered his men almost as though he were a warrior. However, Alexander knew him well by now. He directed his phalanx directly at Darius and as the bristling spears came closer, Darius' puny courage failed, and again he turned and fled. The rest of the battle was almost a mop-up.

This was, in effect, the end of the Persian Empire (two centuries after the conquests of Cyrus, see page 93) for there was to be no more organized resistance. Darius was never to fight again, he would only flee; and Alexander was to meet nothing but local forces for the rest of the war.

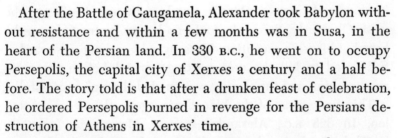

THE END OF ALEXANDER

After the Battle of Gaugamela, Alexander took Babylon without resistance and within a few months was in Susa, in the heart of the Persian land. In 330 B.C., he went on to occupy Persepolis, the capital city of Xerxes a century and a half before. The story told is that after a drunken feast of celebration, he ordered Persepolis burned in revenge for the Persians destruction of Athens in Xerxes' time.

He then made ready to pursue Darius again, who was in Ecbatana (ek-bat'uh-nuh) the capital of Media, 400 miles northwest of Persepolis. Darius waited for no further battles but began to run at once, hastening eastward in wild flight. The satraps with him, feeling they were, after all, better off without their coward-king, murdered him in mid-330 B.C. and left his body for Alexander to find.

For the next two years, Alexander ranged over the eastern reaches of the Persian Empire, fighting satraps and wild tribesmen. These did much better than the organized armies of the Empire had done, but all invariably lost to him in the end. In all his life, Alexander was *never* beaten, by anyone or at any time.

Alexander's successes finally seem to have persuaded him that he was indeed very different from ordinary men, and not bound be either law or custom. Up to Philip's time, the Macedonian monarch had only been a nobleman among noblemen (like the kings described in Homer) but now Alexander was beginning to assume the airs of a Persian king. He began to enjoy flattery and adulation and to expect men to crouch before him in a fashion that the rough Macedonians did not think right.

Conspiracies against him began to spring up among his officers, or, if they did not, Alexander's increasingly fevered mind suspected that they did. In late 330 B.C., while in what is now Afghanistan, he brought one of his generals, Philotas (fih-loh'tas) up for trial on the charge of conspiracy and had him executed. Philotas was the son of Parmenio who was then in charge of troops in Media, nearly a thousand miles to the west. Obviously, Parmenio could no longer be trusted once he heard of his son's execution. Messengers were sent westward at full speed to kill the unsuspecting general before the news reached him, and the slaying was carried through successfully.

This made some of the Macedonian generals even more sullen. In 328 B.C., Alexander was at Maracanda (mar"uh-kan'duh) in the northeastern limits of the Persian Empire. (It is the modern Samarkand.) There he held a banquet and everyone drank a little too much. As was growing to be the custom, a number of men rose to make flattering speeches, telling Alexander how much greater than his father he was. Alexander drank it all in and seemed all the more pleased the more ridicule was thrown on Philip.

One old veteran, Clitus (kligh'tus), could stand it no more at last. He had fought with Philip and he had saved Alexander's life at the Battle of Granicus. Clitus rose to defend Philip, say-

ing that it was Philip who had laid the foundation for Macedonian greatness and that Alexander won his victories with Philip's
army. Alexander, quite drunk, was infuriated at this. He seized
a spear and killed Clitus.

This sobered Alexander and for days afterward, he repented
in wild remorse. That did not bring back Clitus, however. Nor
did it stop the change that was coming over Alexander. He was
not satisfied to be king of Macedonia and general of the
Greeks. He began to see himself as universal monarch over all
men, Greek and barbarian. He married a Persian princess, Roxana, in 327 B.C. and began the training of 30,000 Persians, in
Macedonian fashion, for service in the army.

In that same year, he was invited into India by a ruler of
that area who was fighting a monarch of the Punjab called
Porus. Alexander needed little excuse to plunge into a good
fight and marched southward at once toward the Indus River.
In doing so, he passed beyond the limits of the Persian Empire.
No Persian monarch, not Cyrus and not Darius I, had penetrated so far into India.

In the Punjab, Alexander met the most capable general he
was ever to face. Porus was, according to reports, seven feet
tall and of magnificent appearance. He had a large army
backed by 200 elephants, a situation that was completely un-
precedented for Alexander.

In 326 B.C. the two armies met at the Hydaspes River (high-
das'peez), a tributary of the Indus and Alexander fought the
last of his four great battles in Asia. The elephants were the
greatest danger but he executed a series of clever feints which
threw Porus off-balance and kept him off-balance so that his
elephants never got a chance to get into the battle with full
effectiveness.

Alexander won, but the experience with the elephants was
impressive. In the century that followed, Macedonian monarchs were often to use elephants in warfare, somewhat in the

fashion that modern armies use tanks.

In this battle, Alexander's horse, Bucephalus, which had carried him for thousands of miles, finally died, and Alexander founded a city he named Bucephala in his horse's honor.

After the battle, he asked the haughty, unbending Porus how he expected to be treated. "Like a king!" replied Porus, and so he was. He received back his realm in order that he might rule it as a satrap for Alexander, and Porus was faithful to this charge during his life. (He was assassinated about 321 B.C. by a rival.)

It was now Alexander's intention to go across India to the ocean which marked, according to the geographical notions of the day, the end of the world. At this moment, however, his troops failed him. The Macedonian soldiers were nearly 3000 miles from home. They had followed him for six years, fighting, fighting, fighting. Winning battles was no longer a thrill for anyone but Alexander. His men just wanted to go back.

Alexander sulked for three days and, as later legend has it, wept because there were no more worlds for him to conquer. Reluctantly, he consented to return.

He had a fleet built which sailed down the Indus River, while the army marched along the bank. Again, Alexander had to subdue hostile tribes as he went. At one point, in besieging a city, Alexander lost patience, and leaped from the wall into the city. Only three companions were with him, and before the flabbergasted army could beat their way in to rescue him, he was seriously wounded and almost dead. It was the most serious wound he ever received, but he recovered.

The fleet was sent back from the mouth of the Indus, by way of the Arabian Sea and the Persian Gulf to Babylonia under a Macedonian officer named Nearchus (nee-ahr′kus). It was the first appearance of a western fleet in the Indian Ocean.

In 325 B.C. Alexander and his army marched back overland through the Gedrosian desert (jee-droh′zhee-an) in what is now southern Iran. It was a wrong-headed thing to do, for the desert could not support an army that lived off the land. The Macedonian soldiers underwent incredible tortures of thirst and hunger, marching through the area, and suffered more casualties than in all their fighting. (Some have speculated that Alexander was deliberately punishing his army for their refusal to let him cross India.)

When Alexander got back to Babylonia, he got busy punishing corrupt officials and reorganizing the government. He carried on his grandiose projects of merging Greek and barbarians by ordering 10,000 Greek and Macedonian soldiers to marry Asian women in a mass ceremony.

Furthermore, he forced the Greek cities to recognize him as a god in order that he might more easily rule as a king over men who would refuse to bow down to a ruler who was only a man. The Greek cities, even Athens, accepted Alexander's godhood with much flattery. Only Sparta retained her ancient pride. The ephors said, "If Alexander wishes to be a god, let him" and turned contemptuous backs on the whole matter.

But the shadows were closing in on Alexander the God. While at Ecbatana in late 324 B.C., his dearest friend, Hephaestion (hee-fes'tee-on) died and Alexander was thrown into the deepest melancholy. More and more his men began to fear his dangerous whims.

His plans were growing still more grandiose. He was going to conquer Arabia; or he would sail westward and take Carthage. Preparations were made and the world held its breath.

But nothing came of it after all. In June, 323 B.C., he suddenly fell ill, and there are some who think it was the result of poisoning by those who thought they would feel safer with the great monarch dead. On June 13, 323 B.C., he died.

He was only thirty-three at the time and had only ruled thirteen years. Into his short life, however, he had packed more adventure, more victory, more fame than had ever fallen or ever would fall to any other single man.

The story was later told that Diogenes the Cynic, whom

Alexander had met for a moment at the very beginning of his reign, died on the very same day as Alexander, at the age of almost ninety. This story is probably another of the manufactured coincidences the Greek historians love so well.

14

THE SUCCESSORS OF ALEXANDER

ANTIPATER IN GREECE

Sparta was the one city of Greece that maintained a kind of independence under Philip and Alexander. During the years that Philip was gradually extending his control over Greece, Sparta was ruled by Archidamus III, the son of Agesilaus. He continued to do what he could to oppose Thebes and to regain Sparta's old mastery in the Peloponnesus. He failed and, like his father, ended his days as a mercenary.

The city of Tarentum in Italy needed help against native tribes from the north and appealed to Sparta, the mother-city. Archidamus answered the appeal and died in battle in Italy, on the same day (supposedly) as the independence of Greece perished at Chaeronea.

His son, Agis III, succeeded to one of Sparta's thrones, and began his reign with the answer "If!" to the invading forces of Philip (see page 208). Sparta under his rule refused to join with either Philip or Alexander, and though the world rang with the deeds of Alexander, Agis kept his eyes fixed on the Peloponnesus only. It was as though Sparta had made up its mind to live permanently in the days of the Messenian Wars.

With Alexander off in Asia, Agis began to apply for money and ships to Persia, which, of course, was willing to do anything to raise trouble for Alexander at home. The news of Issus put a temporary stop to this, but as Alexander proceeded to recede farther and farther into the unknown depths of Asia, Agis took heart again.

In 331 B.C. he opened an attack, with much of the Peloponnesus behind him. For a while, he scored successes, with Persian ships and with mercenaries hired with Persian money. Finally, he laid siege to Megalopolis, the one Arcadian city which, out of hatred for Sparta, would not join in the anti-Macedonian uprising.

Sparta pressed the siege but eventually Antipater came down out of the north with a large Macedonian army. The Spartans fought with their old-time courage but they were outnumbered and out-generaled and Agis was killed. Sparta had to yield hostages to Antipater and pay a stiff fine. Nevertheless Antipater, like Philip and Alexander before him, refrained from destroying Sparta itself.

Athens had carefully stayed out of the fighting, but Demosthenes had openly encouraged Sparta and his policy had failed again. His great opponent, Aeschines, felt it was time to attack Demosthenes and destroy his influence forever. In 330 B.C. Athens was awarding a golden crown to Demosthenes in honor of his past services to the city, and Aeschines rose to speak against the award. Aeschines' speech was masterly, but Demosthenes countered with the most magnificent speech he was ever to make — "On the Crown."

So complete was Demosthenes' victory that the humiliated

Aeschines was forced to leave Athens. He retired to Rhodes and spent the rest of his life there, conducting a school for oratory. (A student, in later years, on reading Aeschines' speech against the crown, wondered out loud how Aeschines could possibly have lost the case. "Ah," said Aeschines ruefully, "you will not wonder, after you read Demosthenes' reply.")

When Alexander, in deepest Persia, was told of the fight in the Peloponnesus, he muttered that he was being disturbed over a battle of mice.

And he was right, for from the moment when Alexander crossed into Asia, battles within Greece among the Greek city-states were of no account and didn't matter. These battles between the cities were to continue for another century and a half but history had passed beyond them.

If any wars of importance remained to be fought in Greece they would involve the great powers from outside, to whom Greece was only a convenient battleground.

In fact, with Alexander the Great, the wonderful Hellenic period, which had begun in 776 B.C. (see page 29) and during which the eyes of history are fixed on little Greece, came to an end. The year 323 B.C., the year of Alexander's death, is usually taken as its closing. The next few centuries, in which Greek culture is still dominant but Greece itself has become insignificant, is labeled the "Hellenistic period."

Although Athens had avoided harm by steering clear of Agis' rebellion, additional temptation was to come her way six years afterward.

It came about in this fashion. When Alexander left Babylonia after the Battle of Gaugamela and journeyed to the east to complete his conquest, he left an associate, Harpalus (hahr'puh-lus) behind in charge of the Persian treasury. This Harpalus used for his own benefit, acting on the very good chance that Alexander would not return. When he realized he had guessed wrong and that Alexander was coming back, he fled to Greece with some soldiers, ships and a vast treasure worth many millions of dollars in modern money.

He presented himself at Athens in 324 B.C. and asked for admittance and protection against Macedonia. Demosthenes for once tempered his anti-Macedonian feelings with prudence and argued against Athens' permitting him to enter. Harpalus continued to point out what Athens could do with the money; how eagerly other cities and all of Asia would join her against Alexander, if only she could distribute some of the money properly; and, in the end, despite Demosthenes, he was allowed into the city.

Antipater sent an immediate demand to Athens that Harpalus be given up. Demosthenes argued against this as beneath the city's dignity. Instead, he suggested that Harpalus be arrested, his money stored in the Parthenon for safekeeping and an offer be made to surrender the money to Alexander when Alexander appeared to ask for it.

This was done but there was trouble. Between the time that Harpalus brought the money and the time that it was counted for storage in the Parthenon, half of it had disappeared. It may be that Harpalus lied as to the quantity he had, but would Alexander believe that? Would not Alexander believe that the Athenians had stolen half? Matters were all the worse since Harpalus escaped from Athens (and fled to Crete where he was quickly assassinated).

It seemed that for Athens' own sake, an investigation had better be started and guilty men punished. This was done and a number of men were placed on the list, with Demosthenes at their head. Demosthenes was almost certainly innocent, but guilty men had to be found to satisfy a possibly furious Alexander, and Demosthenes would be the most acceptable sacrifice. Demosthenes was fined an impossible amount and was put in jail when he could not pay. He escaped from jail and fled to the Argolis.

What might have happened next is hard to say, but in the

following year Alexander died, before he had a chance to return and punish Athens. At once (as on the day thirteen years ago when Philip had died) Greece rose in joyful rebellion against the Macedonians. (Aristotle, fearing that the Athenian patriots would remember the fact that he had been tutor to Alexander once, did not wish to tempt Athens to commit another crime against philosophy. He quietly escaped to Euboea and died there in 322 B.C.)

With Athens at the head, a Greek army was formed and against them Antipater led his Macedonian forces. It seemed, however, that the magic of Philip and Alexander was gone, for the Macedonians were badly beaten in Boeotia. Antipater had to retreat to Lamia (lay′mee-uh), just north of Thermopylae and was besieged there through the winter of 323 B.C. by the allied Greek forces. (Because of this, the conflict is known as the "Lamian War.")

Affairs looked so bright that Demosthenes was able to return in triumph to Athens, the hero of his countrymen once more. The city itself paid his fine and for a moment it seemed as though the great orator's perseverance had won through all and that he would end the victor.

But the brightness was an illusion. Reinforcements reached Antipater from Asia and though the Greeks continued to do well for a while, particularly because of the skillful Thessalian cavalry on their side, the end was foregone. In 322 B.C. they suffered a defeat at Crannon (kran′on) in central Thessaly and Greek morale cracked.

Worse still were affairs at sea. The Macedonians had built a fleet of their own and they met the Athenian ships at Amorgos (uh-mawr′gos), an island southeast of Naxos. Here in 322 B.C. the Athenian fleet was destroyed — and for the last time. Until now, every time an Athenian fleet had been destroyed, even at Aegospotami, a new fleet eventually arose out of the shipyards; but no longer. Never again were there to be Athenian ships dominating the sea anywhere. The era that had begun with Themistocles a century and a half earlier, had come to an end.

The Greek alliance fell apart and one by one the city-states submitted to Antipater. Athens submitted, too, in September 322 B.C., and as the price of avoiding an occupation, the Athenians agreed to give up Demosthenes. The orator fled to a small island off the Argolis, however, and Antipater's hirelings followed him there. They tried to lure him out of the temple in which he had taken refuge, but Demosthenes was tired of the long useless fight. He took poison, which he carried with him for just such a purpose, and died in October, 322 B.C.

The fight for Greek freedom was finally lost.

THE DIADOCHI

But what of the great empire built up by Alexander? At his death, there remained of the royal family of Macedon, the following: Alexander's mother, Olympias; his wife, Roxana; a son, Alexander IV, not born until a few months after Alexander's death; a half-sister, Thessalonike (thes"uh-loh-nigh'kee) and a mentally retarded half-brother who was later known as Philip III. None of these could rule and so a regent was required.

Alexander did not name a regent, however. With his last breath, he is supposed to have answered the question of the succession by saying "To the strongest!"

Unfortunately, there was no strongest. There were a number of generals in Alexander's army, all trained by the master, all determined, all capable, all ambitious, none willing to allow any of the others to take over the supreme position. No less than thirty-four held power here and there in Alexander's vast dominion. These generals are called the *Diadochi* (digh-ad'oh-kee) meaning "successors."

Among the Diadochi was Antipater, of course, who was back in Macedon fighting the Greeks. In Asia, the most prominent were Cratarus (krat'er-us), Antigonus (an-tig'oh-nus), Polysperchon (pol"ee-spur'kon), Perdiccas (pur-dik'as), Lysimachus (ligh-sim'uh-kus), Seleucus (see-lyoo'kus) and Eumenes (yoo'mih-neez). In Egypt was Ptolemy (tol'uh-mee).

These generals at once engaged in confused and incessant warfare, like that which had ruined the city-states of Greece, but on a much larger scale. As soon as one seemed to gain the upper hand, the others would combine against him. The wars continued among the sons of the Diadochi, or the *Epigoni* (ee-pig'oh-nee), as they were called, from Greek words meaning "born after."

The wars began with Perdiccas, who had been Alexander's "prime minister" at the time of his death, and who had control of Philip III, Alexander's mentally retarded half-brother. Perdiccas hoped to be accepted as regent of all the empire, but most of the Diadochi would not allow this. Perdiccas led an army against Ptolemy, but the march was unsuccessful. Perdiccas was therefore assassinated by some of his sullen officers in 321 B.C.

General warfare was proceeding in Asia Minor, too. On one side was Eumenes fighting in alliance with Perdiccas. On the other side was Craterus, who had just returned from Greece where he had helped Antipater crush the Greeks in the Lamian War (see page 229). In the battle, Craterus was killed, but Eumenes was not helped thereby since his ally, Perdiccas, had also died. Antigonus defeated Eumenes and took over control of Asia Minor.

Antipater died in 319 B.C. and, passing over his own son Cassander (ka-san'der) for some reason, left the regency of Macedonia and the control of Greece to Polysperchon. Cassander had no intention of accepting this arrangement. He gained the support of most of the Greek cities and took Athens in 317 B.C.

The mother of Alexander the Great, Olympias, took an active part in the fighting against Cassander and had her stepson, Philip III, slain. Cassander marched against Olympias, defeated her and had her executed in 316 B.C. He seized control of Macedonia and imprisoned Alexander's wife, Roxana, and her infant son. Eventually, in 310 B.C., he had both slain.

Of all the family of Alexander, only the half-sister remained. Cassander married her and settled down to a rule of some twenty years. He rebuilt a city at the northwestern base of the Chalcidice and named it Thessalonike for his wife. (Its modern name is Salonika.) He also restored Thebes in 316 B.C. causing it to rise again from the destruction visited upon it by Alexander twenty years before.

Of the Diadochi, the four who remained were Antigonus and Eumenes in Asia Minor, Seleucus in Babylonia and Ptolemy in Egypt. In addition, one of the Epigoni, Cassander, ruled in Macedonia.

This arrangement was upset by Antigonus, the most ambitious of the group. He was still not satisfied with part but wanted the whole. In 316 B.C. he defeated Eumenes in battle and had him executed, then marched into Babylonia, driving out Seleucus. Antigonus now looked out of his one eye (he was called "Antigonus Monophthalmos" [mon"of-thal'mus] or "Antigonus, the One-Eyed") at an empire that was almost his.

However, Seleucus joined Ptolemy and Cassander in a coalition against him. None of the remaining Diadochi wanted Antigonus in supreme control. On his own side, Antigonus had his son, Demetrius (dee-mee'tree-us), a capable general.

In 312 B.C. Demetrius was defeated by Ptolemy at Gaza, but this defeat was not decisive. Demetrius decided to take to the sea, which was then controlled by Ptolemy. He gathered a fleet, captured Athens in 307 B.C. and defeated Ptolemy off Cyprus in 306 B.C. For the moment, Demetrius controlled the seas.

This was the victory Antigonus needed. He was seventy-five years old and he could wait no longer. If he could not have supreme power, he would at least assume the name of "king." At once the surviving Diadochi called themselves kings as well. What had been true in fact became true in name; Alexander's empire was broken into slivers.

As Antigonus was king in Asia Minor, so Ptolemy was king in Egypt, Cassander king in Macedonia, and Seleucus (who had retaken Babylonia from Antigonus in 312 B.C.) was king in Babylonia.

Demetrius, to celebrate his victory over Ptolemy, set up a sculptured figure of a winged Goddess of Victory on the island of Samothrace (sam'oh-thrays) in the northern Aegean. The statue (the "Winged Victory") survives today, with head and arms missing, but with its wings intact.

(Another famous Greek statue of this period still in existence today is an armless carving of Aphrodite found on the island of Melos in 1820. It was carved at some unknown time during the Hellenistic period and is generally known by the Italian name of "Venus de Milo.")

Having beaten Ptolemy's fleet, Demetrius went on to besiege the island of Rhodes, which was an ally of Ptolemy. In doing so, he made use of great siege-machines designed to batter down walls and destroy cities, for war had become a highly mechanized affair. Demetrius stuck to the siege for a year, but the Rhodians resisted stubbornly and, in 304 B.C., Demetrius had to withdraw.

So famous was this siege that Demetrius became known as Demetrius Poliorcetes (pol"ee-awr-see'teez), or "Demetrius the Besieger."

It was now the turn of the Rhodians to build a statue commemorating a victory. They decided to use the material left behind by the besiegers in order to construct a large statue of the Sun-god who, they believed, had saved them.

It took many years to build and was not completed until 280 B.C. When done, it was, according to the descriptions that have survived, 105 feet tall. Looking out over the harbor, as it did, it could be seen by approaching ships from far out at sea.

This statue of the Sun-God is known to us as the "Colossus of Rhodes" and it was listed by the Greeks among the Seven Wonders of the World. Unfortunately, the Colossus of Rhodes did not remain standing for more than half a century. In 224 B.C. it was shaken down by an earthquake and, in after years, the stories about it exaggerated its size. It was supposed to have been so huge that its legs straddled the harbor and that ships passed between those legs to enter. This, alas, is a fairy tale.

After the failure of the siege of Rhodes, Demetrius returned to Athens, which was being blockaded by Cassander of Macedon. Demetrius freed Athens, then went on to wrest most of Greece from Cassander. In 302 B.C. he was voted general-in-chief of the Greek cities, the office once held by Philip and by Alexander.

Cassander, however, sent forces into Asia Minor to attack Demetrius' father, Antigonus. Demetrius was forced to race to Asia Minor to join his father, leaving Greece to fall back into Cassander's hands.

Antigonus and Demetrius were facing all the rest of the Diadochi and the battle was joined at Ipsus (ip'sus) in central Asia Minor in 301 B.C. This battle marks the climax of the use of the elephant as a war-machine. The Diadochi had, in general, been using elephants whenever they could, having learned the trick at the Battle of Hydaspes (see page 221). At Ipsus, nearly 300 elephants fought, some with one army and some with the other.

Antigonus had the fewer elephants and was defeated. Even at the age of eighty-one, he remained fierce and indomitable and at the moment of death was crying "Demetrius will save me!" But Demetrius could not; he barely escaped with his own life.

The Battle of Ipsus ended all hope that Alexander's empire might ever be united again.

But Demetrius Poliocetes was not yet done. He still had his fleet and he waited his chance. Cassander died in 298 B.C. and left only two young sons to succeed him. Neither was capable of holding Macedonia and Demetrius hastened to take advantage of the situation.

In 295 B.C. he laid siege to Athens and once again took it. Using that as his base, Demetrius conquered most of Greece again and then wrested Macedonia from Philip IV, the young son of Cassander. Without much compunction he had the young king killed.

He next entered the Peloponnesus and drove at Sparta. Since her attempt to fight the Macedonians under Agis III, a generation earlier, Sparta had remained motionless. She had not joined in the Lamian War or in any of the efforts occasionally made by the Greeks to free themselves. Yet, although she could not resist Demetrius, she refused (as always) to surrender. At the last moment, Demetrius was called away by emergencies elsewhere and, once again, Sparta was saved an occupation. Whatever charm had saved her against Epaminondas, Philip, Alexander, and Antipater saved her again.

Demetrius' control of Greece and Macedonia did not last long. He was expelled by the forces of Lysimachus, who had been on the winning side at Ipsus and who had been given Antigonus' holdings in Asia Minor. Eventually in 288 B.C., Demetrius was captured in battle and died in captivity in 283 B.C. He left behind a son in Greece, however, another Antigonus, who was later to carry on the fight of his father and grandfather.

In 283 B.C. Ptolemy died a natural death at the age of eighty-four (the Diadochi were very long-lived for some reason). The

two remaining Diadochi, Lysimachus and Seleucus, each
nearly eighty years old, had not yet tired of the eternal struggle. They met in battle at Corupedion (kor"yoo-pee'dee-
on) in Asia Minor, inland from the Ionian coast and there, in
281 B.C., Lysimachus was defeated and killed.

Could Seleucus, even now, have dreamed of supreme
power? It could be. He had a weapon against Egypt. It seems
that Ptolemy had had two sons, of whom the younger succeeded to the throne. The older had to seek his fortune elsewhere. Both sons were called Ptolemy (indeed all Ptolemy's
descendants had the name) and surnames had to be used to
distinguish them. Ptolemy's oldest son was Ptolemy Ceraunus
(see-roh'nus) or "Ptolemy, the Thunderbolt."

Ptolemy Ceraunus had reached Asia Minor and had remained there under the protection of Seleucus who thought he
might be handy as a possible weapon against the new Ptolemy
who sat on the throne of Egypt. Meanwhile, with Ptolemy Ceraunus, Seleucus stretched out his hand toward Macedonia
which, thanks to the defeat of Demetrius Poliorcetes and the
death of Lysimachus, was now in confusion.

However, Ptolemy Ceraunus had his own plans. In 280 B.C.,
he assassinated Seleucus and seized Macedonia for himself.

Thus, nearly half a century after the death of the great Alexander, the last of the Diadochi was finally gone. And what was
the result of fifty years of grueling and senseless warfare? Why,
nothing but to confirm the situation that had existed from the
very moment of Alexander's death.

HELLENISTIC SICILY

The only portion of the Greek world to escape Macedonian
domination entirely were the cities of Sicily and Italy. To them
it was as though Philip and Alexander had never lived. For a

while, the Sicily of Hellenistic times was just like the Sicily of
Hellenic times. The enemy was still Carthage, as it had been in
the days of Xerxes and in Syracuse, and, despite the bright
interlude of Timoleon (see page 192), there were still tyrannies.

Among the democrats in opposition to Syracusan tyranny
was Agathocles (uh-gath'oh-kleez), who began life in poverty
but won his way to wealth through the charm that enabled him
to marry a rich widow.

He was driven out of the city as a result of his political activities but managed to recruit a private army and to fight here
and there, for all the world as though he were another Demetrius. In 317 B.C., he succeeded in seizing control of Syracuse,
and promptly instituted a bloody massacre of the oligarchs
and the supporters of the tyranny.

Of course, he was a tyrant himself in the sense that he was
an absolute ruler. He ruled, however, in such a way as to keep
himself popular with the common people. He was almost
Dionysius (see page 189) reborn after half a century.

The Carthaginians on the other hand wanted no new Dionysius. They sent a large army into Sicily under another
Hamilcar. This one was more successful than the older Hamilcar, who had died at Himera a hundred seventy years before
(see page 111). He won victory after victory and eventually
placed Syracuse itself under siege.

Never had Carthage come so close to conquering all of
Sicily, when Agathocles, out of sheer desperation, thought of a
notion worthy of a Macedonian. In 310 B.C., he slipped out of
Syracuse with a few soldiers, made his way across the sea to
Africa and began raiding the towns near Carthage itself.

The flabbergasted Carthaginians, seeing the Greeks on their
shores for the first (and last) time in history, were helpless.
They had no troops at hand and the raw levies they managed
to scrape up were simply cut down by Agathocles' trained soldiers.

Panicky messages were sent to Hamilcar in Sicily to send troops back to Africa. Hamilcar didn't wish to do that before taking Syracuse, so he attacked hastily, was defeated and killed. That ended Carthaginian hopes for the complete conquest of Sicily.

Eventually, Carthaginian forces did flow back into Africa and the Greeks were defeated. Before that, however, Agathocles had returned to Sicily and resumed the overlordship of Syracuse. In 307 B.C., he followed the new custom that the Macedonian generals were setting up all over the Greek world and called himself king.

Among Agathocles' projects was a possible conquest of southern Italy (something Dionysius had succeeded in doing). At the time, the most prominent city in southern Italy was Tarentum. It was having continuing troubles with native Italian tribes and some thirty years earlier had been forced to appeal to Sparta for help. Archidamus III had answered the call and had died in Italy (see page 225). Now, with the Italian tribes still threatening and with Agathocles lowering over Italy as a new menace, Tarentum appealed to Sparta once more.

But in 289 B.C. Agathocles died before he could carry out his plans and Tarentum seemed to have won through all its dangers.

That, however, was not so, for a new and formidable danger had arisen. There was a city in central Italy named Rome which had over the past century been quietly growing stronger and stronger; so gently, in fact, that its growth had gone almost completely unnoticed by the Greek world, which had its eyes fixed instead on the incredible Alexander and his reckless successors.

By the time of Agathocles' death, Rome had concluded long wars with other central Italian powers and was now master of all the peninsula down to the Greek cities themselves. Tarentum found herself facing not local tribes, but a highly organized nation with an advanced military machine.

Rome was beginning to interfere in the affairs of the cities of southern Italy and formed alliances with some of them. Tarentum took offense at this and when Roman ambassadors appeared in the city, they were rudely insulted.

Rome immediately declared war in 282 B.C. and Tarentum, suddenly sobered, felt the need of help again. It was no use appealing once more to Sparta; the need required stronger measures. Tarentum therefore looked across the Adriatic and chose the strongest Macedonian general it could find. That general was Pyrrhus (pir'us) who, for a brief while, dominates history.

THE MOMENT OF EPIRUS

Pyrrhus was king of Epirus which, under him, for one moment in history became an important military power.

The early history of Epirus is of little importance although the ruling kings claimed to be descended from Pyrrhus, a son of Achilles. Down to the reign of the new Pyrrhus, the only possible claim to fame that Epirus held was the fact that Olympias, Alexander's mother, was a princess of the land and that Alexander was therefore half an Epirot.

After Alexander's death, a cousin of Olympias was seated on the throne of Epirus. He fought against Cassander and was defeated and killed in 313 B.C. His younger son was Pyrrhus, who was thus second cousin of the great Alexander, and the only relative ever to show even a fraction of Alexander's ability.

Pyrrhus' older brother succeeded to the throne of Epirus and for a while Pyrrhus served as soldier of fortune in the armies of the Diadochi. He fought for Demetrius Poliorcetes at Ipsus, for instance, when he was only seventeen.

Pyrrhus became king of Epirus in 295 B.C., but he chafed when at peace. Only war interested him and he needed some vast project to engage him. This came in 281 B.C. in the form of the call from Tarentum and gladly indeed he answered it.

He landed in Tarentum with 25,000 men and a number of elephants, which thus entered Italian warfare for the first time. Pyrrhus viewed the soft life of the Tarentines with contempt. He ordered the theaters closed, suspended all festivals and began drilling the people. The Tarentines were surprised and displeased; they wanted the Romans defeated, but not by going to any trouble themselves. The whole point was for others to do the task. Pyrrhus simply took some of those who grumbled and sent them to Epirus. The rest grew quiet.

Pyrrhus met the Romans at Heraclea (her"uh-klee'uh), a coastal town about thirty-five miles south of Tarentum. He sent his elephants forward and they rolled over the Romans, who had never seen such beasts before. After the victory, however, Pyrrhus viewed the battlefield with some concern. The Romans had not fled. The dead lay there with wounds in front and even the terrifying elephants had not made them turn. This, obviously, was not going to be an easy fight.

He tried to make peace with the Romans, but the Romans would not discuss peace as long as Pyrrhus was in Italy. The war, therefore, continued. In 279 B.C. Pyrrhus met a new Roman army at Ausculum (aws'kyoo-lum) about 100 miles northwest of Tarentum. He won again but this time with even greater difficulty, for the Romans were learning to handle the elephants.

When Pyrrhus viewed the battleground this time, someone tried to congratulate him on the victory. He snapped back bitterly, "One more such victory, and I am lost." It is from this that the expression "Pyrrhic victory" has arisen. It means a victory so narrowly won and at such a cost that it has all the effect of a defeat.

The battles of Heraclea and Ausculum were the first occasion on which the Macedonian phalanx met the Roman legion. The phalanx had deteriorated since Alexander's time, growing heavier and more unwieldy and therefore harder to maneuver. It required level ground, for any serious unevenness upset its close formation and left it helpless. The legion on the other hand was a flexible arrangement which, with properly trained men, could expand outward like a hand or contract inward like a fist. It could take uneven ground in stride.

The phalanx beat the legion in these two battles, partly because of the elephants and partly because of Pyrrhus' ability. The phalanx was never to beat the legion again.

Meanwhile, Syracuse was undergoing serious disorders following the death of Agathocles and the Carthaginian danger was again threatening. The Syracusans called to Pyrrhus, who gladly took his army into Sicily in response.

Sure enough, once Pyrrhus faced Carthaginians rather than Romans, he had an easier time of it. By 277 B.C., he had the Carthaginians penned into the westernmost angle of the island, as Dionysius had done a century earlier. From that angle, however, he could not drive them any more than Dionysius had been able to. What's more, he lacked the fleet that would have made it possible for him to attack Carthage directly, as Agathocles had done a quarter-century earlier. Therefore, he decided to return to Italy, where the Romans had been making steady progress during his absence.

In 275 B.C., Pyrrhus met them for a third battle, at Beneventum (ben"ih-ven'tum) about thirty miles west of Ausculum. This time the Romans were completely ready for the elephants. They used flaming arrows and the elephants, burned and maddened, turned and ran, crushing Pyrrhus' own troops. It was a complete Roman victory.

Pyrrhus made haste to take what troops he had left and got out of Italy, without ceremony. Rome occupied all of southern Italy and from that day forward, Magna Graecia was Roman.

Once back in Epirus, Pyrrhus continued battling, for war

was his only interest. Another call for help came to him. This was from Cleonymus, a Spartan prince who was trying to make himself king.

Pyrrhus invaded the Peloponnesus in 272 B.C. and attacked Sparta. The Spartans resisted, of course, but Pyrrhus had little trouble in destroying almost the entire Spartan army. For the sixth time, however, Sparta was saved an occupation when Pyrrhus turned away because of more pressing problems.

He advanced onward to Argos and was killed in its streets when, according to the story, a woman flung a tile from a rooftop at him. It was an ignoble end for a warrior and, with his death, the importance of Epirus vanished.

THE GAULS

While Pyrrhus was gone in Italy, Ptolemy Ceraunus had consolidated his hold on Macedonia (see page 236) and had reason to congratulate himself on the absence of his warlike rival.

Unfortunately for Ptolemy, disaster was to strike from a new direction and in the shape of a new foe.

It had been nearly a thousand years since Greece had had to suffer the miseries of a major barbarian raid, but now it came. The barbarians in question were the Gauls who had occupied much of the European interior since at least Bronze Age times. Groups of them had been established north of the Danube River for an indefinite period.

Occasionally, because of population pressure or because of movements in response to defeats in war, tribes of Gauls would come flooding southward toward the Mediterranean. Thus, in 390 B.C., Gallic tribes swarmed down the Italian peninsula and took Rome, then a small town of no importance.

Now, a century later, it was the turn of Greece. In 279 B.C., Gallic invaders, under a leader called Brennus (bren′us), poured southward into Macedonia.

Ptolemy Ceraunus found himself suddenly faced with wild hordes against whom he scarcely had time to rally his forces. His army was mowed down and he himself was killed. For a few years there was no government at all in Macedonia, only roving bands of savages whom the various cities held off as well as they could.

Meanwhile, the Gauls, in search of more booty, drove further southward into Greece in 278 B.C. As Athens, two centuries before, had taken the lead in withstanding the Persians, so now she took the lead in withstanding the Gauls. At her side was not Sparta, but the Aetolians. They lived west of Phocis and had been reduced to impotence by the Dorian invasion a thousand years before. After having played no part in Greek history in Hellenic times, they were now rising to prominence.

Together, they made their stand at Thermopylae, and matters turned out exactly as they had once before. The Greeks held firm until traitors showed the invaders the old path through the mountains. This time, fortunately, the Greek army was removed by sea and did not have to suffer the fate of Leonidas and his men.

The Gauls continued moving southward and attacked Delphi, which was a particularly valuable prize because of the treasures it had accumulated over the centuries; treasures which no Greek or Macedonian conqueror would have dared to touch.

Here the Gauls, however, suffered defeat, probably at the hands of the Aetolians. The story is obscure, for in later times the defeat was blamed on the miraculous intervention of the gods. The noise of thunder was said to have terrified the Gauls, and large boulders, dashing down from the mountains, killed many. Of course, there may have been an earthquake.

But whether because of the Aetolians or an earthquake or

the gods, it seems a fact that Brennus was defeated and died and that the Gauls had to leave Greece. Some of them remained in Thrace and some crossed over into Asia Minor.

As for Macedonia, one man who made successful headway against the Gauls, after the first fury of their assault had spent itself was Antigonus Gonatas (gon'uh-tas), possibly meaning "Antigonus, the Knock-Kneed." He was the son of Demetrius Poliorcetes and the grandson of Antigonus Monophthalmos.

In earlier life, he had consoled himself with the beauties of philosophy, studying under Zeno the Stoic (see page 184). Now he grasped the chance of seizing the throne that had eluded his father and grandfather. The old One-Eye and the Besieger would have smiled if they had been alive for Antigonus Gonatas succeeded.

By 276 B.C. he was King of Macedonia. He managed to fight off Pyrrhus of Epirus when that warrior returned from Italy and remained king in reasonable peace for nearly forty years, down to his death in 239 B.C. What's more, his descendants ruled over Macedonia for a century after his death.

15

THE TWILIGHT OF FREEDOM

THE ACHAEAN LEAGUE

Greece, in Hellenistic times, decayed rapidly. The vast conquests of Alexander poured loot into the land, but in the end the chief result of this wealth, unaccompanied by industrial development, led to inflation, in which a few got rich and many grew poor.

The situation was like that during the age of colonization, but then a solution had been found in the development of democracy. Now, in Hellenistic times, foreign domination prevented Greece from adjusting to the new situation freely. Attempts at social revolution were crushed.

Worse yet, the Greek population had a tendency to leave old Greece where the future seemed to hold so little and migrate outward to the new areas, which were larger and richer, and where Macedonian monarchs were ready to subsidize Greek learning and energy at the expense of native populations. As the new Hellenistic monarchies became more Greek, they competed with Greece itself in industry and commerce and Greece suffered the more. Greek population began a steady decline during which what had been good-sized cities became small towns and what had been small towns vanished altogether.

There were a few compensations, however. The outright Macedonian domination had weakened and was not as it had been in the time of Philip and of Antipater. Macedonia had also grown feebler; first because so many of its people had emigrated outward to the newly conquered lands and second because of the devastation of the Gauls.

She was able to maintain garrisons here and there, for instance in Corinth. In 262 B.C. she also occupied Athens and in 255 B.C. she had the Long Walls pulled down again. To be sure, by 255 B.C. Athens had no need for them. She was fighting no wars and would never more fight any.

Still most of Greece (with the help of the Ptolemies in Egypt, who were always anxious to hamper Macedonia) managed to maintain a certain shadowy independence from Macedonia. This independence, however, was not based on the city-state, for that was just about dead. (In all the Greek world, the only city-states of the old style that were in the least prosperous were Syracuse and Rhodes.) Instead, Greek independence rested with leagues of cities.

About 370 B.C. the tribes of Aetolia were organized into an "Aetolian League," which now began to play a part in Greek history.

A second, somewhat more citified and polished league, was founded in the Peloponnesus in 280 B.C. It began with a union of some of the cities of Achaea along the southern shores of the Gulf of Corinth so it was termed the "Achaean League."

For a generation it remained a local organization of no great importance. The man who changed that was Aratus (uh-ray'tus) of Sicyon.

The main object of Aratus was to unite all the Peloponnesus in the Achaean League. He led a daring raid against Corinth in 242 B.C. and, with a few soldiers, captured its central fortress, the Acrocorinth. The Macedonian garrison was expelled and Corinth joined the Achaean League. By 228 B.C. even Athens managed to expel its Macedonian garrison and allied itself to the League, which now stood at the height of its power.

Oddly enough, there was one another power of importance in Greece, aside from the two Leagues (which, in true Greek fashion, were in constant conflict — a conflict that helped only Macedonia) and that was Sparta.

Sparta still clung, even now, to the memory of the days of Agesilaus, a century and a half before, and would not enter any organization of cities it did not lead itself. It was therefore the great enemy of the Achaean League.

To Aratus' concern, Sparta was also beginning to show signs of renewed strength. It suffered as the rest of Greece did from economic dislocation and it contained only 600 Spartiates qualified as full citizens. The remaining Spartans were virtually paupers and it was common for helots (there were still helots) to be allowed to starve to death.

In 245 B.C., a new king, Agis IV, came to power. He was an unusual person, a Spartan revolutionary. He wanted a new deal and suggested that the land be distributed among 4500 citizens and that these should include the perioeci. He said nothing about the slaves, but this was a beginning. However, the few Spartiates who owned everything would not yield. They managed to gain the support of the other king, Leonidas II, and in 241 B.C. seized power, put Agis on trial and had him executed.

However, this did not end attempts at reform in Sparta. In 235 B.C. Leonidas II died and his son, Cleomenes III, became king. He had married the widow of Agis IV, and he had inherited Agis' enlightened plans. He was, moreover, a more forceful person.

He mustered what men he could and led them out to battle in the fashion of Sparta of old. Into Arcadia he went, defeating the Achaean League in several battles, and taking most of Arcadia. With the prestige so gained, he returned to Sparta in 226 B.C., had the ephors executed and put through the necessary economic reforms.

He was now stronger than ever and in 224 B.C. he marched forth and defeated the armies of the Achaean League again, capturing and sacking Megalopolis. He also captured Argos, while Corinth and other cities voluntarily went into alliance with him.

Aratus saw the Achaean League crumbling under his eyes. Rather than see that happen he turned to the common enemy and appealed to Macedonia. In Macedonia, Antigonus Doson (doh'son) — that is "Antigonus the Promiser" — was now king. It was to the Promiser that Aratus appealed and Antigonus promised to deliver gladly and did.

He drove a hard bargain, though. Corinth was to be delivered to a Macedonian garrison; he was himself to be recognized as head of the Achaean League; and the League was to support his armies. It was obvious that this meant delivering Greece over to Macedonia, but Aratus, in his hatred of the Spartans, agreed.

Antigonus marched his army southward and, in 222 B.C., met the Spartans at Sellasia (seh-lay'zhuh) a town five miles north of Sparta itself. Cleomenes and the Spartans fought with old-time valor, but the verdict of Chaeronea a century earlier was repeated. The Macedonians won a complete victory.

At last the charm that had kept Sparta, even in its weakness, free from enemy occupation for a century and a half was broken. Epaminondas, Philip, Alexander, Antipater, Demetrius and Pyrrhus had all turned away from the city walls, but Antigonus Doson, a lesser man than any of them, entered Sparta, restored the ephors and forced Sparta to join the Achaean League.

Cleomenes fled to Egypt but in 219 B.C., unable to stand life after Sparta's defeat, committed suicide. He had done wonders considering the weapons he had; and was not only a brave warrior, but an enlightened ruler. What might he not have done, one wonders, if he had been king in the time of Sparta's greatness? There is reason to argue that Cleomenes, though he died a failure and suicide, was the greatest Spartan of all times.

In 219 B.C. Antigonus Doson died, and Philip V came to the Macedonian throne. Philip managed to strengthen his hold over Greece slowly, especially after 213 B.C. when Aratus died. However, Philip's plans for Greece would not be settled there. Rome was becoming increasingly strong after she had absorbed the Greek cities of southern Italy, and it was plain to Philip that here was an enemy that was to mean far more danger for him than was to be found in all the Greek cities combined.

THE FALL OF SYRACUSE

For a while, though, it seemed (while Philip V held his breath) that Rome, for all its growing strength, might be destroyed. This came about because half a century before the time of Philip, after Rome had defeated Pyrrhus and conquered southern Italy, she had been forced to meet a new enemy, Carthage.

The trouble arose in Sicily, where a Syracusan general, Hiero, grew powerful. He had fought alongside Pyrrhus and now he tried to control some of the Italian mercenary troops that had been plaguing Sicily since they had been brought in by Agathocles. Hiero defeated them, and the Syracusans made him king in 270 B.C. as Hiero II.

In 264 B.C., Hiero renewed the attack on the mercenaries who had fortified themselves in Messana, in the corner of Sicily nearest Italy. The mercenaries called loudly for the help of the new Italian power, Rome, and she responded. Hiero was defeated several times and was wise enough to see that Rome was going to dominate the Mediterranean area. He switched to an alliance with her and maintained it faithfully.

The Carthaginians, who considered Sicily subject to their own interference only, were incensed at the entrance of Roman troops into that area. Thus began the "First Punic War." (It was called "Punic" because the Carthaginians were a Phoenician colony to begin with, and the Latin word for Phoenicians was *Poeni*.)

The war lasted twenty years and both sides suffered tremendous losses. Rome built a fleet, however, and fought Carthage on the sea. In the end, Rome managed to win and in 241 B.C., after 500 years, the Carthaginians were finally expelled from Sicily completely, and for good. The Romans took over in their place but left the eastern half of the island to their ally, Hiero, and Syracuse continued independent.

On the whole, the Greek world was pleased. Carthage was the old enemy who had gone for their throats so many times. Rome was newer, seemed gentler, and more amenable to Greek culture.

The Greeks even admitted Romans to the Eleusinian Mysteries and to the Isthmian games; a formal admission by the Greeks that the Romans were a civilized power and not to be considered barbarian.

Syracuse flourished under Roman domination. The reign of Hiero II is best remembered because he had a kinsman, Archimedes (ahr″kih-mee′deez), who was the greatest of the ancient Greek scientists.

A number of well-known stories are told about Archimedes. He discovered the principle of the lever and explained its workings according to a simple mathematical formula. (He did not discover the lever itself, of course; that was known since prehistoric times.) He could see that there was no theoretical limit to the multiplication of force made possible by a lever and he is reported to have said, "Give me a place to stand on and I will move the world."

Hiero, amused at this, challenged Archimedes to move something heavy; not the world, perhaps, but something heavy. So (the story goes), Archimedes chose a ship at the dock and had it loaded with freight and passengers. He then arranged a pulley device (a kind of lever, in effect) and, using it, pulled the ship, single-handed, out of the sea and up on the shore, with no more effort than he would have expended on pulling a toy boat.

Even better known is the story of the crown. At one time, Hiero asked Archimedes to determine whether a gold crown he had ordered from a jeweler was really all gold or whether it had been dishonestly alloyed with cheaper silver or copper. To determine this, Archimedes had to know both the weight and volume of the crown. To determine the weight was easy, but to determine the volume without beating the crown into a solid shape (unthinkable!) seemed impossible.

One day, Archimedes lowered himself into a full bathtub and noted that water overflowed as he was submerged. It occurred to him that the volume of water that overflowed was equal to the volume of his own body as it replaced the water. This meant he could measure the volume of the crown by lowering it into water and measuring by how much the water level rose. Mad with excitement, he jumped out of the bath and (according to the story) ran naked through the streets of Syracuse to Hiero's palace, crying "Eureka! Eureka!" (I have it! I have it!"). And, indeed, he had what is now called the "principle of buoyancy."

The general peace of Syracuse and of Rome was disturbed, however, by a vengeful Carthage. She had by no means resigned herself to defeat. Carefully, she colonized Spain as a new source of wealth and a new base for attack against Rome. In addition, a general arose, named Hannibal, who proved without doubt to be one of the great war-captains of history.

He marched from Spain to Italy in 218 B.C. (just after Philip V succeeded to the throne of Macedon) and thus began the "Second Punic War." Inside Italy, Hannibal met one superior Roman army after another and by cleverly maneuvering his forces and by taking full advantage of Roman over-confidence, he inflicted three defeats on them, one after another, and each worse than the one before.

The third defeat, in 216 B.C., at Cannae (kan′ee) on the south Adriatic coast, was just about the classic battle of anni-hilation of all time; a perfect example of a weaker army maneu-vering a stronger one to complete destruction. Never in its history was Rome to suffer a defeat quite so crushing.

After Cannae, Rome seemed through. Certainly Philip V of Macedon thought so, for he promptly formed an alliance with Carthage.

Hiero II of Syracuse retained his faith in Rome, and held to the alliance, but he died in 215 B.C. His grandson, Hieronymus (high″er-on′ih-mus), who succeeded to the throne, agreed with Philip V. He, too, felt that Rome was done and hastened to get on the side of Carthage.

However, Rome was *not* through. The years after Cannae were, indeed, her finest, and never did she so closely resemble the Spartans at their height. With stubborn and almost superhu-man determination she continued the fight against Hannibal.

And beleaguered though she was, she still had the strength to deal with Syracuse. In 214 B.C., a Roman fleet appeared to lay siege to Syracuse (the first since the Athenian fleet of two centuries before, see page 152).

Syracuse fought back valiantly for nearly three years, thanks chiefly to Archimedes. That scientist, according to later stories by Greek historians who delighted to tell the tale of Greek brains versus Roman brawn, invented all sorts of ingenious devices to fight off the Romans. There were burning mirrors, grapples, special catapults and so on (the details of which were probably exaggerated with time.) It was said that as soon as a rope or a piece of wood appeared over the walls of Syracuse, the Roman ships began rowing away at top speed, trying to get out of range of the latest device of the deadly Syracusan.

But it was brawn that won out in the end. In 211 B.C. despite all that Archimedes could do, Syracuse was taken by the Romans. The Roman commander had given orders that Archimedes was to be taken alive. However, a soldier came upon him as he was working out some geometrical problem in the sand. The soldier ordered old Archimedes (he was about seventy-five at the time) to come along.

Archimedes cried out, "Don't step on my circles."

And the soldier, who felt he had no time for such nonsense, killed the great man.

Sicily was entirely Roman thereafter, and the history of the Greeks as an independent people in the west, which had begun five centuries earlier in the age of colonization, came to a permanent end.

THE FALL OF MACEDONIA

After Cannae, Philip V was, for a brief moment, in control of Greece. Even the Aetolian League feared invasion by a victorious Carthage and relied on Philip (the ally of Carthage) to protect it against that.

But Rome, despite its mortal duel with Hannibal and the engagement of its fleet at Syracuse, managed to scrape up some troops to send into Greece. These were not enough to control the situation entirely but they did keep Philip from doing more than lending Carthage moral support. He did not quite have the courage to send troops to join Hannibal.

Furthermore, Rome stirred up Greece against Macedonia. She allied herself with the Aetolian League and with Sparta for this purpose. In the end, though, the Carthaginian menace forced Rome to stop short of a complete settlement and what was called the "First Macedonian War" ended in pretty much of a draw.

This Roman-Macedonian conflict reflected itself in the Peloponnesus, where the Achaean League (under the control of Philopoeman [fil″oh-pee′men] of Megalopolis), counting on Macedonian help, and Sparta, counting on Roman help, continued their duel.

In 207 B.C. a Spartan revolutionary, Nabis (nay′bis), deposed the last kings (nine centuries after the Dorian occupation of Sparta) and took control as tyrant. He carried through to completion the reforms of Agis IV and Cleomenes III, abolishing debt and redividing the land. He even freed the slaves and brought the vicious system of helotism to an end.

Meanwhile, the Second Punic War reached its climax. Rome had come across a particularly successful general of her own, Publius Cornelius Scipio (sip′ee-oh). To Scipio, it seemed that the one way to defeat Hannibal was to take a leaf out of the book of old Agathocles, a century earlier, and to carry the war to Carthage itself.

In 202 B.C. he did exactly this. Hannibal was called back by the anguished Carthaginians. At the town of Zama (zay′muh), southwest of Carthage, Scipio met and defeated Hannibal. The Second Punic War was over and Rome was victorious.

Now Rome could turn its attention to all those who in the dark days had turned against her or tried to hasten her fall, and on the top of the list was Philip V of Macedon.

In 200 B.C. Rome had its excuse (it always waited for an excuse, although the excuse was sometimes a very trivial one). This came when the island of Rhodes appealed for help against

Philip. Rome at once declared war ("the Second Macedonian War").

The Roman general Titus Quinctius Flamininus (flam"ih-nigh'nus) worked slowly. He made sure that Greece itself was on his side and would remain quiet. In 197 B.C. the Macedonian phalanx and the Roman legion met again at Cynoscephalae in Thessaly, as in the days of Pyrrhus nearly a century before. The legion won and Philip V, huddled behind his broken army, had to beg for peace. He retained Macedonia but that was all. His control over Greece was destroyed and the Macedonian hegemony, which had descended upon Greece in the time of Philip II a century and a half before, was now lifted permanently.

At the Isthmian games of 197 B.C., Flamininus publicly announced the restoration of their old freedom to all the Greek cities and Greece went wild with joy.

However, the first use the cities made of their freedom was to try to get Rome to help them in their ancient task of destroying one another. The Achaean League persuaded Flamininus to help them destroy Nabis, the feared revolutionary of hated Sparta. Flamininus reluctantly agreed and, despite gallant Spartan resistance, drove Nabis out of Argos (which he had earlier reoccupied). Thus was brought to a final end the long five-century feud between Sparta and Argos. Flamininus prevented the League, however, from taking Sparta itself.

But Flamininus left Greece in 194 B.C. and that gave the Achaean League and Philopoemen their chance. They attacked Sparta, defeated it and forced it to join the Achaean League. Nabis was assassinated by some Aetolians and with that Sparta subsided.

Philopoemen was the last Greek general to win victories in wars between Greek cities and for that reason he came to be called in later times "the last of the Greeks." He met his end, finally, in Messenia, in 184 B.C., when he was trying to put down a revolt there against the Achaean League.

THE END OF THE ACHAEAN LEAGUE

The Greek cities found, however, that in obtaining their freedom from Macedonia, they were really only experiencing a change in masters and were coming under a Roman hegemony. The Aetolian League chafed under that control and looked about for outside support.

None was expected from Philip V, of course, who was never to dare the Romans again. However, in the east was another Macedonian, Antiochus III of the Seleucid Empire. He had made conquests in the east and fancied himself another Alexander. At his court, moreover, was Hannibal, who had never given up his dreams of humbling Rome and who urged Antiochus into western adventures. He offered to lead an army into Italy, if Antiochus would make a gesture in Greece to distract the Romans.

This might possibly have worked, but the Aetolians asked Antiochus to make his main effort in Greece, promising that all Greece would rise against Rome. Of course, this turned out to be untrue. All Greece never rose against an outside enemy. Since the Aetolian League was anti-Roman, the Achaean League was naturally pro-Roman.

Antiochus, however, decided to make Greece the battleground as the Aetolians requested and in 192 B.C. passed over into Greece. There he wasted his time in a foolish pursuit of pleasure and when the determined Romans caught up with him, he found himself smashed at Thermopylae in 191 B.C. and sent tumbling out of Greece and back into Asia.

As a result of Antiochus' defeat, the Aetolian League was made thoroughly subject to Rome. Only the Achaean League retained a dim spark of Greek freedom, and Rome watched narrowly lest the spark grow too bright.

Perseus (pur-syoos), the son of Philip V, planned war against Rome and carefully arranged for help from the Aetolians. In

171 B.C. the "Third Macedonian War" broke out. The Romans finally forced a decisive battle at Pydna (pid'nuh), a town on Macedonia's Aegean coast, in 168 B.C. Again the Macedonians were completely smashed. It was the last battle for the Macedonian phalanx. Perseus fled, but was captured, and sent to Rome. The Macedonian monarchy came to an end.

The Romans were exasperated at the manner in which Greece helped every anti-Roman rising, and decided to carry off a group of Achaean hostages just to make sure there would be no further trouble.

Among the hostages was Polybius (poh-lib'ee-us), who had been born about 201 B.C. in Megalopolis, and who was among the leaders of the Achaean League after the death of Philopoemen.

Polybius became friendly, in Rome, with several of the leading Romans, including Scipio the Younger (grandson by adoption of the Scipio who had defeated Hannibal) and so his treatment in Rome was not harsh. Scipio benefited from this for Polybius was the greatest of the Greek historians of the Hellenistic Age and wrote a history of the Second Punic War in which the older Scipio's feats were duly and favorably recorded.

When the Achaean hostages, including Polybius, were finally released in 151 B.C., Polybius did not remain in Greece long. He hurried to Africa, with a historian's interest, to join his friend Scipio at a new Roman triumph.

Rome retained the desire to put a final end to Carthage, a city which was now helpless but which was never forgiven for having dragged Rome so near to destruction half a century before. Finally, Rome manufactured an excuse to attack Carthage in the "Third Punic War" in 149 B.C.

Carthage, as helpless as Sparta, managed to find means to resist. On sheer stubborn heroism (like their fellow-countrymen of Tyre against Alexander nearly two centuries before, see page 217) they held out for over two years. However, the final destruction of Carthage was inevitable and the end came in 146 B.C.

The city was then leveled to the ground and the people which had disputed the rule of the Mediterranean with Greeks and Romans for six centuries were no more.

The Roman preoccupation with Carthage caused hopes to stir in Greece once more. Macedonia rose in 149 B.C. under someone who pretended to be a son of Perseus, the last king of Macedonia. In the "Fourth Macedonian War," Rome quickly crushed all resistance and, in 148 B.C., converted Macedonia into a Roman province.

Meanwhile the Achaean League seized its chance to pounce upon Sparta once more. The Romans had forbidden any warfare between the cities, but the Achaeans had eyes for nothing but Sparta. Rome, they decided, was too busy with Macedonia to bother.

The exasperated Romans were not too busy, however, and they did bother. An army under Lucius Mummius (mum'ee-us) entered the Peloponnesus. The Achaean League, frightened into immobility, dared not resist, but Mummius did not care. He was not one of those Romans who were, at that time, falling in love with Greek culture. He took Corinth in 146 B.C. It was the wealthiest city in Greece, and although it had made no resistance, he used it as an object lesson. The men were killed, the women and children sold into slavery, the city itself pillaged.

The Achaean League was dissolved, all cities placed under oligarchies. The last miserable spark of Greek freedom was extinguished, although some of the pretense was maintained. It was not until 27 B.C. that Greece was actually made an outright part of the Roman realm as the "Province of Achaea."

16

THE HELLENISTIC MONARCHIES

HELLENISTIC ASIA MINOR

But though twilight closed in on Greece during Hellenistic times, the conquests of Alexander had spread Greek culture throughout the east, and it was actually more powerful and influential in the days of Greek decline than ever it had been in the Athenian noon.

A series of small Hellenistic monarchies arose in Asia Minor, for instance. Of these, one was centered about the city of Pergamum (pur′guh-mum), a city about eighteen miles inland from the coast opposite the island of Lesbos.

North of Pergamum, bordering on the Propontus, was Bithynia (bih-thin'ee-uh). The area had gained virtual independence under the last weak years of Persia. It retained that independence during the lifetime of Alexander (who never sent an
army into that area) and afterward as well. In 278 B.C., its ruler
Nicomedes I (nik"oh-mee'deez) assumed the title of king.

His rule was not secure, however, as there were rivals for the
throne. Seeking for help, it occurred to him to make use of the
Gauls who had been ravaging Macedonia and Greece for some
years (see page 243). He invited a tribe into Asia Minor. They
came, but with ideas of their own. In no time they began pillag-
ing the prosperous and unwarlike towns that lay all about.

For a generation, the Gauls were the terror of western Asia
Minor. It was as though the time of the Cimmerians, four and
a half centuries before (see page 87) had returned. It was
Pergamum that finally settled matters.

In 241 B.C. Attalus I (at'uh-lus) succeeded his father, Eumenes, to the Pergamene throne, and it was with him that the
kingdom's greatness began. Attalus fought and defeated the
Gauls in 235 B.C., ending their menace and receiving the name
of Attalus Soter (soh'ter) or "Attalus, the Savior" in consequence.

In honor of his victory, Attalus had a statue, "The Dying
Gaul" erected in Athens. It is often miscalled "The Dying
Gladiator" and is one of the most famous surviving pieces of
Hellenistic art.

The Gauls were penned into a region of central Asia Minor
which came to be known as Galatia (ga-lay'shee-uh) in consequence. They were quickly civilized once they were made to
settle down.

Attalus I, like his contemporary, Hiero, in Syracuse, recognized Rome to be the coming power and allied himself with
her. Under his son, Eumenes II, who succeeded in 197 B.C.,
Pergamum reached its height. It gained territory (with Rome's

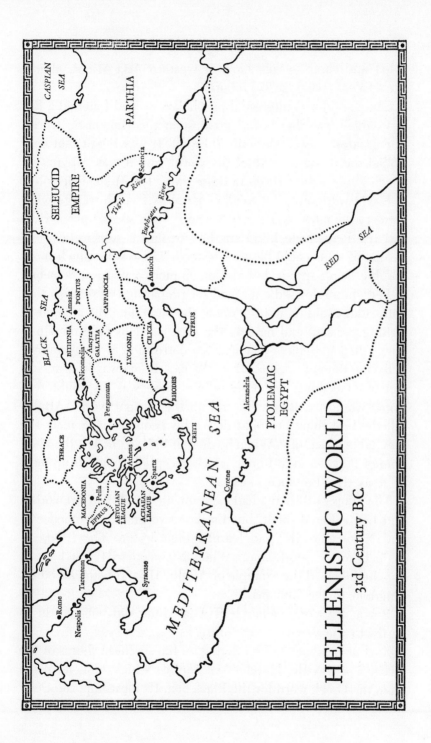

HELLENISTIC WORLD
3rd Century B.C.

help) and came to rule most of western Asia Minor, almost like a Lydia (see page 87) reborn.

Eumenes II was interested in scholarship and founded a library which was the second greatest in the Hellenistic world. The greatest was at Alexandria, Egypt. It was Egypt that controlled the papyrus trade of the world, and it was papyrus on which books were written in those days. The Hellenistic rulers of Egypt were reluctant to allow papyrus (which was growing scarcer) to move too freely toward their second-place rival and the Pergamene librarians had to find a substitute.

Animal skins could be used instead. These were much more durable than papyrus, but also much more expensive. Someone in Pergamum devised a method for preparing the skins so that both sides could be written upon, thus doubling the amount of writing per skin and halving the expense. This type of skin is now called "parchment" which is a corruption of "Pergamum."

By the time of Attalus III in 138 B.C., Rome was in firm control of Macedonia and Greece and there was no doubt that Rome would eventually control all the ancient world. Attalus felt the best thing he could do for his people was to meet the inevitable peacefully. When he died in 133 B.C., he left the kingdom of Pergamum to Rome, which accepted it and set up most of it as the "Province of Asia."

The kings of Bithynia had experimented with anti-Romanism and had suffered for it, but the last two kings, Nicomedes II and Nicomedes III, had learned their lesson. They, too, remained firmly pro-Roman. When Nicomedes III died in 74 B.C., he followed the example of Attalus III and bequeathed his kingdom to the Romans.

But at least one monarch of Asia Minor did not give in so easily to the wave of the future.

East of Bithynia and bordering on the southern shores of the Black Sea was the kingdom of Pontus, which took its name from the Greek word for the Black Sea. Its most important city was Trapezus, the coastal town which had been reached by Xenophon's Ten Thousand.

The first to call himself king of Pontus was Mithridates I (mith"rih-day'teez) who assumed the title in 301 B.C. For two and a half centuries afterward his successors ruled the kingdom. The last of the line was Mithridates VI, who ruled for over half a century, from 120 to 63 B.C. He was a capable man who extended the territory of Pontus over the neighboring Hellenistic kingdoms.

In expanding his influence, Mithridates came into conflict with Rome, of course, and war was bound to come. Mithridates struck the first blow in 88 B.C. Surprisingly enough, he had large initial successes, swept up most of Asia Minor, actually defeated the Roman armies, and massacred Roman citizens.

He then crossed the Aegean Sea and entered Greece. Athens took no part in the warfare — she was long past such things — but she could still make a political decision. She decided to support Mithridates and allowed him to enter the city.

But the Romans had lost ground only because after their final conquest of Carthage and Macedonia, they had allowed themselves the luxury of a bloody civil war. That war had come to a temporary halt now, leaving Lucius Cornelius Sulla (sul'uh) in control. At the head of new Roman armies, Sulla entered Greece in 87 B.C., took Athens and pillaged it thoroughly. Athens never made another political decision after that.

In 86 B.C., Sulla met Mithridates at the fateful field of Chaeronea and defeated him. Mithridates had to flee to Asia and the Romans followed him. In 84 B.C., Mithridates was forced to make peace on Roman terms.

Twice more, he rose in furious battles against the Romans, and twice more he was defeated. In 65 B.C., he received his third and final defeat at the hands of Gnaeus Pompeius Magnus, better known, in English, as Pompey (pom'pee) and in 63 B.C., Mithridates killed himself.

After that, all of Asia Minor was under firm Roman control, though parts of it retained a nominal independence for some years to come.

THE SELEUCID EMPIRE

The portion of Alexander's empire that lay east of Asia Minor fell to Seleucus. His realm was based chiefly on Syria and Babylonia so that it was almost a rebirth of the old Chaldean Empire of two and a half centuries before (see page 90). The vast Iranian regions to the north and east were more or less under his control so that on the map he seemed to be heir to most of Alexander's empire. He was therefore known as Seleucus Nicator (nigh-kay'tor), or "Seleucus, the Conqueror."

In 312 B.C., Seleucus built himself a new capital on the Tigris River, not many miles from Babylon, which is on the Euphrates. He named it Seleucia (see-lyoo'shee-uh) after himself. As Seleucia grew, Babylon declined.

Babylon had been full of fame and glory since it first ruled an empire in the time of the Hebrew patriarch, Abraham. But Alexander's death was the last event of importance with which it was connected. By the beginning of the Christian Era, Babylon was as dead as Nineveh.

In 300 B.C., Seleucus also founded a city in northern Syria. He named it for his father, Antiochus, and the city is known to us as Antioch (an'tee-ok).

Seleucus' great-great-great-grandson attempted to turn the Judaeans away from Judaism and force them to accept Greek culture. In 168 B.C., he declared Judaism illegal and the Jews, consequently, revolted. Under the leadership of a family we know as the Maccabes (mak'uh-beez) they succeeded, against great odds, in establishing an independent Judaean kingdom in 164 B.C.

The Maccabean kingdom was strongly Hellenistic itself. Two of its kings bore the Greek name Aristobulus (a-ris″toh-byoo′lus) and in 103 B.C. a king named Alexander ruled over Judaea. The last of the Maccabees was named Antigonus.

The Seleucid Empire continued to decline after the Judaean revolt. About 141 B.C. it lost Babylonia to eastern invaders and Antioch became sole capital of the empire. In 64 B.C., the Roman general, Pompey, fresh from his destruction of Mithridates, collected the miserable remnant that was left of the vast empire of Seleucus Nicator and made it a Roman province. The next year, 63 B.C., Judaea was made a Roman province.

ALEXANDRIA

The most successful of all the Hellenistic kingdoms was that established over Egypt by Alexander's general, Ptolemy, whose descendants were to rule Egypt for nearly three centuries. The first Ptolemy helped the Rhodians defeat Demetrius Poliorcetes (see page 233) and the Rhodians, in gratitude, named him "Ptolemy Soter" (Ptolemy, the Savior). It is by this name that he is known in history.

Ptolemy Soter laid the groundwork for a university in his capital, Alexandria; one to which he invited the scholars of the Greek world by promise of financial support and an opportunity for uninterrupted study. The university was dedicated to the Muses, the Greek goddesses of learning, so it is known to us as the "Museum."

This was the most famous institution of learning in all the ancient world and attached to it was the largest and finest library ever collected in the days before printing. Alexandria became one of the most famous of all Greek-speaking cities and remained the center of ancient learning for a period of some seven centuries.

Greek science had remained alive during all the turbulences following the death of Alexander. Aristotle's school, the Lyceum, continued vigorously for a century. Because Aristotle had given lectures while walking about the garden, his followers at this school were called the "Peripatetics" (the walkabouts).

One of the peripatetics was Theophrastus (thee″ohfras′tus), who was born on Lesbos about 372 B.C. He studied under Plato, then became an associate of Aristotle. When Aristotle died, he left his library to Theophrastus, who took charge of the Lyceum and extended Aristotle's biological work.

Theophrastus concentrated chiefly on the plant world and painstakingly described over 500 plant species, thus founding the science of botany. He remained in charge of the Lyceum until his death in 287 B.C.

Succeeding Theophrastus was Strato (stray′toh) of Lampsacus. He performed important experiments in physics and had correct views on such matters as vacuums, the motion of falling bodies, and levers.

After Strato's death, the Lyceum declined, however. Strato himself had received an education at Alexandria and the movement of Greek science was away from Athens and toward the new capital of the Ptolemies, where the openhanded monarchs stood ready to subsidize learning.

One of the early members of Alexandria's Museum was Euclid (yoo′klid) whose name is permanently linked to geometry, for he wrote a textbook ("Elements") on the subject that has been standard, with some modifications of course, ever since.

As a mathematician, however, Euclid's fame is not due to his own research, for few of the theorems in his textbook are his own. Many were adapted from the work of Eudoxus (see page 185). What Euclid did, and what made him great, was that he took all the knowledge that had been accumulated in mathematics by the Greeks and codified two and a half centuries of work into a single systematized structure.

In particular, he evolved, as a starting point, a series of axioms and postulates that were admirable for their brevity and elegance. He then arranged proof after proof in a manner so logical as almost to defy improvement.

Practically nothing is known of Euclid's life, however, except that he worked at Alexandria about 300 B.C. One story about him (which is also told about other ancient mathematicians) is that he was trying to explain geometry to Ptolemy. When the king asked Euclid to make his demonstrations easier, Euclid answered uncompromisingly, "There is no royal road to knowledge."

A mathematician who followed Euclid by fifty years or so, was Appollonius (ap″uh-loh′nee-us) of Perga (per′guh), a town on the coast of southern Asia Minor. He dealt with the curves that were to be found at the intersection of a plane and a cone (the "conic sections"). These include the circle, the ellipse, the parabola and the hyperbola.

The world grew wider in the Hellenistic era and some Greeks became great travelers. The greatest perhaps was Pytheas (pith′ee-us) of Massalia who was a contemporary of Alexander the Great and who searched for new worlds in the far west, while Alexander penetrated the east.

Pytheas moved out into the Atlantic and from his reports it seems quite likely that he reached the British Isles and Iceland, exploring Europe's northern waters even to the Baltic Sea. In the Atlantic Ocean, he was able to observe the tides (which are not marked in the land-locked Mediterranean) and suggested they were caused by the moon; an observation in which he was 2000 years ahead of his time.

Another geographer was Dicaearchus (digh″see-ahr′kus) of

Messana, who studied under Aristotle and was a close friend of Theophrastus. He made use of the reports brought back by the far-ranging armies of Alexander and his successors to draw better maps of the ancient world than had existed before. He was the first to use lines of latitude on his maps.

However, without budging from home, Eratosthenes (ehr″uh-tos′thuh-neez) of Cyrene performed a greater geographical feat than either Pytheas or Dicaearchus. Eratosthenes, who was in charge of the Library at Alexandria about 250 B.C. and who was a close friend of Archimedes, did nothing less than measure the size of the planet.

He took note of the fact that on the day of the summer solstice (June 21), the sun was directly overhead in Syene (sigh-ee′nee) in southern Egypt at the same time that it was 7 degrees from the zenith in Alexandria. This difference could only be due to the curvature of the earth's surface between Syene and Alexandria. Knowing the actual north-south distance between the two cities, it was easy to calculate the circumference of the earth by Euclid's geometry. Eratosthenes' figure is believed to have been 25,000 miles, which is correct.

Eratosthenes also attempted to set up a scientific chronology, in which all events were dated from the Trojan War. He was the first man in history to concern himself with accurate dating.

Greek science was not strong in its applied aspects, for in ancient times, physical labor was in the hands of slaves and there was little need felt to relieve that labor. (Besides, interesting one's self in what concerned slaves was beneath the dignity of a free man, it was felt.)

Even so, occasional Greeks could not help but be engineers. Archimedes was one of these, with his levers and pulleys. Another was a Greek inventor, Ctesibius (teh-sib′ee-us), who was born in Alexandria about 285 B.C. He used weights of water and jets of compressed air to move machinery. His most famous invention was of an improved water clock, in which water, dripping into a container at a steady rate, raised a float which held a pointer that marked a position on a drum. From that position, the hour could be read. Such clocks were the best available timepieces in the ancient world.

In addition to the Museum and the Library, which proved so successful, Ptolemy Soter also conceived the notion of building a structure to house a beacon that might serve to guide sailors into Alexandria's harbor at night. He hired a Greek architect, Sostratus (sos'truh-tus) of Cnidus, to build the structure on an island just off Alexandria. The island was named Pharos (fay'ros) and that was the name given the structure as well.

The structure had a base 100 feet square and at its top a beacon was kept perpetually lit. The admiring Greeks considered it one of the Seven Wonders of the World. It remained standing for 1500 years and then it was partially destroyed by an earthquake and was allowed to fall into ruins. (In fact, of the Seven Wonders, only the pyramids of Egypt still survive.)

THE PTOLEMIES

In 285 B.C. Ptolemy Soter abdicated in favor of his second son. (His oldest son, Ptolemy Ceraunus went to Macedonia and his death, see page 242.)

Ptolemy II adopted the old Egyptian custom whereby rulers married their sisters because no other family was noble enough to supply a wife. He carried on his father's patronage of science and literature.

In 246 B.C., Ptolemy II was succeeded by Ptolemy III whose wife was Berenice (ber"eh-nigh'see) of Cyrene. There is a legend to the effect that Berenice cut off her hair and hung it up in the temple of Venus, dedicating it to the goddess in the hope that she would bring her husband home from the wars victorious.

The hair disappeared (probably stolen) and the court astronomer, Conon of Samos, at once announced that it had been raised to heaven by the goddess and pointed out some faint stars which he said were the dedicated hair. Those stars now form the small constellation "Coma Berenices," which is Latin for "Berenice's hair."

With three capable kings in a row, Egypt had had a century of good rule; more, perhaps, than it had ever had in one piece at any time in its long history, before or since. Unfortunately, this did not last. After Ptolemy III, all the rulers that followed were weak and incapable so that Ptolemaic Egypt gradually decayed.

With it, there was a growing decay of Greek science. Only one scientist of first rank brightened this period and he did not work at Alexandria. He was Hipparchus of Nicaea, born about 190 B.C. and perhaps the greatest astronomer of antiquity. He worked at an observatory on the island of Rhodes.

Rhodes had been unimportant in Hellenic times but after the death of Alexander, it gained its independence and, by engaging in commerce while the rest of the Hellenistic world ruined itself with war, made itself rich and prosperous. The successful resistance to the siege by Demetrius began a century and a half during which it was the most prosperous city-state in a world in which city-states were dead and dying. After the fall of Syracuse in 211 B.C. (see page 253), Rhodes was the only prosperous city-state remaining.

In Hipparchus' time, however, this was coming to an end. In 167 B.C., after the Third Macedonian War, Rome deliberately forced the flow of commerce elsewhere in order to ruin Rhodes. Rhodes was then made to become a Roman ally and satellite in 164 B.C. After that, she slowly sank into insignificance again.

Hipparchus carried on the work of Aristarchus (see page 187) in determining the distance of the moon and the sun, but he did not adopt Aristarchus' notion of an earth revolving about the sun. In fact, he worked out in full detail a universe in which all heavenly bodies revolved about the earth, making use of careful, detailed mathematics. It was Hipparchus who placed the "geocentric theory" on a firm basis; firm enough to have it last seventeen centuries before being overthrown, once and for all, in favor of Aristarchus' sun-centered "heliocentric theory."

In 134 B.C. Hipparchus observed a star in the constellation Scorpio, of which he could find no record in previous observations. This was a serious matter, for there was the definite belief (endorsed by Aristotle) that the heavens were permanent and unchangeable. Hipparchus could not easily tell whether this star was an example of the contrary because of the unsystematic nature of previous observations. He decided then that future astronomers would not suffer similar difficulties. He proceeded to record the exact positions of a little over a thousand of the brighter stars. This was the first accurate star map.

In doing this, Hipparchus plotted the stars by latitude and longitude, a system which was later transferred to maps of the earth. Hipparchus also divided the stars into degrees of brightness (first magnitude, second magnitude and so on) a system which is still used. Then, too, by studying old observations, he discovered the "precession of the equinoxes" as a result of which the point in the sky toward which the earth's north pole points slowly shifts from year to year.

Following Hipparchus came a much inferior astronomer, Posidonius (pos-ih-doh'nee-us) of Apamea (ap"uh-mee'uh), a Syrian city near Antioch. About 100 B.C. he repeated Eratosthenes' experiment determining the size of the earth. He used a star instead of the sun which was, in itself, a worthwhile change. However, for some reason, he obtained 18,000 miles as the earth's circumference, a figure which was far too small.

By 50 B.C. Rome was overshadowing the Hellenistic world like a colossus. It had taken Macedonia and Egypt, was in the process of taking Asia Minor, bit by bit, and soon took what was left of the Seleucid Empire.

Yet still Egypt itself remained under the Ptolemies. Alone it survived of the great Macedonian conquests of nearly three centuries before.

There then arose in Egypt one last great Hellenistic monarch, someone we might term "the last of the Macedonians." This was not a man, either, but a woman. She was Cleopatra.

Cleopatra was not an Egyptian, remember, but a Macedonian. Nor is Cleopatra an Egyptian name. It is a Greek one, meaning "famous father," that is, "noble descent." It was a common name among Macedonian women. When Philip II divorced Olympias to marry a young woman (see page 209), that young woman's name was Cleopatra.

The Cleopatra who was the last of the Macedonians was born in 69 B.C. Her father, Ptolemy XI Auletes (oh-lee′teez) or "Ptolemy, the Flute-Player" died in 51 B.C. and two young sons were, in theory, to be kings next. Cleopatra, their older sister, had the help of a Roman in her own bid, however; the help of the greatest Roman of them all, in fact — Caius Julius Caesar (see′zer).

The Roman civil wars had continued after Sulla's time and Greece was occasionally a battlefield. Thus, Caesar went to war with Pompey (the conqueror of Mithridates) and pursued him to Greece in 48 B.C. There, he defeated him in Pharsalia (fahr-sayl′yuh) a district in Thessaly.

Pompey then tried to flee to Egypt, but he was promptly assassinated there by Egyptians who wanted no trouble with Caesar. Sure enough, Caesar came following soon after. In Egypt, he met Cleopatra and found her beautiful. He saw to it that her brothers shared the throne with her and eventually brought her back to Rome with him.

In 44 B.C. Caesar was assassinated and the civil war began

again. Quietly, Cleopatra slipped back to Egypt where she felt she would be out of harm's way. She disposed of her brothers and became sole occupant of the throne.

But a former associate of Caesar, Marcus Antonius (better known, in English, as Mark Antony) was traveling eastward in pursuit of Caesar's assassins. These he overtook in Macedonia and defeated them in 42 B.C. at Philippi, a city that the great Philip had built three centuries earlier. In 41 B.C., Mark Antony met Cleopatra and he, too, fell in love with her.

In fact, he forgot his duties in his desire to stay with her and live a life of pleasure. Not so Caesar's capable nephew and adopted son, Caius Octavianus (commonly known, in English, as Octavian) who was making himself powerful at home, gaining strength in Rome as Mark Antony lost strength in Egypt.

Eventually, there had to be a showdown between the two. In 31 B.C. the fleet of Cleopatra and Mark Antony met that of Octavian off Actium (ak'shee-um), a city on the west coast of Greece, about fifty miles north of the Gulf of Corinth. For the last time, Hellenistic power faced that of Rome, and it is rather fitting that it should have happened off the Greek coast.

At the height of the battle, Cleopatra panicked and fled with her ships. Mark Antony at once deserted his own men and pursued her. The battle was lost and Octavian was master. Back in Egypt, Mark Antony, hearing the false report that Cleopatra was dead, killed himself in 30 B.C.

Octavian, following after him, led his army into Alexandria. Cleopatra faced him and made one last attempt to win a Roman with her charm. Octavian, however, was not the type to be charmed by anybody. He made it quite clear she was to come back to Rome with him as a conquered enemy. She had only one card to play and she played it. According to the traditional story, a poisonous snake was smuggled to her and she killed herself with its bite.

Egypt was promptly annexed to Rome and thus, in 30 B.C., the last of the Hellenistic kingdoms was gone. Two and a half centuries after the first clash between Greek and Roman in the time of Pyrrhus, Rome had finally swallowed and absorbed all the Greek world. Even those Greek cities still surviving in the Crimea on the northern shore of the Black Sea accepted Roman overlordship.

As for Octavian, he renamed himself Augustus and, although he kept the forms of the Roman republic, made himself into what amounted to a king. He called himself "Imperator" which means simply "leader." This word becomes "emperor" in English and with Augustus, in 31 B.C. (the year of the Battle of Actium), the history of all the ancient world fades into that of the "Roman Empire."

17

ROME AND CONSTANTINOPLE

THE ROMAN PEACE

Yet with the Hellenistic monarchies gone, Greek culture did not disappear. It was, in fact, stronger than ever. Rome itself had absorbed Greek thought and by the time Augustus established the Roman Empire, Rome itself had become a Hellenistic realm and the greatest of all.

But Greece itself continued to decay. The Roman Empire brought two centuries of absolute peace to the Mediterranean world (the "Pax Romana," or "Roman Peace") but for Greece it was the peace of death. In its period of expansion, Rome had treated Greece with reckless cruelty. The destruction of Corinth, the deliberate ruin of Rhodes, the sack of Athens, the battles of the Roman civil war on Greek soil had made Greece a wasteland.

The Greek geographer, Strabo (stray'boh), has left a description of Greece in the time of Augustus. It is a melancholy picture of ruined towns and depopulated areas.

Yet even at this time, the beginnings of a new and great force made itself felt in Greece. In Judaea, a prophet had arisen — Jesus Chirst ("Joshua, the Messiah"). He gathered a few disciples who began to consider Jesus the manifestation of God in human form.

(The western world now numbers the years from the time of Jesus' birth. Thus, the battle of Marathon was fought in 490 B.C. — Before Christ. The years since Jesus' birth are written with the initials A.D. This stands for "Anno Domini" or "The Year of our Lord.")

Jesus was put to death by crucifixion in A.D. 29 but the disciples continued in their belief. The followers of Christ ("Christians") underwent persecution in Judaea as heretics, and one of the most active persecutors was a Jew named Saul, who had been born in the Greek-speaking city of Tarsus, on the southern shores of Asia Minor.

Several years after the death of Jesus, Saul experienced a sudden conversion and became as firm a Christian as before he had been a persecutor. He changed his name to Paul and began to preach Christianity to the non-Jews, particularly to the Greeks.

About A.D. 44, Paul traveled to Antioch, then to Cyprus and Asia Minor. Later, he visited Macedonia and Greece itself, preaching in Corinth. In A.D. 53, he preached in Athens. Finally, in A.D. 62 he sailed westward to Rome and there met his death.

During his missionary years, Paul addressed a number of letters (or "epistles") to the men he had converted among the Greeks. They appear in the Bible under the names of the inhabitants of the cities to which they are addressed. Two are to the Corinthians, the men of Corinth.

Three epistles are addressed to the cities of Thessalonica and

Philippi in Macedonia; two are "to the Thessalonians" and one "to the Philippians." Others are to cities in Asia Minor, one "to the Ephesians," one "to the Galatians" and one "to the Colossians." This last epistle was to a church in the town of Colossae (koh-los'ee), a town in inland Asia Minor, about 120 miles east of Miletus.

According to tradition, Paul died a martyr in the first Roman persecution of Christianity under the Emperor Nero (nee'roh), who ruled A.D. 54 to A.D. 68.

Nero was one of those emperors who, now that Greece was nearly dead, loved to make much of the land and to go through a pretense of living once again the old great days. He had, as his dearest wish, the desire to join in the celebration of the Eleusinian Mysteries but did not dare because he had had his mother executed!

The Emperor Hadrian (hay'dree-an), who reigned from 117 to 138 carried the Roman love for a dead Greece to its extreme. He visited Athens in 125. There he presided at festivals, was initiated in the Eleusinian Mysteries, and had its temples completed, enlarged and beautified. He also built a canal through the isthmus and allowed what was left of the Greek towns (villages, rather) certain "liberties" in imitation of the old days.

As Greece slowly decayed, Greek science withered. A few last names remain to be mentioned.

Sosigenes (soh-sij'ih-neez) was an Alexandrian astronomer who flourished in the time of Julius Caesar. He helped Caesar construct a new calendar for the Roman dominions, the so-called "Julian calendar." In this calendar, three years of every four have 365 days, while every fourth year has an added 366th day. It is this calendar (slightly improved fifteen centuries later) which survives and is in use in the world today.

In the time of Nero, a Greek physician, Dioscorides (digh"os-kor'ih-deez), traveled with the Roman armies and studied the new plants he encountered, particularly with regard to their medicinal properties.

Then there is Hero (hee'ro), a Greek engineer who worked at Alexandria near the beginning of the period of the Roman Empire. He is famous for his invention of a hollow sphere to which two bent tubes were attached. When water was boiled in the sphere, the steam escaped through the tubes and drove the sphere into a rapid rotation. This is a simple "steam engine."

Hero used the energy of steam to open doors and work statues in temples. These, however, were just devices by means of which priests might impose on gullible worshipers, or marvels with which to amuse the idle. The idea of using the energy of steam to substitute for the strained and aching muscles of human slaves did not seem to concern anyone.

The last of the Greek astronomers was Claudius Ptolemaeus, commonly known as Ptolemy in English. He was no relative of the Macedonian kings of Egypt, however. He lived about 150.

Ptolemy adopted the system of the universe which Hipparchus had worked out (see page 271) and added his own improvements. His chief importance lies in the fact that whereas Hipparchus' books all perished, those of Ptolemy survived. For fourteen centuries afterward, Ptolemy's books were the basic textbooks of astronomy, and the system of an earth-centered universe is called the "Ptolemaic system" in consequence.

Ptolemy also wrote on geography and he accepted Posidonius' figure of 18,000 miles as the circumference of the earth (see page 271) instead of Eratosthenes' correct figure of 25,000. The smaller figure persisted into early modern times and, indeed, when Columbus offered to sail westward to reach Asia, he counted on a 3000-mile voyage on the basis of Ptolemy's figures. Had he known that it was 11,000 miles to Asia he might not have made his journey.

The last of the Greek biologists was Galen (gay'len) who was born in Pergamum about 130. In 164, he settled in Rome where, for a time, he was court physician to the emperors.

Galen's best work was in anatomy. Since the dissection of human beings had fallen into disrepute, Galen worked on animals. He developed an overall theory of the workings of the human body that was the most elaborate the ancient world had to offer and that remained the basis of medical science for thirteen centuries after his death.

The last Greek mathematician of any importance was Diophantus (digh"oh-fan'tus), who worked in Alexandria about 275. He turned from the Greek specialty of geometry and made the first advances toward algebra.

Greek science was influenced by the learning of other lands also (as, indeed, it had always been). The Greeks in Egypt picked up the ancient lore of that land with regard to the study of the structure of substances, and the methods of changing one substance into another. The Greeks called this science *khemeia* (perhaps from the Egyptian name of their own country, Khem.) This science was the ancestor of our own chemistry. About 300, a Greek practitioner of khemeia, Zosimus (zoh'sih-mus) wrote a series of volumes summarizing Greek knowledge in this field.

Among the Greek historians of Roman times was Diodorus Siculus (digh"oh-doh'rus sik'yoo-lus) who lived in the time of Julius Caesar. He wrote a history in forty books of which only the first to the fourth, and the eleventh to the twentieth survive. Much of the information we have about the Diadochi comes from Diodorus.

A much better writer was Plutarch (ploo'tahrk) of Chaeronea. He was born about 46 and is best known for his biographies. Anxious to show that the Greeks had had their great men as well as the Romans, he wrote a series of "Parallel Lives" in which a Greek is compared to and contrasted with a Roman. Thus, Alexander the Great and Julius Caesar are written up in parallel, and their similarities and differences discussed. Plutarch's style is so pleasing that his book, with its gossipy stories about great historical figures, remains good reading to this day.

Another biographer was Arrian (ar'ee-an) of Nicomedia. He was born about 96 and his most important work is a biography of Alexander the Great. This was based on the firsthand work of Ptolemy Soter (which is now lost) and is the most reliable story we have of the deeds of the great Alexander.

Finally, there is Diogenes Laertius (lay-ur'shee-us), concerning whom we know nothing except that he lived about 230. He put together a collection of lives and sayings of the ancient philosophers. It is very little more than a scrapbook really and not very good, but it is important because most of it survived and it is all we have left concerning many of the greatest leaders of Greek thought.

THE TRIUMPH OF CHRISTIANITY

Greek philosophy maintained its importance during the period of the Roman Peace. Stoicism in particular (see page 184) achieved a peak of popularity.

It was most successfully taught to the Roman world by a Greek philosopher, Epictetus (ep"ik-tee'tus). He was born in Hierapolis (high"er-ap'oh-lis), a town of inland Asia Minor, about 60. He was a slave in early life, but was freed and spent his adult years at Nicopolis (nih-kop'oh-lis.). This town, its name meaning "City of Victory," had been founded by Augustus a century before near the site of the Battle of Actium (see page 273).

Like Socrates, Epictetus did not commit his teaching to writing. His disciples, however (Arrian was one), carried his views far and wide.

The Emperor Marcus Aurelius (mahr'kus oh-ree'lee-us),

who reigned from 161 to 180, believed in and acted upon the stoic doctrine and is called the "Stoic Emperor" in consequence. He was one of the most kindly and civilized men ever to be in a position of absolute power. Nevertheless, his reign marked the end of the good days of the Roman Empire.

After Marcus Aurelius, a series of cruel or incompetent emperors followed. Uncivilized tribes attacked the borders of the Empire; the Roman legions set up puppet emperors and revolts and civil wars became common. In short, the Roman Peace was over, and the Empire entered a long decline.

Partly because of this decline and the increasing hardships that resulted, the people of the ancient world found the dry beliefs of stoicism, and of Greek philosophy generally, to be unsatisfying. They needed something more emotional, something that provided a higher goal than could be attained in this world and that promised more in the way of glorious release from a hard life both before and after death.

The Mystery Religions were one answer, but from out of the non-Greek east there came a series of religions that offered even more excitement and hope than did the Greek Mysteries. These included the worship of Isis (igh'sis) picked up from Egypt, Cybele (sib'uh-lee) from Asia Minor and Mithras (mith'ras) from Persia.

The answer of Greek philosophy to the increasing importance of these oriental religions was made by Plotinus (ploh-tigh'nus) who was born in Egypt about 205. His teachings began with Platonism, the philosophy of Plato, but joined to it many mystical notions resembling those in the oriental religions. Thus "neo-Platonism" became a kind of halfway house between Greek philosophy and eastern mystery cults.

Neo-Platonism, however, had little of the force and appeal of the revolutionary new religion that was sweeping the Roman world. Men like Paul and those who came after him might die for their beliefs, but they continued to preach the gospel, and Christianity continued to gain strength until half the population of the Empire was Christian. Finally, in 313, Constantine I, who reigned from 306 to 337, adopted Christianity as the official religion of the Roman Empire.

Paganism made one last attempt at a comeback. In 361, Julian (jool'yan), a nephew of Constantine, became emperor. Although raised a Christian, he was an admirer of the ancients. His dream was to restore the days of Plato and once he became an emperor he tried to do this.

He declared religious freedom and removed Christianity from its position as official religion of the Empire. He had himself initiated into the Eleusinian Mysteries and walked through Athens in ancient costume talking to philosophers.

But, of course, this could not work. The supremacy of Greek philosophy could not be brought back to life any more than Plato himself could be brought back from the dead. Julian died in battle in 363 and Christianity was re-established as the official religion. Christianity has remained the dominant religion of the western world ever since.

With Christianity again in official power, paganism fast approached its end. Followers of the two ways of thought clashed in bitter riots here and there in the Empire. In A.D. 415, such riots brought about serious damage to the Library at Alexandria. That ended Alexandria as a center of Greek learning and Greek science, too, came to an end.

Other ancient symbols of Greek culture also petered out. The Olympian games were held for the last time in 393. Then, by an edict of the emperor, Theodosius I (thee"oh-doh'shee-us), they were brought to an end after almost twelve centuries of existence. The great statue of Zeus, which Phidias had made eight centuries before, was carried off and was destroyed in a fire in 476.

The various competing religions gradually died out; and the old temples were pulled down or converted into churches. The Parthenon, for instance, was converted into a church and the statue of Athena was removed and somehow disposed of.

The last touch came in 529, when the Emperor Justinian (jus-tin′ee-an) closed the Academy in Athens; the Academy which had been founded by Plato nine centuries before. The pagan teachers had to leave for Persia (the old, old enemy had now become a refuge) and the last scrap of pre-Christian Greek life was wiped out.

And yet Greece still remained. The books it had produced, its art and architecture, its traditions, were all still there. If the Mediterranean world was now Christian; Christianity, especially in the eastern part of the Roman Empire, was built on a Greek foundation. Greek culture had been altered by Christianity but not destroyed.

In fact, the decline of the Roman Empire liberated the eastern portion and allowed the Greek variety of Christianity to gain a special importance. It happened this way.

The Roman Empire had been going steadily downhill after the time of Marcus Aurelius and, in order to keep it working at all, the Emperor Diocletian (digh″oh-klee′shan), who reigned from 284 to 305, decided it needed more than one man in charge. In 285, he divided the Empire into two halves, a Western and an Eastern. He placed a colleague in charge of the Western Empire, while he took care of the Eastern Empire.

Theoretically, the two emperors cooperated and together ruled over a single realm. Indeed, sometimes an emperor gained control of both halves even after Diocletian's time. However, more and more it seemed the division was a natural one. The dividing line was the Adriatic Sea. The western half, including Italy, spoke Latin and was strongly Roman in its traditions. The eastern half, including Greece, spoke Greek and was strongly Greek in its traditions.

Constantine I, the first Christian emperor, ruled the whole Empire but recognized the eastern half to be the richer and more valuable. He decided to make his capital there. He rebuilt and enlarged the old city of Byzantium on the Bosporus and renamed it Constantinople ("Constantine's city") for himself. It became his capital in 330 and became the largest and most powerful Greek-speaking city of all time.

The last emperor to rule all the whole realm was the Theodosius who ended the Olympian Games. After his death in 395, the Empire was permanently divided.

Over the next century the Roman Empire suffered repeatedly from barbarian invasions and, in 476, Romulus Augustulus, the last of the Western Emperors, was forced to abdicate. No emperor reigned in Rome thereafter and this is usually referred to as the "fall of the Roman Empire."

However, the Eastern Roman Empire weathered the storm and remained in being, with a line of emperors that was to stretch in unbroken succession for nearly a thousand more years.

It had broken with the west politically, however, and more and more went its own way. Even its Christianity went its own way. In the west, Christians accepted the leadership of the Bishop of Rome, who came to be known as the Pope.

The Christians of the Eastern Roman Empire, however, looked to the Patriarch of Constantinople as their spiritual leader. There were continuing quarrels between the two branches of the church and, finally, in 1054, they came to a complete parting of the ways. From that time, the western church was the "Roman Catholic," the eastern Church was the "Greek Orthodox."

Both groups labored to convert the pagans of the north, both before and after the final split. The Greek Orthodox church won its greatest victory when it converted not only the Bulgarians and Serbs of the Balkan peninsula, but also the Russians in the great plains north of the Black Sea. The Russians have remained Orthodox ever since and this helped separate them from Catholic western Europe, a fact which has had important consequences down to the present day.

THE COMING OF ISLAM

The Eastern Roman Empire was not all Greek in tradition. Portions of it, such as Egypt and Syria, had traditions of their own stretching far back in time, and Greek culture overlay this old tradition but thinly. The Egyptians and Syrians even differed in their versions of Christianity and did not believe all the dogmas held by Constantinople and the thoroughly Greek areas of Greece and Asia Minor.

Foreign invaders therefore found it comparatively easy to occupy Syria and Egypt. The inhabitants there tended to view the invaders as not so bad after all in comparison with the government at Constantinople.

This was first demonstrated in connection with a renewal of an ancient danger from the East. The Parthian kingdom lying east of Syria had never been conquered by the Romans but it fell through civil war. In 226, a new line of monarchs rose to power. These were Persians termed Sassanids (sas'uh-nidz), because the grandfather of the first king of the line had been named Sassan.

What followed was virtually a recreation of the Persian Empire as it had been six centuries before, except that the western-most portion of that old realm was under Roman control.

For four centuries, Romans and Persians fought frequent wars without either gaining a decisive victory. Then, in 590, Chosroes II (koz'roh-eez) came to the Persian throne. His wars against the Eastern Roman Empire were astonishingly successful. In 603, he began the conquest of Asia Minor. In 614 he took Syria, in 615 Judaea, in 616 Egypt. By 617, he was just across the narrow strait of the Bosporus, within a mile of Constantinople itself.

Virtually all that was left of the Eastern Roman Empire was mainland Greece, Sicily, and a strip of African coast. It was as though Xerxes were alive again and Greece was at his mercy once more.

In 610, Heraclius (her"uh-kligh'us) had become the Roman emperor. For ten years, he made preparations and then he struck. He had made the daring decision to carry the war to the enemy. Using his fleet (the Persians had none), Heraclius carried an army to Issus in 622. For the next five years, he was a new Alexander, marching through the heart of Persia and defeating its armies. The lost provinces were regained by 630.

However, the bitter war had weakened both sides fatally. Even while it was going on, a new prophet, Mohammed (moh-ham'ed), was establishing a new religion, Islam (is'lum), in the Arabian peninsula. Mohammed died in 632 and the Arabs who, till then, had not figured prominently in history, burst out of their peninsula in a career of conquest.

They defeated the forces of the Eastern Roman Empire at Yarmuk (yahr-mook') a tributary of the Jordan River, in 636. The worn-out Empire and the dispirited Heraclius could not rise to meet this new challenge.

After spending the next decade in defeating and conquering the Sassanid Empire, the Arabs turned on Africa. In 642, they took Alexandria and if anything was left of the great Library, that was then destroyed. By 670, the rest of North Africa was taken.

The Arab conquest wiped out the layer of Greek culture that had overspread Syria and Egypt. Islam replaced Christianity in those regions and Arabic replaced the Greek language.

However, Greek culture did not die. The Arabs felt its facination as the Romans had. The Arabs adopted the Greek *khemeia* and gave it the name of "alchemy." They translated the works

of Aristotle, Euclid, Galen and Ptolemy into Arabic, studying
them and writing commentaries of their own. They preserved
Greek learning at a time when it had almost been forgotten in
barbarous western Europe.

Indeed, when learning revived in western Europe after 1000,
it was spurred onward largely by those same books of Greek
lore, which were then translated from Arabic into Latin.

What was left of the Eastern Roman Empire after the Arabic
conquest consisted chiefly of the Balkan Peninsula, Asia Minor,
and Sicily. It still called itself the "Roman Empire"; in fact, it
did so to the very end. However, it was thoroughly Greek in
tradition and in the time of Heraclius, Greek had finally become the official language in place of Latin.

Western Europeans throughout the Middle Ages called the
realm ruled by Constantinople the "Greek Empire" and there
was some justice to this. Later historians began to call the Eastern Roman Empire of the time of Heraclius and afterward the
"Byzantine Empire" (biz'un-tine) after Byzantium, the old
name of Constantinople, and that is the name by which it is
most commonly known today.

The Byzantine Empire withstood the Arab attacks upon its
center. In 673, the Arabs laid siege to Constantinople and for
five years blockaded it by land and sea. Here again, as at the
siege of Syracuse by the Romans nearly five centuries earlier, it
was Greek brain versus non-Greek brawn.

The new Archimedes, according to tradition, was an alche-
mist named Callinicus (kal″ih-nigh′kus), a refugee from Syria
or Egypt. He invented an inflammable mixture which, once set
on fire, would remain burning fiercely even if doused in water.
The exact composition is not known but it probably contained
an inflammable liquid such as naphtha, potassium nitrate to
supply oxygen, and quicklime which, growing hot on contact
with water, keeps the mixture burning despite the presence of
water.

This time brain defeated brawn. Greek Fire burned the Arab

ships and in the end, the Arabs were forced to raise the siege. The Byzantine armies regained Asia Minor, but Syria, Egypt and north Africa were lost forever.

Warfare between Greeks and Arabs continued for four more centuries, but it was a border affair with no striking victories on either side. The only important losses by the Greek world were certain islands. Sicily was taken, for instance, by Islamic forces from Africa in 827. Greek culture finally came to an end in that island and in southern Italy, after it had been dominant for fifteen centuries (even under the Romans.) Eventually, Sicily was restored to Christianity, but that was by forces from western Europe, and the island has been western in culture ever since.

A new danger arose from the north. Beginning shortly after 700, tribes speaking Slavic languages began invasions of the Balkan peninsula and established themselves in Thrace and Macedonia. There was constant fighting between them and the Byzantine Empire. They were finally and disastrously defeated in 1014 by the Byzantine emperor, Basil II. Slavic peoples remained in the regions north of Greece (to this day, in fact) but they accepted the Greek version of Christianity and remained eastern in culture.

Under Basil II, the Byzantine Empire reached the peak of its power but, alas, that was not to last long.

THE CRUSADES

About 1000, a new group of nomads poured southward out of central Asia. They were the Turks. The particular tribe of Turks which first achieved prominence considered themselves to be descended from an ancestor named Seljuk (sel'jook) so that they are known as the Seljuk Turks. They spread havoc over the Islamic lands, but adopted Islam as a religion.

With the fury of the convert, they next turned on the Byzantine Empire. The Byzantine emperor at the time was Romanus IV (roh-may'nus). He defeated the Seljuk Turks several times, but in 1071 he faced them in battle at the eastern borders of his realm and was disastrously defeated. The Turks poured westward and occupied the interior of Asia Minor, confining Greek domination to the coast.

This was the beginning of the process that wiped out Greek culture in Asia Minor permanently, leaving it Turkish to this day. After 1071, in fact, the Greek world was reduced to what it had been at the very beginning of the era of colonization, eighteen centuries before. (The Turks, by the way, called their dominions in Asia Minor, "Rum" (room). This was their way of saying "Rome," for they considered themselves to have conquered the Roman Empire.)

The Byzantine Empire was now in serious trouble and it had to seek for help among the nations of the west. This they did with great reluctance for the Byzantines considered the westerners barbaric and heretical.

The westerners had an equally bad opinion of the Byzantines and were not in the least concerned to save them. However, they were annoyed with the Seljuk Turks, for the Turks had taken over Syria from the tolerant Arabs and were now mistreating western Christians who were undertaking pilgrimages to Jerusalem. The westerners were therefore in a mood to respond to the Byzantine appeal.

The result was a two-hundred-year period, beginning in 1096, during which western armies periodically marched or sailed eastward to fight the Turks. These movements are called the Crusades, from a Latin word for "cross," since the westerners were fighting for the cross; that is, for Christianity.

More and more the Byzantine Empire (or what was left of

it) fell under the influence of western soldiers and, even more, of western traders, particularly the Italian traders of Venice and Genoa.

After 1000, a number of areas of Greece were renamed by these Italian traders, and the Italian names became familiar to the west. Some still linger today. The Peloponnesus, for instance, became Morea (moh-ree′uh) from a Latin word for mulberry leaf, because that was what the irregular outlines of the peninsula seemed to resemble.

Naupactus, the city on the northern shore of the Gulf of Corinth where Athens had once settled Spartan helots (see page 126), came to be called Lepanto (lee-pan′toh). The Gulf of Corinth consequently became the Gulf of Lepanto. Again, a city on Crete, with the Greek name of Herakleion, was renamed Candia (kan′dee-uh) by Venetian traders and the name was applied to the entire island of Crete. Corcyra became Corfu (kawr-foo′) and so on.

But the Crusaders, while helping the Byzantines defeat the Turks, visited upon the Greek people a great disaster.

This came about because one band of crusaders (making up what is now known as the "Fourth Crusade") were persuaded by the Venetians (whose ships they were using) to attack Constantinople instead of proceeding toward Syria. Without Venetian ships, the crusaders could go nowhere and after some thought, they began to think of the loot that might fall to them and they agreed.

The Byzantine emperor at this time was a weakling named Alexius IV who thought he could use the crusaders in his private battles. He merely paved the way for destruction and what with force, guile, and treachery, the crusaders captured the great capital in 1204.

The chief tragedy was this —

Nowadays, printing has made it possible for many thousands of every book to exist. In the days before printing, however, even the greatest book could only exist in a few hundreds of copies, for each copy had to be painstakingly copied by hand.

Gradually in the disorders that followed the decline of the Roman Empire, the few copies of the books in which Greek learning and literature was enshrined were lost. Christian mobs destroyed a number. The barbarians who took over the Western Empire destroyed what was left there. The Islamic armies wiped out the libraries in places like Antioch, Alexandria and Carthage, though they saved some of the more important scientific books.

In short, by 1204, the only place where the entire body of Greek learning existed, still intact, was Constantinople. As a result of the crusaders' conquest, however, Constantinople was ruthlessly pillaged and destroyed and almost all the great treasures of ancient Greek learning were lost forever. It is because of that sack, for instance, that we have only seven plays left out of the better than one hundred written by Sophocles.

The tragedy of 1204 can never be undone and for all of time, only bits and pieces of the marvelous Greek world can be known to us.

18

THE OTTOMAN EMPIRE

THE FALL OF CONSTANTINOPLE

For two generations, Greece was dominated by westerners who established the so-called "Latin Empire." In western feudal style, they parceled out pieces to the various important chieftains. Northeastern Greece became the Kingdom of Thessalonica (with Cassander's city, established fifteen centuries before, see page 232, as the capital.) The Peloponnesus became the Principality of Achaea, while Attica, Boeotia and Phocis made up the Duchy of Athens.

The Greeks, however, were not entirely under western control. A member of the old royal family was in control of northwestern Greece and called his dominion the Despotate of Epirus (thus bringing back a breath of Pyrrhus, see page 239).

A relative, by marriage, of the royal family set up a realm in western Asia Minor, on land reconquered from the Turks during the period of the Crusades. Its capital was at Nicaea and it was called the Empire of Nicaea. Its territory was like ancient Bithynia restored to life.

Finally, along the southeast coast of the Black Sea was a thin rim of Greek land which included the cities of Sinope and Trapezus plus a few Greek towns that still survived on the Crimean peninsula, north of the Black Sea. The city of Trapezus had by then become known as Trebizond (treb'ih-zond) so the realm was the Empire of Trebizond.

The Latin Empire never had much vigor and it was in growing danger from the rather capable rulers of Epirus. In 1222, the Despot of Epirus conquered the Kingdom of Thessalonica, for instance.

However, Constantinople fell to Nicaea, and not to Epirus. Michael Paleologus (pay''lee-ol'oh-gus) became Emperor of Nicaea in 1259. He allied himself with the Bulgarians and the Genoans and waited for a moment when the Venetian fleet (which guarded Latin Constantinople) was absent. Then, in a surprise stroke, he captured Constantinople in 1261.

He became Michael VIII and the Byzantine Empire was ruled by Greeks again. For the remaining two centuries of its history, all Byzantine Emperors were descendants of Michael.

However, the Byzantine Empire was a crippled shadow of anything it had been before. Epirus and Trebizond remained under independent rule, while Venice retained Crete, the Aegean islands, the Duchy of Athens and much of the Peloponnesus.

Athens, indeed, never became Byzantine again. Shortly after 1300, a band of cut-throat adventurers arrived in Greece from the west. Many of them were from a region in eastern Spain called Catalonia, so that the band is known as the Catalan Grand Company. In 1311, they managed to seize control of the Duchy of Athens, which then remained in the grip of one western faction or another until the final defeat of the Christians at the hands of the Turks.

By 1290, a new group of Turks had come into prominence. Their first important leader was Osman (os-mahn') or, in Arabic, Othman (ooth-mahn'). His followers were therefore called the Osmanli Turks or the Ottoman Turks.

By 1338, the Ottoman Turks had taken almost all of Asia Minor, wiping out the territory that had once been the Empire of Nicaea. In 1345, the Ottoman Turks were called into Europe by the Byzantine emperor, John VI, who wanted their help against a rival. This proved to be colossal mistake. By 1354, the Turks had been permanently established in Europe (and they control a small portion of the continent to the present day).

Quickly, the Turks began spreading through the Balkan peninsula. At the time, the dominant people of the peninsula were the Slav-speaking Serbs. They had built a strong state, north of Greece, under Stephen Dushan (doo'shahn) who began his reign in 1331. He had conquered Epirus, Macedonia and Thessaly and was even preparing to attack Constantinople.

Perhaps he might have been able to stop the Turks, but in 1355 he died and his realm began crumbling. It was in 1389 that Serbs and Turks confronted each other at last at Kossovo (koh'soh-voh) in what is now southern Yugoslavia. The Turks won an overwhelming victory and the entire Balkan Peninsula lay at their feet.

All that was left of the Byzantine realm would have fallen to the Turks but for the unexpected appearance of a mighty enemy in the east.

A nomad leader named Timur (tih-moor') had come to power in 1360 and had begun a career of conquest. He was called "Timur Lenk" ("Timur the Lame") and in English, this became Tamerlane (tam'er-layn).

In lightning strokes, he conquered all of central Asia and

made his capital at Samarkand (sam'er-kand), the ancient Maracanda, where Alexander had killed Clitus seventeen centuries before. Tamerlane extended his dominions in every direction, penetrating Russia as far as Moscow, invading India and capturing Delhi.

Finally, in 1402, when already seventy years old, he invaded Asia Minor. The Turkish sultan, Bajazet (baj"uh-zet'), met Tamerlane near Angora (ang-gawr'uh) in central Asia Minor. (Under its earlier name, Ancyra [an-sigh'ruh], this city had been the capital of Galatia once.)

At the battle, Bajazet was completely defeated and taken prisoner. The victorious Tamerlane ravaged Asia Minor, and brought Sardis — once the capital of Lydia 2000 years before — to its final destruction. However, when Tamerlane died, in 1405, his broad realm collapsed at once.

The attack by Tamerlane had so disrupted the Ottoman Empire, that Constantinople was given an additional half-century of life. But during that half-century, the Ottoman Turks recovered their strength in full.

In 1451, Mohammed II became sultan of the Ottoman Empire and he made ready to settle matters with Constantinople once and for all. On May 29, 1453, after a five-month siege, Constantinople was taken by the Turks and Constantine XI, the last of the Roman emperors in a series that had begun with Augustus fifteen centuries earlier, died in action, fighting valiantly.

Constantinople became permanently Turkish and its name changed again. The Greeks, in traveling to Constantinople would say they were going "eis ten polin" meaning "to the city." The Turks seized on this phrase, made it into Istanbul (is"tan-bool') and made it the capital of the Ottoman Empire.

In 1456, Mohammed took the Duchy of Athens from its western rulers and in 1460, the Peloponnesus. In 1461, he took the Empire of Trebizond, too. The city where Xenophon's army had reached the sea, nearly nineteen centuries before, had become the last scrap of independent Greek dominion.

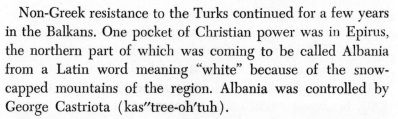

THE TURKISH NIGHT

Non-Greek resistance to the Turks continued for a few years in the Balkans. One pocket of Christian power was in Epirus, the northern part of which was coming to be called Albania from a Latin word meaning "white" because of the snow-capped mountains of the region. Albania was controlled by George Castriota (kas"tree-oh'tuh).

Castriota was in the very homeland of the maternal ancestors of Alexander the Great and he called himself by the Turkish name of "Iskander Bey" ("Lord Alexander"). This became corrupted to Scanderbeg (skan'der-beg). While he lived, he held the Turks at bay, but after he died in 1467, Albania was conquered and attached to the Ottoman Empire.

That left only the Greek islands in Christian hands, but these were western Christians. By 1566 the struggle centered around the Venetian-controlled islands of Crete and Cyprus, with the Greek population there (and elsewhere in Greece) generally favoring the Turks over the westerners. This is not surprising. The Turks tolerated the Orthodox form of Christianity, whereas the western Catholics labored to convert their Orthodox subjects to Catholicism. The westerners also imposed harsher taxes than the Turks did.

The Greeks of Cyprus were generally delighted, therefore, when the Venetians were forced out of Cyprus in 1571 and the Turks took over.

This Turkish victory was counterbalanced by a defeat that same year. A great battle took place between an Ottoman fleet and a Christian fleet (chiefly Spanish) in the Gulf of Lepanto (or Corinth, to use its Greek name). It was the last important battle to be fought between oar-propelled ships, and it was an important Christian victory. The Ottoman Turks recovered from the Battle of Lepanto and remained strong for a considerable period of time to come, but the battle clearly showed that the Turks had passed their peak and that the future lay with the rising strength of western Europe.

A century after Lepanto, the Turks made one last attempt at conquest. At sea, they took Crete from the Venetians in 1669. On land they advanced to the northwest and in 1683 stood on the outskirts of Vienna, so that Austria seemed on the point of falling.

Both Venetians and Austrians counterattacked successfully. The Venetians invaded the Peloponnesus and a Venetian fleet stood off Athens. This was the occasion for a great tragedy. The Turks defending Athens stored gunpowder in, of all places, the Parthenon, which, till then, after standing for 2000 years, was still intact. In 1687, a Venetian cannonball struck the building, exploded the gunpowder and destroyed the most magnificent building of all time. Only the roofless pillars remain to us as a sad memorial to the vanished glory of Greece.

When the Turks were forced to sign a peace in 1699 (the first peace they ever consented to make with Christian power) the Venetians were ceded the Peloponnesus. This was only temporary, for the Peloponnesian Greeks soon learned that the hand of the Venetian was heavier than that of the Turk. They welcomed the reconquest of the area by the Turks in 1718.

Greece, under Turkey, slowly recovered in numbers and strength. Under Turkish tolerance and inefficiency they retained their language and religion. Some could even grow wealthy and powerful. This was particularly true of the descendants of the old Byzantine nobility who lived in a district of Istanbul called Phanar.

After 1699 when the Turks found that they would have to

engage in diplomatic relationships with the western nations and could no longer rely on superior military strength, they turned to these Phanariot Greeks. From then on, the Phanariots practically ran the Turkish foreign service and on many occasions were the actual power behind the throne.

However, all through the 1700's, the Ottoman Empire declined and became prey to increasing inefficiency and corruption. Increasingly, the Greeks began to dream of freedom from the Turks — not at the price of coming under the domination of the west, but of a true freedom. They wanted an independent land of Greece, ruled by Greeks.

This dream became stronger as Russia, throughout the period, had engaged in a series of wars with Turkey and had conquered all the Turkish regions north of the Black Sea. This pointed up Turkish weakness and also provided the Greeks with a new possibility of foreign aid. Since the Russians were Orthodox in religion, the Greeks found them far more acceptable than ever the Venetians had been.

With Russian encouragement, Greek bands rose in revolution against the Turks in 1821. Thanks to Russian help, they seized control of the Peloponnesus, then of the regions north of the Gulf of Corinth. Many westerners were moved by the Greek victories, for to them the Greeks were still the people of Themistocles and Leonidas. The great English poet, George Gordon, Lord Byron, for instance, was an extravagant admirer of the ancient Greeks and he went to Greece to join its revolutionary forces. He met his end there, for in 1824, at the age of 36, he died of malaria at Missolonghi (mis″oh-long′gee), a town in Aetolia.

But the Turks rallied and, in particular, called for the help of their fellow-religionists in Egypt, which was then under the strong rule of Mehemet Ali (meh-met′ ah-lee′). The Turks and Egyptians retook Athens on June 5, 1827 and began to ravage the Peloponnesus. The revolution seemed about over.

By that time, though, western sympathy for the Greeks was simply overpowering. Great Britain and France allied themselves with Russia and all three ordered Turkey to cease hostilities. Turkey refused. The combined British-French-Russian fleet engaged the Turkish-Egyptian fleet at Navarino (nah-vah-ree'noh) on October 20, 1827, therefore, and simply wiped it out. (Navarino is the Italian name of Pylos, where the great battle over Sphacteria had been fought twenty-two centuries before, see page 147.)

The war was not ended immediately, but Turkey found itself facing the inevitable. In 1829, she reluctantly accepted a peace which allowed Greek self-rule. At first this was supposed to be under a vague Turkish overlordship, but by 1832 Greece's outright independence was recognized.

At the time, Greece consisted only of the region south of Thermopylae, plus the island of Euboea. Athens, of course, became the capital of Greece; the free capital of a free Greek realm for the first time since the days of Demosthenes over twenty-one centuries before.

MODERN GREECE

The new kingdom had a population of about 800,000, which constituted only one-fifth of the Greek-speaking people of that corner of the world. There were 200,000 Greeks in the British-owned Ionian islands and fully 3,000,000 still living in territory controlled by the Turks. For nearly a century, the great drive behind Greek policies was the effort to bring these other Greeks, and the land they occupied, into the kingdom.

Greek efforts in this direction were supported by Russia, which wanted the Ottoman Empire weakened for its own purposes (Russia dreamed of occupying Istanbul). Greece was opposed by Great Britain, which wanted a strong Ottoman Empire that would act as a brake on Russian ambitions in Asia.

In 1854, Great Britain and France joined in the Crimean War against Russia. Since Greek sympathies were on the side of Russia, a British fleet occupied the Piraeus to prevent the Greeks from seizing the opportunity to attack Turkish territory. Later in 1862, Great Britain made up for this by ceding to Greece the Ionian Islands, which she had held since Napoleonic times.

But Greece's next chance came in 1875 when Russia went to war with the Turks again. After a stiff three-year struggle, the Russians won (though they did not occupy Istanbul as they had hoped they would). At the last minute, however, the British stepped in to prevent the Russians from destroying the Ottoman Empire altogether. Great Britain rewarded itself for its kindness to the Turks by taking control of Cyprus away from them.

All Greece could do (after the great hopes that had been aroused by the Turkish defeat) was to gain Thessaly and part of Epirus in 1881.

Meanwhile, the Greek-speaking island of Crete was rising in a series of rebellions against the Turkish masters. In 1897, the Greek government tried to come to the assistance of the Cretan rebels and were badly defeated by the Turks. Nevertheless, western intervention forced the Ottoman Empire to grant self-rule to Crete and in 1908, Crete became part of the kingdom of Greece.

There was an unexpected bonus in this for out of Crete came Eleutherios Venizelos (veh″nih-zay′los) who was to be the most capable statesman modern Greece had yet seen. In 1909, he rose to power in Athens and promptly began to concern himself with the Balkan Peninsula.

During the 1800's, Turkish defeats had led to the gradual formation of a series of kingdoms in the northern Balkans.

These were Montenegro, Serbia, Bulgaria and Rumania. They were separated from Greece by a band of territory that was still Turkish and that included Albania, Macedonia and Thrace. All the Balkan kingdoms had designs on this Turkish territory and they hated each other, as a result, even more than they detested the Turks.

Venizelos, with Russian encouragement, managed to get the Balkan powers to pull together. They formed an alliance and, in 1912, attacked the Ottoman Empire. The Turks met a speedy defeat and as soon as that was taken care of, the Balkan kingdoms were free to hate each other again. In a second war, Bulgaria found itself ranged against the other Balkan powers and, in 1913, was defeated.

As a result of these two Balkan Wars, the Ottoman Empire was virtually ejected from Europe, six centuries after she had entered. The European dominions of the Ottoman Empire shrank to a small area about the size of New Hampshire, centered about the cities of Istanbul and Edirne (eh-dihr'neh). (Edirne is the Turkish name of Adrianople [ay"dree-an-oh'pul], a town named for the Roman emperor, Hadrian, who had founded it eighteen centuries before.) That area is still Turkish today.

As for Greece it gained the Chalcidice, along with parts of Epirus and Macedonia, as well as most of the Aegean Islands. Her area and population nearly doubled. The other Balkan nations also gained territory and an independent Albania came into being.

The great catastrophe of World War I struck Europe in August, 1914. In this war, Great Britain, France and Russia (the "Allies") were lined up on one side; Germany and Austria-Hungary (the "Central Powers") on the other. The Ottoman Empire joined the Central Powers in November, 1914, and Bulgaria, Greece's northern neighbor, joined them in October, 1915.

Greece was sympathetic to Russia as always and Bulgaria

was a traditional enemy, so that there was every impulse for Greece to join the Allies, particularly since Venizelos was strongly in favor of the Allied cause. In fact she finally did so in 1917, against the desires of her pro-German king, Constantine I, who was compelled to abdicate.

As it happened, this was a great stroke of fortune for Greece, for the Allies won the war in 1918, and Greece found itself on the winning side. She gained the north shore of the Aegean Sea ("west Thrace") from Bulgaria as a result. (North of Greece, Serbia and Montenegro were joined and, with added territory, became Yugoslavia).

Nor was Thrace all. On Turkey's Aegean shore was the city of Izmir (iz-mir'). This was the Turkish name for Smyrna, the city that had been destroyed by Alyattes of Lydia twenty-five centuries before (see page 302) but that had been re-founded by Antigonus Monophthalmos.

About half the city's population was Greek, and the Greeks therefore claimed it as the spoils of war. The Allies were swayed by Greek arguments and in the peace treaty that followed World War I, Izmir and the region about it had been awarded to Greece. In consequence, a Greek army landed in Asia Minor in 1919 to take control.

But in 1920, the Greeks had foolishly turned out the capable Venizelos and called back their incompetent king, Constantine. Constantine dreamed of great conquests and saw himself as a new Alexander or, at the very least, as another Agesilaus. Why should not the Greeks take over the eastern shores of the Aegean Sea and make it a Greek lake once more as it had once been for over 2000 years from 900 B.C. to A.D. 1300.

In 1921, therefore, Constantine ordered the Greek army to drive toward the east and crush the Turks. However, Turkey was reorganizing itself. After over two centuries of almost continual losses in war under an increasingly inefficient monarchy, things began to change. An energetic general, Mustafa Kemal (moos-tah-fah' keh-mahl') reorganized the army.

At Angora (where five hundred years before, Tamerlane had crushed the Turks) Kemal's army met the Greeks in August, 1921, and stopped them cold. In 1922, the Turks moved to the counter-offensive. The Greek armies, deep in hostile territory, broke and retreated in wild haste. On September 9, 1922, the Turks took Izmir which, in the process, was largely burned.

Both nations then set about settling matters. In Greece, Constantine was forced to abdicate, and Venizelos was called back. In Turkey, the Sultan was forced to abdicate and the Ottoman Empire came to an end after six centuries of power. In its place was the Republic of Turkey under Mustafa Kemal.

Greece and Turkey then came to a final agreement by which the entire east coast of the Aegean Sea remained Turkish. In addition, arrangements were made for a compulsory exchange of population so that Greeks living in Turkey would be returned to Greece and Turks living in Greece would be returned to Turkey.

This meant that, for the first time in nearly 3000 years, there would be no Greek-speaking people on the eastern Aegean shores, but it also meant a possible peace between Greek and Turk after 1000 years of warfare. It was done.

AFTER WORLD WAR I

Even after World War I, there remained Greek-speaking islands that were not Greek. Great Britain was still in possession of Cyprus, which she had gained in 1878. In addition, Italy had fought a victorious war with Turkey in 1911 and, as part of the spoil, had gained the island of Rhodes and a number of smaller islands in the neighborhood. There were about a dozen islands altogether and these were therefore called the Dodecanese (doh-dek'uh-nees), meaning "twelve islands."

The Dodecanese voted for union with Greece after World

War I, but in 1922, Italy had come under the control of the
Fascist leader, Benito Mussolini, who was dedicated to a policy of gaining territory, not losing it. Mussolini became the
chief enemy of Greece, in fact. In 1936, Greece too joined the
increasing number of European nations that were abandoning
democracy in favor of dictatorship. The Greek dictator was
John Metaxas (mih-tak'sas).

The menace of Mussolini came closer in those years, especially after he had allied himself with Adolf Hitler, the far more
powerful and dangerous dictator of a Germany that had completely recovered from her defeat in World War I.

In April, 1939, Mussolini invaded and occupied Albania without a fight and was poised on Greece's northwestern frontier.
Half a year later, in September, World War II began.

The Germans won stunning victories in Europe during the
first year of war, crushing France completely, and in June,
1940, Italy felt it was safe to join the German side. Mussolini
was anxious to achieve some great warlike feat to match those
of Hitler. In October, 1940, therefore, with no provocation
whatever, he ordered his armies to invade Greece.

To his surprise and to the surprise of the whole world (except perhaps the Greeks themselves) it was as though the ancient days had returned. The outnumbered Greeks dug stubbornly into the mountains of Epirus and stopped the Italians
cold. Mounting a counter-offensive, they drove the Italians
back into Albania. Metaxas died in January, 1941, with the
Greeks slowly tiring, but still maintaining their advantage.

However, this battle, somehow reminiscent of the Greeks
versus Persia, did not have the same ending. An enemy far
stronger than the Italian dictator was in the field. In March,
1941, the German army occupied Bulgaria; in April it destroyed the Yugoslavian armies and drove southward toward
Greece.

The British (who were the only nation left in the field at that
moment against the all-conquering Germans) tried to send

help, but it was not enough. Both Greeks and British fell back and on April 27, 1941, the German flag flew over the Acropolis.

Nevertheless, the war was not over. In July, 1941, Germany made the supreme error of invading Russia. (Russia had had a revolution during World War I, had adopted a Communist form of government, and now called itself the Soviet Union.) Hitler expected another easy victory but did not get it. Then, in December, 1941, the Japanese attacked Pearl Harbor and the United States was in the war, against Germany as well as against Japan.

With the Soviet Union and the United States both among her enemies, Germany could no longer hope to win. On every front, the German forces were slowly beaten back.

On July 26, 1943, Mussolini was forced to resign and within six weeks, Italy was out of the war. On October 13, 1944, Allied forces entered Greece and the Greek flag flew once more over the Acropolis. In 1945 came the end for the dictators. Mussolini was captured by Italian guerrilla fighters and was executed on April 28, 1945. Hitler committed suicide in the ruins of Berlin on May 1. By May 8, the war in Europe was over.

As an aftermath of the war, Rhodes and the Dodecanese were ceded by Italy to Greece.

The end of the war did not, however, bring peace to Greece. As the Nazi tyranny was lifted from Europe through the exertions of the Soviet army on the east and the Anglo-American army on the west and south, a new question arose. Were the liberated nations to form governments patterned on the British-American style or on the Soviet style?

The Soviet army had occupied the Balkan peninsula north of Greece, and Albania, Yugoslavia and Bulgaria, Greece's three northern neighbors all had Soviet-style governments. What of Greece?

For four years after the end of Hitler, this question had no certain answer, for civil war raged in Greece. Greek guerrilla forces, sympathetic to the Soviet Union, were strong in the north, where they received help from Greece's northern neighbors. The government at Athens, meanwhile, was pro-British and received help from Great Britain.

Great Britain, however, intent on her own recovery from her great exertions during World War II, felt she could not support the Greek government indefinitely. The United States, richer and stronger, must take over. On March 12, 1947, President Harry Truman of the United States agreed to do so and by this "Truman Doctrine" the Greek guerrillas were placed at a disadvantage.

In addition, Yugoslavia quarreled with the Soviet Union in 1948 and refused to help the Greek guerrillas further. Finally, in 1949, the guerrillas gave up the struggle and Greece was at peace, with a government that ranged itself on the western side.

The government at Athens entered the 1950's, then, in control of all Greek-speaking areas, with one exception. That was Cyprus which was still, after seventy years, under British control.

Cyprus, however, was a special problem. It was not entirely Greek, as Crete and Corfu were, for instance. Of the 600,000 people living on Cyprus, about 100,000 were Turkish in speech and in sympathy. Furthermore Cyprus is relatively far from Greece for it is 300 miles east of Rhodes, the easternmost possession of Greece. On the other hand, it is only fifty miles off the southern coast of Turkey.

After World War II, there was a strong movement in Cyprus for union with Greece (or *enosis*) but this was strongly opposed by the Turkish minority and by Turkey itself. The Turks suggested, instead, that Cyprus be partitioned, with a Greek portion to join Greece and a Turkish portion to join Turkey. The Greek Cypriots, however, would not hear of partition for a moment.

Riots and disorders of all sorts racked the island from 1955 on, with the British unable for a while to find any solution that would please everyone. Finally, the decision was reached to make Cyprus independent, a nation to itself, with a Greek president and a Turkish vice-president. The Greek Cypriots would run the government but the Turkish Cypriots would have a form of veto so that they could not be oppressed.

On August 16, 1960, then, Cyprus became an independent republic. Archbishop Makarios, the leading Orthodox churchman on the island was president, and Fazil Kutchuk was vice-president. Cyprus was accepted into the United Nations and all seemed well.

* * * * *

It would be pleasant if, on that note of peace and understanding, this history of Greece could be brought to a close — but it cannot.

In 1963, President Makarios tried to alter the Cyprus constitution in order to decrease the power of the Turkish minority, which, he said, was hampering the government's functioning by its veto power.

In December, Turkish Cypriots erupted in riots. Through early 1964, the riots worsened and the British were forced to send in troops. These were replaced after a few months by United Nations troops and now an uneasy truce rests on the island.

History is a story without an end. Almost at its opening Greek history dealt with the battle between Europe and Asia, between the men on one side of the Aegean Sea and the men on the other. It was Greece and Troy; then Greece and Persia; then Greece and the Ottoman Empire and — it continues.

TABLE OF DATES

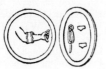

B.C.

3000 (or earlier) Crete enters Bronze Age

2000 (or earlier) Greeks enter Greece

1700 Knossos leveled by earthquake

1400 Mycenaeans destroy Knossos. End of Minoan Age

1184 Trojan War

1150 Thessalians occupy Thessaly

1120 Boeotians occupy Boeotia

1100 Dorians invade Peloponnesus. End of Mycenaean Age

1068 Death of Codrus, legendary last king of Athens

1000 Greeks begin to colonize coast of Asia Minor

850 Legendary establishment of Spartan constitution by Lycurgus; Homer writes *Iliad*.

814 Carthage founded by Phoenicians

776 First Olympian Games; opening of Hellenic period

753 Legendary date of founding of Rome

750 Argos under King Pheidon; Hesiod writes *Works and Days*.

738 Phrygia under King Midas

735 Corcyra settled by Corinthians

734 Syracuse founded by Corinthians

730 First Messenian War begins

721 Sybaris founded

710 Croton founded

700 Attica unified; Cimmerians invade Asia Minor

687 Gyges established kingdom of Lydia

685 Second Messenian War begins

683 Archon becomes annual office at Athens

671 Assyria conquers Egypt

660 Byzantium founded and Black Sea colonization begins; Neapolis and Massalia founded. Saitic Egypt breaks free of Assyria.

640 Theagenes, tyrant of Megara

635 Naucratis founded

632 Cylon attempts to found tyranny in Athens; Curse of the Alcmaeonidae

625 Periander, tyrant of Corinth

621 Draco of Athens draws up law code

617 Alyattes becomes king of Lydia; ends Cimmerian menace

612 Destruction of Nineveh and fall of Assyria

610 Thrasybulus, tyrant of Miletus

605 Nebuchadrezzar becomes king of Chaldea

600 Thales establishes Greek philosophy; Cleisthenes, tyrant of Sicyon; Alyattes occupies Greek cities of Asia Minor; Birth of Cyrus

594 Solon, archon of Athens

590 First Sacred War

589 Pittacus, tyrant of Lesbos

586 Nebuchadrezzar destroys Jerusalem; Death of Periander

585 Battle between Media and Lydia stopped by solar eclipse

582 Pythian games founded; Birth of Pythagoras

570 Athens conquers Salamis

562 Death of Nebuchadrezzar

561 Pisistratus becomes tyrant of Athens; Sparta under Chilon establishes supremacy over Arcadia

560 Death of Solon; Croesus becomes king of Lydia

550 Cyrus conquers Media, establishes Persian Empire

546 Cyrus conquers Lydia

544 Abdera founded

540 Greek fleet defeated off Sardinia by Carthaginians and Etruscans; end of period of Greek colonization

538 Cyrus conquers Chaldea

535 Polycrates, tyrant of Samos

530 Death of Cyrus; Birth of Aristides

529 Pythagoras migrates to Italy

527 Death of Pisistratus; Birth of Themistocles

525 Cambyses conquers Egypt; Birth of Aeschylus

522 Death of Polycrates; Death of Cambyses

521 Darius I becomes king of Persia
520 Cleomenes I becomes king of Sparta
514 Hipparchus, tyrant of Athens, assassinated
512 Darius conquers Thrace
510 Hippias, tyrant of Athens, expelled; Croton defeats Sybaris
507 Cleisthenes establishes Athenian democracy
500 Birth of Phidias; Birth of Anaxagoras
499 Ionian Greeks revolt against Persia
498 Athenians and Ionians burn Sardis
495 Birth of Sophocles
494 Persians sack Miletus and Ionian revolt ends; Cleomenes I defeats Argos
492 Mardonius of Persia reconquers Thrace
490 Athenians defeat Persians at Marathon; Birth of Pericles
489 Death of Miltiades; Death of Cleomenes I
486 Death of Darius I
485 Gelon becomes tyrant of Syracuse
484 Egypt rebels against Persia; Birth of Herodotus; Birth of Euripides
483 Silver mines discovered in Attica
482 Aristides ostracized
481 Congress of Greek cities at Corinth
480 Spartans die at Thermopylae; Greek fleet defeats Persians at Salamis; Syracusans defeat Carthaginians at Himera
479 Greeks defeat Persians at Plataea and Mycale
478 Confederation of Delos founded; Death of Gelon
477 Cimon at head of Athenian fleet
474 Syracusans defeat Etruscans at Cyme
472 Themistocles ostracized
471 Death of Pausanias; Birth of Thucydides
470 Birth of Democritus
469 Birth of Socrates

468 Cimon defeats Persians at Eurymedon; Death of Aristides
464 Earthquake levels Sparta; Third Messenian War; Death of Xerxes
461 Cimon ostracized
460 Pericles comes to power in Athens
458 Long Walls of Athens completed
457 Sparta defeats Athens at Tanagra
456 Death of Aeschylus
454 Athenian forces in Egypt destroyed
450 Death of Cimon; Birth of Alcibiades
449 Second Sacred War
448 Birth of Aristophanes
447 Parthenon begun; Thebans defeat Athenians at Coronea
443 Athens founds Thurii
436 Athens founds Amphipolis; Birth of Isocrates
434 Birth of Xenophon
431 Beginning of Peloponnesian War
430 Plague strikes Athens; Birth of Dionysius; Herodotus writing his history
429 Death of Pericles
428 Death of Anaxagoras
427 Birth of Plato
425 Athenians take Spartans at Sphacteria
424 Spartans take Amphipolis; Death of Herodotus
422 Death of Brasidas and Cleon
421 Peace of Nicias
415 Athens launches expedition against Syracuse
413 Athenian forces wiped out at Syracuse. Death of Nicias
412 Birth of Diogenes
407 Lysander leads Spartan fleet
405 Spartans defeat Athenians at Aegospotami; Death of Sophocles
404 Peloponnesian War ends; Long Walls pulled down; Thirty Tyrants rule Athens; Death of Alcibiades
403 Athenian democracy restored
401 Battle of Cunaxa; Retreat of the Ten Thousand

399	Socrates executed; Agesilaus II becomes king of Sparta
398	Birth of Antipater
396	Agesilaus invades Asia Minor
394	Spartan fleet defeated at Cnidus; Athens regains sea power
393	Long Walls rebuilt
390	Iphicrates destroys Spartan column
387	Plato founds Academy; Peace of Antalcidas
384	Birth of Aristotle; Birth of Demosthenes
383	Syracuse controls 5/6 of Sicily
382	Birth of Philip of Macedon
378	Pelopidas of Thebes seizes Cadmea from Spartans
377	Mausolus comes to power in Caria
371	Epaminondas of Thebes defeats Spartans at Leuctra
370	Jason of Pherae assassinated; Megalopolis founded
369	Messene founded
367	Death of Dionysius; Philip of Macedon taken as hostage to Thebes
364	Death of Pelopidas
362	Thebes defeats Sparta at Mantinea; Death of Epaminondas
361	Birth of Agathocles
360	Death of Agesilaus II
359	Philip II in control of Macedon; marries Olympias
358	Philip II takes Amphipolis
356	Birth of Alexander the Great; Temple of Artemis at Ephesus burnt
355	Death of Xenophon; Third Sacred War
353	Philip II conquers Thessaly; Death of Mausolus
352	Philip II conquers Thrace
351	Demosthenes' First Philippic
348	Philip II conquers Olynthus
344	Demosthenes' Second Philippic
343	Timoleon goes to Sicily
342	Aristotle tutors Alexander; Birth of Epicurus
341	Demothenes' Third Philippic
338	Philip II defeats Athens and Thebes at Chaeronea; Death of Isocrates
337	Death of Timoleon; Birth of

	Demetrius Poliorcetes; Philip II divorces Olympias
336	Assassination of Philip II; Alexander becomes king
335	Alexander destroys Thebes; Aristotle founds Lyceum
334	Alexander invades Persia; victorious at Granicus
333	Alexander defeats Persians at Issus; takes Tyre
332	Alexander takes Egypt
331	Alexander founds Alexandria; defeats Persians at Gaugamela. Antipater defeats Agis II of Sparta
330	Alexander burns Persepolis; Demosthenes' speech "On the Crown"
326	Alexander defeats Porus at Hydaspes
324	Harpalus at Athens; Demosthenes banished
323	Death of Alexander the Great; Death of Diogenes; Lamian war
322	Antipater defeats Athens; Death of Demosthenes; Death of Aristotle
319	Death of Antipater
318	Birth of Pyrrhus
317	Agathocles in control of Syracuse
316	Cassander in control of Macedonia; founds Thessalonika; Antigonus founds Nicaea; Death of Olympias
312	Seleucus founds Seleucia
310	Agathocles invades Africa; Zeno establishes school at Athens
306	Epicurus begins teaching at Athens
305	Demetrius Poliorcetes fails in siege of Rhodes
301	Battle of Ipsus; Death of Antigonus Monophthalmos
300	Euclid at Alexandria; Seleucus founds Antioch
298	Death of Cassander
295	Pyrrhus becomes king of Epirus
290	Aetolian League founded
289	Death of Agathocles
287	Birth of Archimedes
283	Death of Demetrius Poliorcetes and of Ptolemy Soter; Kingdom of Pergamum founded

282 Tarentum at war with Rome; appeals to Pyrrhus

280 Achaean League founded; Colossus of Rhodes completed; Ptolemy Ceraunus in control of Macedonia; Death of Seleucus; Pyrrhus defeats Romans at Heraclea

279 Pyrrhus defeats Romans at Ausculum; Gauls invade Macedonia; Death of Ptolemy Ceraunus

278 Gauls defeated at Delphi; Nicomedes I of Bithynia invites Gauls into Asia Minor

277 Pyrrhus clears almost all of Sicily of Carthaginians

276 Antigonus Gonatas in control of Macedonia

275 Romans defeat Pyrrhus at Beneventum

272 Death of Pyrrhus; Birth of Aratus

270 Hiero II becomes king of Syracuse

255 Long Walls of Athens pulled down again

253 Birth of Philopoemon

251 Aratus in control of Achaean League

250 Eratosthenes in charge of Library at Alexandria

249 Kingdom of Parthia founded

245 Agis IV becomes king of Sparta

241 Death of Agis IV; Rome expels Carthage from Sicily

235 Attalus I of Pergamum defeats Gauls; Cleomenes III becomes king of Sparta

229 Antigonus Doson becomes king of Macedonia; Rome crushes Illyrian pirates

228 Athens in alliance with Rome

226 Cleomenes III reforms Sparta

224 Earthquake destroys Colossus of Rhodes: Cleomenes III captures Megalopolis

221 Antigonus Doson defeats Sparta at Sellasia; Cleomenes III exiled

219 Death of Cleomenes III and of Antigonus Doson; Philip V becomes king of Macedon

216 Hannibal of Carthage defeats Rome at Cannae

215 Death of Hiero II

213 Death of Aratus

211 Rome conquers Syracuse; Death of Archimedes

210 Philopoemen defeats Sparta

207 Nabis ends Spartan monarchy; seizes control of Sparta; ends helotism

202 Philopoemen defeats Nabis; Rome defeats Carthage at Zama

201 Birth of Polybius

197 Rome defeats Macedon at Cynoscephalae; Greek cities given "freedom" by Rome

191 Rome defeats Antiochus III at Thermopylae

190 Rome defeats Antiochus III at Magnesia

184 Death of Philopoemen

179 Death of Philip V

168 Rome defeats Macedon at Pydna; End of Macedonian monarchy

167 Rhodes' prosperity ruined by Rome; Hipparchus making observations at Rhodes

164 Maccabaean kingdom of Judaea established

148 Macedon becomes Roman province

146 Rome destroys Carthage; dissolves Achaean League; sacks Corinth

134 Hipparchus prepares first star map

133 Pergamum becomes Roman province

88 Mithridates VI of Pontus wins victories in Asia Minor over Rome

87 Sulla defeats Mithridates; sacks Athens

75 Cyrene annexed by Rome

74 Bithynia becomes Roman province

69 Birth of Cleopatra

65 Pontus becomes Roman province

64 Syria becomes Roman province; Seleucid Empire at end

63 Judaea becomes Roman province; Death of Mithridates

58 Cyprus annexed by Rome

48 Caesar defeats Pompey at Pharsalia; meets Cleopatra

44 Caesar assassinated

42	Mark Antony defeats Caesar's assassins at Philippi	617	Sassanid Empire takes Syria and Egypt
41	Mark Antony meets Cleopatra	630	Heraclius defeats Sassanids, restores Byzantine dominions
31	Cleopatra and Mark Antony defeated at Actium by Octavian; Octavian, as Augustus, founds Roman Empire	636	Arabs take Syria
		642	Arabs conquer Sassanid Empire; take Alexandria
30	Egypt becomes Roman province; Death of Mark Antony and of Cleopatra	673	Arabs besiege Constantinople; driven off by Greek fire
		827	Arabs take Sicily
27	Greece becomes Roman province	1014	Basil II defeats Bulgarians
25	Galatia becomes Roman province	1054	Final split between Greek Orthodox and Roman Catholic churches

A.D.

		1071	Seljuk Turks defeat Byzantines; occupy most of Asia Minor
100	Epictetus teaching at Nicopolis; Plutarch writing his biographies	1096	Beginning of Crusades
		1204	Crusaders sack Constantinople; set up Latin Empire
120	Arrian writes biography of Alexander	1261	Michael Paleologus recaptures Constantinople
125	Hadrian beautifies Athens; founds Adrianople	1303	Pharos of Alexandria destroyed by earthquake
150	Ptolemy summarizes Greek astronomy	1311	Catalan Grand Company in control of Athens
180	Death of Marcus Aurelius; Beginning of decline of Roman Empire	1338	Ottoman Turks in control of Asia Minor
190	Galen summarizes Greek biology	1354	Ottoman Turks establish first foothold in Europe
226	Sassanid Empire founded	1389	Ottoman Turks defeat Serbs at Kossovo; control Balkan peninsula
230	Diogenes Laertius writing of Greek philosophers		
240	Plotinus founds neo-Platonism	1402	Tamerlane defeats Ottoman Turks at Angora
275	Diophantus works on algebra	1451	Mohammed II becomes Turkish sultan
300	Zosimus summarizes Greek chemistry		
313	Christianity becomes state religion of Roman Empire	1453	Mohammed II captures Constantinople
330	Constantine establishes Byzantium (Constantinople) as his capital	1456	Mohammed II takes Athens
		1460	Mohammed II takes Mistra
		1461	Mohammed II takes Trebizond
		1467	Mohammed II takes Albania
361	Julian tries to re-establish paganism but fails	1481	Mohammed II fails to take Rhodes
394	Theodosius ends Olympian games	1522	Suleiman the Magnificent becomes Turkish sultan; captures Rhodes
395	Death of Theodosius; Roman Empire permanently divided		
		1565	Suleiman defeated at Malta
415	Hypatia killed at Alexandria; Library destroyed	1571	Ottoman Turks capture Cyprus from Venetians; defeated at Lepanto by Spaniards
426	Parthenon converted into Christian church		
		1669	Ottoman Turks take Crete from Venetians
476	Fall of Western Roman Empire		
529	Justinian shuts down Academy	1687	Parthenon blown up by Venetian bombardment
610	Heraclius becomes Byzantine Emperor		
		1699	Ottoman Turks forced to sign

peace treaty; turn to Phanariot Greeks to handle their dealings with west

1718 Ottoman Turks reconquer Peloponnesus from Venetians

1797 Great Britain annexes Ionian islands

1821 Greeks revolt against Turks

1824 Lord Byron dies at Missolonghi

1827 Western fleet destroys Turkish-Egyptian fleet at Navarino

1829 Greece wins independence of Ottoman Empire

1854 Great Britain occupies Piraeus

1862 George I king of Greece; Great Britain cedes Ionian islands to Greece

1878 Great Britain occupies Cyprus

1881 Greece annexes Thessaly

1908 Greece annexes Crete

1909 Venizelos rises to power in Greece

1911 Italy defeats Ottoman Turks; takes Rhodes

1912 Greece annexes Chalcidice after Balkan War

1913 Constantine I becomes king of Greece

1917 Greece joins Allies in World War I; Constantine I exiled

1919 Greece annexes West Thrace after World War I; occupies Izmir. Venizelos out of power and Constantine recalled

1921 Greece invades Turkey

1922 Turkey defeats Greece, takes and burns Izmir; Constantine exiled again; George II, king of Greece

1923 Mussolini bombards Corfu

1924 George II exiled

1935 George II recalled

1936 Metaxas dictator of Greece

1939 Italy occupies Albania

1940 Italy invades Greece; Greek army counterattacks successfully

1941 Hitler invades Greece; Germany occupies Greece and takes Crete

1944 Greece liberated by western Allies

1945 Greece annexes Rhodes

1947 Truman Doctrine. The United States supports Greek government in civil war

1949 Greek civil war ends; pro-western government victorious

1960 Cyprus becomes independent nation

1963 Greek-Turkish fighting erupts in Cyprus

1964 United Nation Troops enforce truce in Cyprus

INDEX

Miltiades (the younger), 102
  death of, 105
Minoan Age, 4
Minos, 4, 18, 42
Missolonghi, 298
Mithras, 281
Mithridates I, 263
Mithridates VI, 263
Mohammed, 286
Mohammed II, 295
Money, 57-58
Morea, 290
Mummius, Lucius, 258
Museum of Alexandria, 265-269
Mussolini, Benito, 304-305
Mycale, battle of, 121
Mycenae, 5, 125
  Schliemann and, 9
  fall of, 17
Mycenaean Age, 7-11
  end of, 17
Mystery religions, 71, 281

Nabis, 254
  assassination of, 255
Nabopolasser, 90
Naples, 36
Naucratis, 40, 66
Naupactus, 126, 290
Navarino, battle of, 299
Naxos, 101
  rebellion of, 129
Neapolis, 36
Nearchus, 222
Nebuchadrezzar, 90
  death of, 93
Nemea, 28
Nemean games, 28
Neo-platonism, 281
Nero, 277
Nestor, 50
Nicaea, Empire of, 293
Nicias, 146, 148
  Peace of, 150
  Sicilian expedition and, 153
  death of, 156
Nicomedes I, 260
Nicomedes II, 262
Nicomedes III, 262
Nicopolis, 280
Nineveh, 38
  fall of, 90
Ninus, 38
Nisaea, 148
"No," 40
Numbers, theory of, 67

Obelisks, 41
Octavian, 273
Odysseus, 8, 24, 33, 70
Odyssey, 8, 24, 26, 70
Oedipus in Colonus, 134
Oligarchy, 23
Olympia, 27
Olympiad, 27
  First, 27, 29
Olympian Games, 26-28, 49
  end of, 282
Olympias, 200, 239
  divorce of, 209
  death of, 232
Olympus, Mt., 27
Olynthus, 201
  Macedonian conquest of, 205
On, 41
"On the Crown," 226
Oracle, Delphic, 26
Orchomenus, 20
Ostracism, 106
  end of, 152

Paeonia, 200
Papyrus, 262
Parchment, 262
Parmenides, 117
Parmenio, 215, 217
  death of, 220
Parnassus, Mt., 25
Paros, 105
Parthenon, 132
  conversion to church, 282
  destruction of, 297
Parthia, 285
Paul (Saul), 276-277
Pausanias (the general), 119, 128
  death of, 124
Pausanias (the king), 163
Pelopidas, 176, 194-195
Peloponnesian War, 142 ff.
  history of, 144
Peloponnesus, 5, 10, 53-55, 290
  Spartan domination over, 53-55
  Venetians and, 297
Pelops, 5, 27
Peltasts, 174
Penelope, 24
Peoples of the Sea, 15, 37, 85
Perdiccas II, 149
Perdiccas III, 195, 199
Perdiccas (the general), 231
Perga, 267
Pergamum, 259-262